P9-DXD-472

All We Leave Behind

All We Leave Behind

A REPORTER'S JOURNEY
INTO THE LIVES OF OTHERS

Carol Off

RANDOM HOUSE CANADA

PUBLISHED BY RANDOM HOUSE CANADA
Copyright © 2017 Carol Off

www.penguinrandomhouse.ca

Random House Canada and colophon are registered trademarks.

Extracts from Richard Wagamese's "The Canada Poem," from the book *Runaway Dreams*,
published by permission of Ronsdale Press.

LIBRARY AND ARCHIVES CANADA CATALOGUING IN PUBLICATION

Off, Carol, author
All we leave behind : a reporter's journey into the lives of
others / Carol Off.
Includes index.
Issued in print and electronic formats.

ISBN 978-0-345-81683-2
eBook ISBN 978-0-345-81144-8

1. Off, Carol. 2. Aryubwal, Asad—Family. 3. Journalists—Canada.
4. Families—Afghanistan. 5. Immigrants. 6. Refugees. I. Title.
DS371.415.O34 2017   305.9'069140922581   C2016-906066-7

Text design by Colin Jaworski
Cover photos: *top* (tile from the Shrine of Hazrat Ali) © Jane Sweeney;
bottom (tile from the Ancient Blue Mosque in Mazar-i-Sharif) © Scott Peterson, both Getty Images
Image credits: Photo on page 267 courtesy Lana Šlezić;
All other photos courtesy Carol Off and the Aryubwal family

Printed and bound in the United States of America
2 4 6 8 9 7 5 3 1

Penguin
Random House
RANDOM HOUSE CANADA

For Chloe Alice and Clara Mae,
that they may always have the freedom,
and the courage, to speak their minds.

. . . and in the end it is all we carry forward and all we leave behind. Our story. Everything we own.

—FROM "THE CANADA POEM," BY RICHARD WAGAMESE

Contents

Introduction

KARACHI, PAKISTAN
SEPTEMBER 5, 1986

I WAS RUNNING THROUGH THE DARKNESS across the tarmac of Jinnah International Airport, weaving to avoid armed soldiers but carrying on with single-minded purpose through the bedlam and towards the gunfire, fuelled entirely by adrenalin. And at that moment I had my earliest and, perhaps, most important morality lesson about journalism: Be careful what you wish for.

Members of the Abu Nidal Palestinian terrorist organization had gained access to a runway early that morning and boarded Pan Am Flight 73 bound for Frankfurt, then New York City. The jumbo jet was taking on fuel and passengers for its return journey when the hijackers, dressed as airport service workers, took control. I had just flown into Karachi, but I was already headed towards downtown, unaware of the event that would change so many people's lives, including mine.

My taxi lumbered into the city as first light penetrated the smog, revealing shapes and figures that were foreign and exotic to me. It was my first trip abroad as a journalist and I wanted to absorb the otherness of everything, to feel a sense of adventure, but instead I was intimidated. Why on earth had I decided to come here? I had no idea what to do as a reporter in a distant country. And I was freelance, on my own dime, gambling that this venture might relaunch my faltering career. I said a prayer—*please make something happen.*

It was at that moment, I figured out later, that four terrorists boarded the aircraft, armed with assault rifles and a briefcase full of grenades, their waists girded with plastic explosives. By way of opening talks with the Pakistanis, they shot an American passenger and threw his dead body onto the runway.

A message from the news desk of CBC Radio in Toronto was waiting for me when I checked into the hotel. There were preliminary reports of a hijacking. The news department knew that I had just arrived. Could I return to Karachi airport? I gathered up whatever kit I presumed necessary to cover a hostage-taking and hailed a cab.

At the airport, negotiations between the hijackers and Pakistani authorities went on all day and into the night. I passed on the scraps of news that airport personnel shared with reporters and eventually had a half-dozen agencies, including the CBC, relying on my dispatches. One senior airport manager was surprisingly forthcoming during media briefings and we learned that the terrorists were growing more agitated, their demands less coherent, as night fell.

When the auxiliary power unit on the plane shut down without warning, plunging everything into darkness, the gunmen panicked, detonated their grenades and fired off their weapons. Flight attendants, who had stayed on duty through the entire ordeal even as the pilots fled through the cockpit window, frantically tried to save as many lives as they could. A senior purser, an Indian woman who had been trying to comfort and console passengers for the previous seventeen hours, managed to get one emergency exit open before the hijackers shot her in the head. The remaining crew members coaxed bewildered hostages down an inflatable slide into the uncertain night. Other passengers attempted to jump to safety from an emergency hatch where the slide had failed to open. Many of them were injured.

Authorities on the ground had been caught off guard by the sudden exodus and no one was outside the aircraft to help. With little guidance, people scurried in every direction, some holding children or trying to support the wounded as they sought refuge from the explosions and the shooting. It was impossible to tell who was firing or in what direction. Soldiers frantically hunted for the hijackers, passengers ran for cover, and I sprinted across the tarmac towards it all with my tape recorder rolling.

From the earlier media briefings I knew that Pakistani commandos had been preparing for some kind of a raid. But they were nowhere to be seen and it fell to regular army troops to try and gain control. I caught sight of someone lying in the back of an army vehicle whom I presumed to be a wounded passenger. The soldiers allowed me to crawl into the wagon where I attempted to interview the man: "Are you hurt?" It turned out that the person I thought was a victim was actually one of the hijackers who had just been apprehended. I sat in the truck for a brief moment, bewildered, face to face with the terrorist, while the soldiers laughed. To say that I was in over my head would be an understatement.

By the time the carnage ended, there were 20 bodies lined up in Karachi's morgue, 120 people in hospital, and 239 other passengers and crew members whose lives had been permanently scarred. All the hijackers were captured and would face death sentences that would eventually be commuted to life in prison. Neerja Bhanot, the purser who had been fatally shot while trying to help the hostages through the emergency hatch, would be celebrated in India as a national hero. The Pakistanis would spend decades trying to account for how they could have allowed this act of terrorism to happen.

I had come to Pakistan hoping to feel the heat of foreign journalism, to cover stories of consequence, of life and death. I know I'm not personally responsible for the hijacking of Pan Am Flight 73 or the massacre that took place inside the jumbo jet—still, I'm uncomfortable when I remember that silent prayer. Because drama is what I had wanted. It's what I had hoped for. The lesson I learned that day is that journalists all too often have their best moments when other people are having their worst.

Only a handful of foreign reporters had gained access to the airport that morning, before the Pakistani army arrived and closed it. Among them was a veteran journalist from the *Financial Times*, John Elliott, who took me under his wing and showed me, among other things, how to make international calls from a public phone (it was in the days before the widespread use of mobiles). When a policeman nabbed me on the tarmac, John barked, "Leave her alone! She's a journalist!" The gun-wielding officer—who had full authority to stop people—actually recoiled as if I were red hot.

This was my first real experience of the entitlement that comes with the profession, the access to places the public can't go. I would make ample use of it in the years to come, learning the term for "journalist" in other languages and employing it like a tool to pry open doors in dozens of different countries, along with all the other devices of the business: the flak jacket emblazoned with the word PRESS; the accreditation that puts you on the other side of the yellow police tape; the photo ID that gains you access to the inner sanctums of the powerful and influential. It gives you permission to call strangers in the middle of the night or even arrive at their door, to question authority, to demand accountability from people in charge.

More important, it gives you admission into the lives of others, into their most tragic, emotional and often degrading experiences. It permits—or even compels—you to ask personal questions, to probe, to intrude at the moment when people are coping with calamity. And it presumes that everyone has a story that they want to have told, if only someone would ask.

The next day, journalists were allowed to see the state of the plane and the airstrip, strewn with shoes, purses and the other detritus of people's lives. Looking at the flight number, I realized that this was the aircraft that had brought me here from New York City, stopping in Mumbai along the way to take on more people, and then carrying on to Karachi, my destination. It had been getting ready for a flight through Frankfurt and back to the US with 379 passengers and crew members on board, each of them settling in for a long journey, each with plans for the days following arrival at their destinations. One moment I had been among such travellers, and then I was a reporter, covering an event in which I could easily have been victim rather than observer.

What was my responsibility as a journalist to the people who had been aboard Pan Am Flight 73? What was my obligation to those whose lives I'd entered? To that point I had learned that it was to get the facts straight, spell the names correctly, present all sides, tell the story fairly and make sure that what you report is in the public interest. Show respect and civility but don't get personal. Be engaged, of course, but disinterested; a journalist mustn't be invested in the outcome of events. Above all else, avoid unnecessary involvement in the lives of people who are subjects in your stories. Impartiality is the key to objectivity. Hang in, get your story, leave and don't look back.

As a freelancer I had arrived in Pakistan with only a few vague commitments from news agencies that had agreed to accept material from me "on spec." I had one firm promise from the CBC Radio program *Sunday Morning* to buy an interview with Benazir Bhutto—if I got it. This was a big "if" since Bhutto had been arrested and thrown into prison weeks earlier. Her nemesis, Pakistani president Mohammad Zia-ul-Haq, had engineered her incarceration to prevent her from running for the office of prime minister in the upcoming elections.

Since she had abandoned a comfortable existence in London to become a politician in Pakistan, Bhutto had been drawing crowds in the tens of thousands. And she had captured the imaginations of more than just Pakistanis: she had become celebrated in the Western media. Benazir was just thirty-three years old, beautiful and charismatic, an unmarried woman courageously pursuing power in a man's world that was also very dangerous.

Her father, Zulfikar Ali Bhutto, had served as the ninth prime minister of Pakistan and also for a term as president. He had been deposed by General Zia-ul-Haq, who prosecuted and executed him in 1979. Now, seven years later, his daughter wanted to follow in his footsteps and fulfill his ambitions by challenging the man who'd orchestrated her father's destruction. I had timed my arrival to coincide with a scheduled court appearance. Benazir's sister told me before I'd left Toronto that, if I got to Pakistan, I had a slight chance of an encounter with Benazir in mid-September when she would get out of prison long enough to stand before a magistrate.

Foreign reporters had flooded into the country as a result of the Pan Am hijacking but their interest in that story quickly waned. Assignment editors instructed them to find something else to cover. American news agencies were especially keen to get a piece of the compelling Bhutto saga—dazzling, Oxford-educated daughter of executed politician seeks to fill his shoes. While I had the inside track on the story of the hijacking, now I was competing with approximately two hundred journalists lined up to cover her day in court. I figured I didn't have a chance in any contest with the American networks but, once again, fate intervened.

President Zia understood the optics. The case against Bhutto was paper thin and now there was going to be too much scrutiny of this trial. Without warning, he declared an amnesty for political prisoners that allowed for Benazir's release. Now there would be no trial, and since I had pre-arranged an interview through her sister, I suddenly found myself at the head of a long, aggressive queue.

Benazir's house was in the suburbs of Karachi where the wealthiest and most powerful people in Sindh province live quite comfortably. Despite her privilege, Bhutto's Pakistan People's Party (PPP) was wildly popular with poor farm families who could never dream of living in such a neighbourhood. When I arrived, the mansion was sur-rounded by her supporters, an assembly of mostly emaciated women, camped on the sprawling lawn and hoping to catch a glimpse of their hero. The PPP slogan was "bread, clothing, shelter"—all essentials that the sophisticated daughter of a wealthy landowner could take for granted. And yet she was a near god-like figure to some of the most marginalized people in the country who believed that she understood them and their needs.

I waited in a small room near the front entry hall where I overheard a terse conversation between Bhutto's handler and another journalist, a woman from Agence France-Presse. The reporter explained that she had just come from an interview with Corazon Aquino, the first female president of the Philippines and a self-proclaimed housewife who had entered politics when her husband was assassinated. The reporter at the door wanted to talk to Benazir Bhutto in order to complete her feature article about women who have been unexpectedly thrust into public office. She wouldn't take no for an answer. I caught a glimpse of a slender woman with thick dark hair who could have easily been mistaken for one of the loyal followers camped in the yard, except she was wearing cargo pants and a T-shirt. Just as the handler was closing the door in her face, declaring that Bhutto's schedule was full, I suggested that she could join my interview.

We had just a few minutes to discuss strategy so I quickly told my new collaborator that I planned to challenge Benazir on her claims that she was being persecuted by Pakistani authorities. I had seen Bhutto at an impromptu press conference the night before, just after she had been released, and she had seemed too fresh and effervescent to have been a recent jailbird. I questioned how much she had really suffered. The AFP reporter listened patiently and then volunteered her own assessment: she herself had been captured and imprisoned for a month by the North Vietnamese during the war in Southeast Asia and had suffered immensely. Then she described the feeling of elation that comes at the moment of release, the need to recover something of the old self. Perhaps Bhutto was experiencing something of the same? She proposed a different line of inquiry. Was Bhutto really where she wanted to be? Was she prepared? Did she really enjoy politics? Did she really want power? Or was this a role that had been imposed upon her by an idealistic dad? There were stories that Benazir's father had doted on her as a child, that he had groomed his daughter from an early age for a life of politics. Benazir had visited him in prison many times before his execution and he had made it clear that she would inherit the organization he had founded, the Pakistan People's Party. It was her destiny. But was this the life she would have chosen for herself?

I never encountered this reporter again nor did I make note of her name, though I figured out years later that she was probably Kate Webb, an Australian journalist with a formidable reputation as a ground-breaking war correspondent who died in 2007. In this brief encounter, she had a profound effect on me. This was my first high-profile inter-view and I thought I had come prepared, but now I realized my woeful inadequacy. What did I know about what Bhutto had gone through in prison? What did I know about politics and destiny, the intrigues of South Asia? What the hell was I doing here?

During the interview (I abandoned my queries about whether she had suffered in prison), Benazir responded to my earnest probes with dull, rehearsed answers. But she was clearly unprepared for some of my colleague's questions. "Do you really want this life for yourself?" asked my new friend. "A life of politics?" Benazir's white silk headscarf slipped from her dark hair and she stared into the distance thoughtfully as she responded. "Sometimes when I'm in prison I imagine that I pass through the walls and go walking. I go to the souks and bazaars. I go shopping. I look at all the beautiful saris and jewellery. When someone shouts, 'There is Benazir Bhutto!' the others say, 'It can't be her. Benazir Bhutto is in jail.' And they all leave me alone."

I saw in that interview how a question should be a key, sliding into the most reluctant lock and opening a portal on a private mind. Even the most guarded subject becomes vulnerable to the skilled locksmith and it was fascinating to see the effect of such a probe on someone as impenetrable as Benazir Bhutto. But while her answers were revealing, she was careful not to expose herself to any danger. Benazir knew how to protect herself. What about the ordinary person, perhaps unsophisticated, under stress, judgement altered by emotion? What is a reporter's responsibility when people, unaware of consequences, tell us more than they should?

I'd been little more than a tourist on previous visits to the subcontinent and it had become my obsession to access the other side of the glass, to be on the inside. Pakistan was in the midst of major change, possibly cataclysmic. And that's where I wanted to be. The Bhutto interview was intended to be only an entrée before I made my way to northern Pakistan, near the border with Afghanistan, where I would be able to feel the heat of conflict.

In the fall of 1986, Pakistan was the corridor for the largest covert military operation in the history of the United States, a campaign designed by President Ronald Reagan and his overzealous CIA chief, William J. Casey, to bring the Soviet Union to its knees. The forward operating base for the war was northern Pakistan where the CIA, with additional backing from the Saudi royal family, was equipping an army of Islamist fighters.

The Soviets had impetuously invaded Afghanistan in 1979 and were now struggling to control a population that had demonstrated from time immemorial that they didn't take well to invasions. Fierce but poorly armed guerrilla fighters known as mujahidin made up the bulk of the Afghan resistance force. Jimmy Carter's administration had provided some support to them but Reagan saw the dogged determination of what he called "freedom fighters" as an opportunity to defeat the "evil empire." The USSR was already bleeding in Afghanistan: now the White House believed there was an opportunity to help create a fatal hemorrhage with a well-subsidized Islamic military. Reagan regarded his Afghan operation as a holy war against godless Communists and he embraced the mujahidin as his allies.

Not long after interviewing Bhutto, I left Karachi and headed north to Peshawar, capital of North-West Frontier Province and close to the Afghan border. Roads were clogged with convoys of trucks, their contents concealed, but many were believed to be laden with covert supplies and weapons for the Afghan fighters. No one knew the extent of US involvement at the time since the White House was attempting to keep its contribution under wraps. But when the US is engaged in a multi-billion-dollar operation that sprawls all over the Asian subcontinent it doesn't stay secret for very long. Enterprising reporters told stories of the American-supplied guns, bombs and rocket-propelled grenade launchers that arrived in Peshawar regularly. The weapons were loaded onto pickup trucks for transport to the jihadist training camps along the porous border with Afghanistan. Hundreds of millions of dollars' worth of arms—that would eventually defeat the Soviets—made their way into Afghanistan on the backs of mules.

The ranks of mujahidin warriors swelled with the constant arrival of foreign fighters, Arabs from all over the Middle East, eager to take part in the holy war and profit from the generosity of Washington and the House of Saud. These jihadists joined the Afghan freedom fighters in the training facilities along the border while their commanders hung out in Peshawar meeting with foreign benefactors.

Peshawar was an edgy, at times sinister city, headquarters for Washington's clandestine operation. Along with the US dollars, weapons and foreign fighters passing through Peshawar, I encountered—or heard tell of—a disturbing assortment of shady financiers, criminal gang members and drug dealers. Money and weapons entered Afghanistan while opium from the Afghan poppy fields made its way back out, using the same mountain supply routes and even hitching rides on the return trip of the same mule caravans. The illicit cargo was mostly destined for the heroin market in the United States, where, ironically, the president's wife, Nancy Reagan, had launched her "war on drugs."

Peshawar was also home to one of the rare establishments that legally sold alcohol in Pakistan—the famous Dean's Hotel. The room where you made the purchase had no windows to ensure that Pakistanis wouldn't see the booze and the degenerate Westerners who were buying it. As a customer you were required to fill out a detailed form, providing your father's name and swearing you were not a Muslim and that you would never, ever share your alcohol with anyone of the Islamic faith. Dean's was just one of the hangouts in the city for a rogues' gallery of war profiteers, carpetbaggers, gunrunners and some of the most cynical foreign journalists I would ever meet. Over drinks of counterfeit Scotch whisky, I heard tales of secret agents who were apparently lurking around every corner in Peshawar. Many of the stories were probably apocryphal—like the one about two hapless Russian spies who had fallen out of a tree near the US consulate—but they all stoked the imagination of a journalistic neophyte.

Peshawar was where you could get the Soviet-US war news from a Western perspective and learn about the key players in this drama. There was Gulbuddin Hekmatyar, an Afghan commander believed to be an agent of Pakistani intelligence (in one way or another, they all were); Burhanuddin Rabbani, a scholar turned warrior chief who would one day fight his way to the Afghan presidency; Ahmad Shah Massoud, the "Lion of Panjshir," a charismatic mujahidin who spoke foreign languages; and Abdul Rasul Sayyaf, an Afghan but also the darling of the Saudis, who'd already acquired a nasty reputation for violence even before a civil war that would one day make him notorious. All of these men were profiting immensely from the covert US operation in the region while another raft of Afghan mercenaries were on Moscow's payroll, performing the same proxy task for the Kremlin. Chief among the names tossed about was that of General Rashid Dostum, an ethnic Uzbek whose private army would help the Soviets hang on to northern Afghanistan for much longer than anyone anticipated.

In 1986, only the best-informed insiders were tracking some other characters who would, in the next decade, come to dominate the gossip and intrigue that swirled through those smoky rooms in Peshawar. A tall Saudi construction magnate named Osama bin Laden was playing on the fringes of the great game then unfolding in the hills and valleys of Afghanistan even as he became a conduit for arms, fighters and money from the Middle East. And less well known was Mohammed Omar, a mujahidin who would later become a mullah and inspire a group of pious youngsters to take up arms as the Taliban. For most Westerners, including many regarded as authorities on the region, people like bin Laden and Mullah Omar were marginal figures whose activities were not expected to amount to much. These characters would all become familiar to me over the next fifteen years, intimately associated with wars that would kill a million and a half people. But at the time they were just names in an unfolding drama that I wanted to report on, though I barely understood it.

The human effect of Reagan's escalating Cold War tactics wasn't as obvious in the centre of Peshawar as it was in the refugee camps for displaced Afghans that sprawled over the barren countryside around the city. Huddled in abject poverty and hopelessness, more than three million Afghans had come seeking assistance that was ultimately controlled by militia leaders and agents of the various political factions who profited from the conflicts that were causing their distress.

These settlements were a breeding ground for the kind of radicalism that feeds on desperation. Young men and boys, wearied by their impotence, turned to their religion—or a distorted version of Islam—for empowerment. Radical imams established religious schools called madrassas where children and teenagers found comfort in a revolutionary doctrine—the ideology of violent jihad against the nonbelievers who, ironically, were paying for the food, medicine and weapons that enabled their hopeful militancy.

The camps were the size of cities, fetid and filthy, containing so many people there wasn't a moment's privacy. The inhabitants barely had enough water to drink, so sanitation was water wasted. They sheltered from the beating sun in flimsy tents and tarps while aid workers struggled to supply them with basic medicine. As a nurse guided me through a makeshift hospital, the sights and smells were so overwhelming that I fainted, becoming an added burden to those who were trying to deal with a real human crisis. Even today, having visited dozens of the world's most shameful slums and shantytowns over the past decades, I have yet to see anything that affected me as much as those Pakistani settlements.

It was here that I really saw the consequences of the proxy war between the United States and the USSR, especially in the faces of the women who struggled against impossible odds. They cared for their families as best they could though there didn't seem to be any future for them and so many of their children had missing limbs. The Soviets would drop brightly coloured bomblets all over the Afghan countryside, knowing that young people would presume they were toys to be played with and not explosives that would detonate once handled. It was one of the Red Army's strategies for getting Afghan families to desert their villages, knowing that the mothers would take their children to Pakistan for treatment.

The women were the keepers of the family stories, each one compelling, filled with tragedy and struggle. For me, the wretchedness in these camps was the true narrative of Afghanistan's war. But I soon learned that there was little appetite in newsrooms for tales of the human misery metastasizing in these settlements. For news editors, these sorrowful scenes were the same as those that played out on the fringes of combat everywhere for all time. No one cared. Had more journalists looked more closely into those camps before dismissing them, they may have caught a glimpse into the future of a war that would one day change the world.

I didn't realize it at the time either. But what I saw in northern Pakistan in 1986 was the beginning of a conflict that would dominate the early decades of a new millennium. The army of jihadist fighters trained and financed by the CIA, the weapons, the madrassas, the sprawling refugee camps, the post-colonial disparities of the subcontinent and the seething resentment against the United States would one day help a handful of men to fly jumbo jets into tall towers in lower Manhattan and alter the course of modern history. I was witnessing the prologue for just about all of the international stories I would cover for years to come, climaxing in a global refugee crisis that remains one of the most overwhelming human tragedies of our time. The story of people displaced by war would eventually become not a sidebar to be ignored by newsrooms but the main event.

For years after this first visit to Pakistan, the lessons learned in Karachi remained my journalistic bedrock—objectivity, detachment, disengagement. Until an older, and presumably wiser, version of myself returned to the region in 2002. That's when I met a man who agreed to be the subject of a story—someone to help put a human face on Afghanistan's crisis. Asad Aryubwal did just that. But then he and his family did something else. They turned my assumptions about journalism upside down. They forced me to rethink the rules and question the morality of my profession, to unlearn lessons that began with that fateful dash across the Karachi airport tarmac.

I

George W's Warlords

KABUL, AFGHANISTAN
JANUARY 2002

THE TURBOPROP TOUCHED DOWN ON what had once been a smooth asphalt surface and we bumped along over cracks and potholes before coming to a final stop on the runway. During our descent, all I could see of the countryside was the devastation of wars that had been going on in Afghanistan without interruption for twenty-three years. On the ground, the landscape appeared even more barren, almost lunar.

It had been just four months since the events of 9/11. The site of the World Trade Center in Manhattan was now a heap of debris and never-to-be-recovered bodies but also a shrine—"Ground Zero" had already taken root in the vernacular of journalism. Here, in Kabul, we were about to enter what many now recognized as the real Ground Zero—Afghanistan, where the seeds of terror that blossomed in America had been germinating long before September 2001.

International travel protocols had changed, nowhere more conspicuously than in airports where people now regarded it as almost an homage to those who had died on September 11 in New York, Virginia and

Pennsylvania to have their bags and ID scrutinized at length. Since our plane had just landed in what I would have thought to be one of the most sensitive, security-conscious airports in the world, I anticipated a long delay.

The passengers were told to deplane and wait on the tarmac, some distance away from the battered building that served as Kabul's international terminal. We surrendered our passports and landing cards to two Afghan men in blue jumpsuits who then climbed into a rusting Honda parked in a field beside the runway. I presumed the agents would drive the vehicle to the customs office to process our papers, then return to escort us to the terminal. As we stood in the cold January sleet, we were all hoping it wouldn't take too long.

I was no longer the solitary greenhorn radio reporter of 1986, paying my own way and relying mostly on my own scant resources, but was now a credentialed CBC television journalist travelling with a team. Heather Abbott was the producer for our little crew; Brian Kelly was the cameraman. Both are Canadians, though Brian lives in London. We had met up in Islamabad for this shoot and arranged passage to Afghanistan on a World Food Programme flight, one of the few ways that civilians could get there—unless they had the money to charter their own plane. We were a part of the legions of journalists worldwide who had been on the road for months, covering the fallout from the September 11 attacks. I had learned to be patient with passport security agents.

It soon became apparent that the battered Honda wasn't going anywhere because the vehicle *was* the customs office. The men pored over our documents, passed them back and forth across the front seat of the car, and then stamped our visas into the passports, using the dashboard as a countertop. They brought them back to us and we were free to carry on to the terminal to collect our bags.

In Islamabad, we had been enjoying the warm days and cool nights of a typical winter in that city. But just ninety minutes of flying time later, we were high on a plateau of the Hindu Kush Mountains, in freezing cold Kabul, where January brings sub-zero temperatures and often heavy snow. The first thing I did after reclaiming my gear was to rummage through it for the Gore-Tex jacket that I would all but live in for the duration of our trip.

Before this visit to Afghanistan, the most depressing post-war environment I had witnessed was in Bosnia in the 1990s. I thought nowhere could have been more shattered than Sarajevo after nearly four years of unbroken siege. But here I was seeing the result of decades of annihilation, first from the military might of superpowers and then from the unique savagery of civil war. Every village on the airport road leading to the city had been smashed apart, its buildings flattened. Snow showers soaked the grey-and-tan-coloured land that had once flourished with orchards and vineyards. Boys in dirt-smeared shalwar kameez dug up what remained of the roots of grapevines and apricot trees to sell as firewood and they sheltered themselves from the elements inside the rusted shells of abandoned armoured vehicles along the roadside.

As with so many other people, I was trying to understand the root causes of 9/11; not just what had happened but why. I had gone to Ground Zero in lower Manhattan; then to Washington as President George W. Bush declared his holy war; on to Egypt and the home of a medical doctor, Ayman al-Zawahiri, who was al-Qaeda's second in command and was considered the mastermind behind the 9/11 attacks. I had gleaned some insights from those places, but all roads of inquiry led to the Asian subcontinent, to Afghanistan and Pakistan.

We were here to report on the fallout from events that I had covered in 1986, when the US proxy war against the Soviet Union had forced millions of Afghans into Pakistani refugee camps. A few years later, Ronald Reagan did manage to bring the Cold War to an end, largely through his multi-billion-dollar partnership with the mujahidin. But even before the last Soviet soldier had retreated from Afghan soil, returning to Russia in humiliating defeat, the Americans had also packed their bags and skipped town, leaving behind a rapidly disintegrating state. Now the US was back, hunting down those responsible for the violent events on their own soil.

"Blowback" is a term that refers to the unintended consequences of covert military operations. In the 1980s, Washington had armed and trained the mujahidin to defeat the USSR. But soon after that victory, Afghanistan became, literally and figuratively, a minefield under the loose control of ardent warriors who had vast arsenals of weapons and a mishmash of competing interests. Afghan commanders, whose names I had heard on that first trip to Pakistan—Hekmatyar, Massoud, Sayyaf, Rabbani, Dostum—all vied for power as they evolved from freedom fighters into callous warlords. In the early 1990s, as the United States abandoned Afghanistan, the mujahidin turned their private armies and their foreign-funded weapons on each other and all but destroyed their own country through civil war. In the rubble of a failed state, the fanatical Taliban movement seized control, instituting an Islamic Emirate and establishing a comfortable home base for the Taliban's ideological ally, al-Qaeda.

Long before al-Qaeda's attack on the United States, CIA operatives had warned the White House and the Pentagon about dangerous developments in Afghanistan. A few agents had gone so far as to counsel their political masters that the country was still an American problem. It was becoming an important base for terror operations aimed at targets in the West. Now, in the wake of 9/11, some of the same intelligence agents were emerging from retirement to go public with the heretical assertion that the United States had, in many important ways, brought 9/11 on itself by ignoring Afghanistan as it slipped from chaos into the control of terrorists.

The two most underestimated characters from the 1980s, the leader of the Taliban, Mullah Omar, and the tall, reclusive Arab, Osama bin Laden, had gone on to change the course of modern history. Ayman al-Zawahiri had helped to plan the 9/11 attacks on the United States, providing tactical support from al-Qaeda's fortified caves deep in the Hindu Kush Mountains. His success was only possible because the United States had allowed it. Now the Americans were facing the consequences of blowback head-on.

As we drove into downtown Kabul, it was impossible to determine what had been destroyed by which conflict. Soviet invasion. Insurgency against the Russians. Civil war. Or the American military forces that had just swept through Afghanistan—an avenging hurricane that drove the Taliban from power. Every phase had left its wounds on the city.

Streets ran thick with mud and garbage; the beggars were listless and the markets were a sea of bright blue burqa–clad women who were still too unsure of the security in the city to risk exposing their faces, even though the Taliban enforcers of strict Koranic law had been expelled. We checked into the Mustafa Hotel, a low-rise structure that had been an office building before its owners began to see the allure in catering to hordes of foreigners like us, arriving daily, loaded down with gear and cash, looking for a safe place to hang a satellite dish. The building was now a rudimentary guesthouse catering mostly to journalists.

The much-coveted top floor had been claimed as a CBC bureau and that's where we dropped our twenty-five pieces of luggage, almost all of it TV equipment. Then we went to lunch at the Herat Restaurant, a massive Greyhound bus station–style venue where woolly tribesmen and out-of-work warriors shared long tables with a handful of hapless Westerners such as ourselves.

The city was crawling with foreign reporters. This was the heyday of the celebrity journalist. Correspondents and the famous anchors of TV news shows in Europe and America arrived and departed daily on chartered planes or military aircraft. The so-called triumvirate of traditional US news coverage—CBS, NBC, ABC—were in a fierce competition for audiences as the all-news channels of CNN and Fox began to eclipse them in the important ratings game. Dan Rather from CBS touched down in Afghanistan in late November 2001 and stayed around long enough to say "Good evening from Kabul" as he appeared to be anchoring the news from a war zone (the fighting in Kabul had ended by this point). He presented the latest bulletins from the country and then conducted a dull interview with the Afghan foreign minister before turning to other developments, including the death of Beatle George Harrison. NBC's Tom Brokaw, who had been about to retire before the events of 9/11 gave him a shot in the arm, showed up to tell Americans how amazing the US troops were and how they would bring freedom to Afghanistan. ABC's Peter Jennings, to his credit, stayed away, aware from his own experience in the field that celebrity can be a handicap in covering such a crisis.

Many other TV personalities didn't see it as Jennings did. Dan Rather felt he had ownership of the story since he had covered the mujahidin story for CBS years earlier and had famously appeared on camera dressed as a freedom fighter (the incident won him the nickname Gunga Dan). When asked why he would leave the comfort of the anchor desk for a field assignment in a war zone, Rather declared that "danger is my business."

Geraldo Rivera of Fox News presented an emotional report from Tora Bora, near the Pakistani border, where he claimed he was walking on the "sacred ground" where US soldiers had been killed. He had the wrong location, though, and when it was later pointed out to him, Geraldo claimed that, in the "fog of war," he had conflated two deadly events, unaware that the incident he claimed to have confused with Tora Bora happened three days after he was there.

The celebrity news coverage infuriated the real war reporters and foreign bureau regulars who saw it as grandstanding. Eight journalists had already died in the US-led war in Afghanistan, four of them killed in an ambush on a highway north of Kabul. None of the deceased were Americans.

My usual morning routine was to climb out onto the flat roof of our building and watch the dawn break over the foothills of the Hindu Kush, a rare moment of tranquility in Kabul. One early morning, I caught a glimpse of Peter Arnett standing on another rooftop nearby. The quiet was broken by his familiar voice with the unmistakable New Zealand accent, well known to anyone who followed his audacious coverage from Baghdad during the Gulf War. Arnett was talking on a portable satellite telephone, perhaps the most coveted piece of equipment for journalists at the time. Shamelessly I eavesdropped to find out what important bulletin he was filing to his CNN editors only to discover he was in the middle of what seemed to be a rather personal conversation with someone in a distant time zone.

Before coming to Kabul, Heather and I had spent some days in Islamabad awaiting Brian's arrival and meeting with people who we thought might prepare us for Afghanistan. Canadian Kathy Gannon was a senior correspondent for Associated Press and was one of the most informed journalists in the region. She's also the most generous, willing to impart her wisdom and understanding to reporters like us who needed to get up to speed quickly. Kathy served tea and gave us the lay of the land as we stretched out on the comfortable oversized pillows in her living room. The harsh Islamabad sun filtered through towering fern trees outside the windows.

It wasn't only Washington that had neglected Afghanistan during its years of anarchy. Most reporters, including us, had ignored the story as well. The collapse of the Soviet Empire in the early 1990s had sparked an eruption of nasty civil wars in countries such as Rwanda and the former Yugoslavia, conflicts that had monopolized the always limited news agency interest in foreign coverage. Other than reading the occasional *New Yorker* feature, I had not paid much attention to the region that had taught me so many early lessons. But Kathy had lived and worked in Pakistan and Afghanistan through all those years and she could have told anyone who cared to listen that something big was brewing.

Kathy came to Pakistan as a freelance journalist in 1985. She didn't just pass through the area as I did a year later but settled there, putting out her shingle as a reporter for hire while living as frugally as possible. The story that captured her attention was that of the sprawling refugee camps on the outskirts of Peshawar. Through interviews with those

Afghans, Kathy learned the scope of the devastating war raging just over the border and she wanted to see it for herself. It was difficult for a woman to gain the trust of the mujahidin leaders but they allowed her to join them on their long treks into the battlefields of Afghanistan where she saw first-hand the battle between peasant warriors and the Soviets.

Kathy is one of a number of groundbreaking women journalists who made reputations for themselves in what was, in the 1980s, still considered a man's world. I'd had my own taste of this bias when I returned to Canada from Pakistan and learned it was the CBC's general policy not to dispatch female reporters to war. The public broadcaster wasn't alone. Foreign editors from every Canadian news agency I approached took pains to assure me that they wouldn't send a woman into conflict because it was far too dangerous for members of what was still to be regarded as the weaker sex. One editor (I talked to nine of them) went further, suggesting that a female presence was a magnet for trouble; she would jeopardize the security of everyone else in a news crew.

But a great many women were going to the world's hotspots to cover the news. Ann Medina broke through the CBC's resistance to become the bureau chief in Beirut in the 1980s. Hilary Brown, another Canadian, was among the last reporters to leave during the fall of Saigon. If news agencies wouldn't hire them, the women went as freelancers, Kathy Gannon among them. She ignored the sexist attitude of Western news editors; she was far more preoccupied with convincing the mujahidin that she was competent as she hiked along with them through narrow mountain passages, following battle-hardened warriors as they escorted mule caravans piled with weapons. Kathy never allowed her hosts to see her falter.

Reporters like Kathy and Kate Webb, the woman I met at Benazir Bhutto's house, proved that their resourcefulness and stamina matched the capability of any man. And no one at CBC had hesitated for a moment before sending Heather and me into Afghanistan.

Kathy briefed us at length, charting a course through the intrigues of US-Afghan relations, telling us whom to trust, warning us whom to avoid and giving some advice on how to conduct ourselves as women in a country with some medieval attitudes about gender roles and differences. Heather is tall, lithe, blond-haired and blue-eyed: she would turn heads anywhere, and she was especially conspicuous in Afghanistan. Neither of us would blend into the Afghan landscape easily.

Western women working in Afghanistan had taken to wearing hijabs or headscarves, but Kathy advised that it was required only in specific circumstances—for security or strategy. Covering your head allows you to appear, at least from a distance or in the passenger seats of vehicles, as though you are an Afghan woman and can permit you to move through the streets a bit more unobtrusively. Up close and in person, we would fool no one. Even so, wearing a hijab sometimes helped to get access to a situation or an interview and she said it was always advisable to travel with a shawl or kerchief stuffed in a bag that could quickly transform a woman from infidel to dutiful. But Kathy also assured us that since we were not Muslims, only fundamentalists would expect us to follow a strict Islamic dress code. In fact, progressive Afghans I met actually resented the efforts of Western women to accommodate religious conservatives.

Heather and I were in the middle of the pack in terms of experience with conflict reporting. Our last big assignment together had been in Sudan where we covered the role of a Canadian oil company in the ethnic cleansing of south-Sudanese villages. Heather had been fearless on that assignment, gaining us access to the oil fields when the Khartoum government wasn't allowing any reporters into the area. She then discovered a clandestine backdoor route into southern Sudan, where we were able to report on the horrors unfolding in the countryside, the attacks on civilian villages by Sudan's helicopter gunships, the massacres, and the complicity of foreign companies. Heather and I worked well together and discovered a common willingness to take cautious risks.

Our cameraman Brian Kelly had more experience than most in war zones. He knew how to work discreetly, to dress and act in a manner that would allow him to be productive anywhere, gathering visual scenes and sequences of breathtaking power and drama without drawing attention to himself. Brian is of average build with a salt-and-pepper beard and rimless glasses. People who meet him in the field have an uncanny feeling that they know him from somewhere—he projects a kind of familiarity that crosses cultural barriers.

Brian had learned the hard way that taking the wrong turn in a war zone or failing to leave a situation at the right moment can be catastrophic. To this day, he's haunted by a tragedy from his time covering the civil war in Lebanon. Brian was filming for his friend Clark Todd, the London correspondent for CTV News and a veteran of many crises. Reporting from a village in the volatile Chouf Mountains in 1983, they came under mortar fire. Clark suffered a serious chest wound, probably from shrapnel. As the bombardment continued and intensified, it became apparent that the village was about to be overrun. Brian and the rest of the crew realized that if they stayed where they were, they would undoubtedly be murdered by the Christian Lebanese militiamen who were attacking them. Clark, still conscious, insisted that they should leave and that he would stay behind. Although he assured them he'd be fine, he died there and his body wasn't recovered for another week, the remains so badly decomposed he could only be identified by his clothing. While Brian grieved, the network hung him out to dry—publicly implying that he'd deserted a dying colleague.

Brian never fully recovered from the trauma of his friend's death, and the unfairness of the accusation that he was somehow culpable. But the experience had turned an adventure-seeking young man into a shrewd and vigilant observer with well-tuned instincts for spotting trouble before it crystallized into crisis. We would trust him with our lives.

The story we were hoping to cover was that of the rapidly growing power and influence of Afghanistan's warlords—something that was being made possible largely because Washington was bankrolling them. The warlords had spent the civil war years of the early 1990s fighting each other. But in late 1996 they formed a loose coalition to become the Afghan Northern Alliance. They had one common goal: to destroy the most autocratic regime the country had known since the Communists, the Taliban. After five years of effort, the alliance had been unsuccessful in driving the Taliban from power. But with the events of 9/11, everything changed for the warlords.

Rather than deploy American troops, US president George W. Bush was happy to commission Afghanistan's warlords to do most of the ground fighting, in collaboration with American special forces. The Bush White House put Afghan commanders on CIA and Defense department payrolls just as the Reagan administration had engaged the mujahidin. For President Bush, the warlords and their militias were much cheaper and less politically fraught than US soldiers, and the Afghans shared a common enemy with the Americans—the Taliban, along with its client, al-Qaeda. With Washington's involvement, the warlords hit the jackpot, raking in tens of millions of US dollars in cash that arrived in military transport vehicles, suitcases and sometimes just plastic grocery sacks.

Rashid Dostum—a man who had shifted allegiances more often than some people change their socks—was a principal commander with the Northern Alliance and he quickly became the darling of the Bush administration. The White House may or may not have understood that General Dostum's one-time allegiance to Moscow had been the reason why the Soviet Union was able to resist Reagan's covert operations in Afghanistan for as long as it did. But now the Pentagon embraced Dostum as a hero. Defense Secretary Donald Rumsfeld gleefully released photos that showed members of the US Army's 5th Special Forces Group riding horseback alongside the Northern Alliance as they stormed across the windy foothills of northern Afghanistan, with General Dostum in the lead. Rumsfeld claimed that Taliban fighters spontaneously threw down their weapons and ran away or surrendered to Dostum and the Northern Alliance when they saw what appeared to be the cavalry coming. The Taliban capitulation probably had more to do with the terrifying and deadly barrage of US bombs that had been pummelling enemy positions for days before Dostum arrived.

In the wake of 9/11, the White House had launched what appeared to be a kind of medieval Crusade against radical Islam, a perception that the Bush administration did little to discourage. While the image played well among Republicans in particular, a solid majority of Americans supported the Afghan invasion and many of them believed that it was actually the tenets of the Muslim faith that had inspired the devastating attack. President Bush knew he had wide latitude to demonize the enemy, though he grudgingly agreed to change the name of the US mission from Operation Infinite Justice to Operation Enduring Freedom when a number of prominent American Muslims complained Infinite Justice sounded like a holy war.

What Bush and Rumsfeld did not want to discuss with the media were the shady backgrounds of their warlord heroes, many of whom had long rap sheets of atrocities. The warlords stood accused of horrendous crimes committed against Afghans during the country's civil war but the White House didn't seem bothered. It wouldn't even acknowledge allegations of more recent crimes; news reports that General Dostum and his men, while working with US forces, had massacred possibly thousands of jihadist fighters who had surrendered as prisoners of war. Heather, Brian and I were determined to find out who the White House's warlords really were, and what they had done, before and after the Americans arrived.

We needed to hire a local person as our fixer, someone who could translate native languages and make connections for us. Our CBC colleagues, Kas Roussy and Céline Galipeau, were leaving Kabul and we were hoping to inherit the man who had been working with them. But their employee had already been lured away by another TV crew. Kas and Céline knew that without good local staff we would be lost in Afghanistan and they took the time to find us someone before they departed Kabul for another assignment.

Kas and Céline set up an appointment with Sher Shah Sarbaz but when they met him, they had their doubts. He arrived for the job interview in threadbare shalwar kameez, and wearing a traditional flat-topped woollen cap known as a *pakol*. He sported a thick, unkempt black beard and looked very much like a mujahidin. In fact, he resembled a younger version of the most famous of Afghanistan's freedom fighters, the Lion of Panjshir, Ahmad Shah Massoud. Sher Shah's English was good, but Kas and Céline were concerned that his appearance would compromise our access to NATO and US compounds where the authorities are often uncomfortable in the presence of Afghans who look too authentic. Sher Shah didn't look much different from most men on the streets of Kabul, but that was just the problem: the occupying armies didn't trust most people on the streets.

Kas and Céline switched to speaking in French during the interview in order to privately discuss his demeanour, but Sher Shah interrupted, assuring them in flawless French that they wouldn't be disappointed if he were hired. He got the job. When Heather and I met him, he was clean-shaven and wearing blue jeans. He explained that he had only just returned to Kabul from Pakistan when he went for the job interview. He had been travelling by road, which was only safe to do dressed as he had been and with a full beard. Sher Shah was a qualified pilot who could have been working for Ariana, the Afghan domestic airline. But he made much better wages using his language skills to assist foreign reporters and he knew how to work his connections to get access to the most difficult locations. In the time that we worked with him, Sher Shah would show up in various guises, depending on what the circumstances called for. Sometimes he looked like any man on you'd see in Kabul, other times like someone who would easily blend in on the streets of Toronto. He was a chameleon.

We told Sher Shah we were interested in meeting with some of the warlords who seemed to be thriving under American control of Afghanistan. He suggested we interview Burhanuddin Rabbani, a Northern Alliance commander who had been the last president of Afghanistan before the Taliban took over. Rabbani was believed responsible for ordering attacks on civilian populations during the civil war, most notoriously for a well-documented massacre of Shia Muslims. But he was now among those warlords benefiting from the large amounts of cash arriving regularly from the United States. At Sher Shah's request, Rabbani's media handler dropped by our hotel and we told him we wanted to set up a sit-down, on-camera interview with his boss. He gave our bureau office a quick once-over and, having determined that we were serious, told us we should be at the presidential palace at three o'clock. We thought it odd that the interview would take place in the office of the president but we learned that Rabbani was occupying the Arg, as the presidential residence is called, and refused to move.

Officially, Hamid Karzai was Afghanistan's interim leader, appointed at an international conference in Bonn just weeks earlier. But Rabbani had been Afghanistan's president before the Taliban seized power in 1996 and now that the Taliban was gone he believed he was the rightful resident of the Arg. The US was planning to hold an election as soon as the dust settled and it fully expected that Karzai would then be ceremoniously voted in as president. The snag was that Rabbani refused to go along with the plan. The Americans were paying almost all the bills but it was evident they still weren't calling all the shots.

Rabbani's record of war crimes wasn't the reason the US rejected his claims to the presidency. In fact, the Americans would have financed him in some other government position as it was doing with most of the former mujahidin leaders. The problem for the US was that Rabbani wasn't their man. He didn't speak English nor did he look the part of the "new Afghanistan" that the Americans were trying to project. Hamid Karzai, on the other hand, was a diplomat; a smooth and capable operator. He was thirty years younger than Rabbani and strikingly handsome with chiselled features and carefully groomed whiskers. He was always seen in his trademark *chapan* coat of green, gold and purple stripes, worn casually draped over his shoulders as a cape. Karzai's nonspecific Afghan look played well in the West and fashionistas even marketed the Karzai signature *karakul* hat, until their clients discovered it was made from the wool of aborted lamb fetuses. Rabbani, on the other hand, wore a turban, and had a billowy white beard and a fierce warrior countenance. No fashion company was copying his clothing style. But he was of particular interest to us because he was a seasoned warlord who also happened to be ensconced in the President's Office, at least for now.

Our drive to the palace was painstakingly slow, due to the snow-covered streets and heavy traffic. Since the US occupation, Kabul was perpetually snarled with cars and trucks, some military, many hired by the NGOs and journalists who needed rugged vehicles and drivers who could negotiate the many US Army checkpoints. Everywhere in Kabul, there were posters and pictures celebrating Ahmad Shah Massoud, the Lion of Panjshir, who symbolized for many Afghans their resistance to the Soviets and to the Taliban. With his world-weary expression and his traditional *pakol* cap, images of Massoud had appeared spontaneously in public places as soon as the Taliban fled the city. While Karzai and Rabbani vied for control of the Arg, many people thought Massoud would have been the ideal leader. But Massoud had been dead for several months, presumably murdered by al-Qaeda.

The timing of Massoud's assassination, just two days before 9/11, could not have been a coincidence. There has never been a proper investigation, but the assumption is that Osama bin Laden wanted Massoud dead before the attack on the United States. The al-Qaeda leader feared, quite rightly, that the Lion of Panjshir would expel bin Laden's terrorist network from the country. In death, Massoud was becoming more mythical by the day, compared by some Western journalists to Cuba's revolutionary freedom fighter, Che Guevara. Many Afghans spoke about his commitment to a multi-ethnic Afghanistan, the equality of women, human rights and democratic institutions and free elections. People who had visited Massoud in Panjshir province, northeast of Kabul, said his house had been filled with books and he'd been able to converse with US ambassadors as easily as tribal chiefs. Osama bin Laden hated him; and for reasons no one has ever been able to explain, Ronald Reagan and the CIA didn't like him either, preferring to back an America-bashing extremist by the name of Gulbuddin Hekmatyar. Very few of the hundreds of millions of dollars the US supplied to mujahidin jihadists during the war against the Soviets ever made it into the hands of Massoud and his allies. Many wonder where the world would be today if the US had backed him instead.

When we got to the palace, Rabbani's security personnel spent hours checking our equipment before the interview. (Massoud had been killed by two men posing as journalists.) Even so, they failed to find Brian's pocket knife or to even notice my little camera, a common hiding place for explosives. It didn't surprise me to learn, years later, that Rabbani was assassinated in his own home by visitors posing as peace envoys from the Taliban. The killers had concealed explosives in their turbans.

Although Rabbani claimed to support equal rights for women, Sher Shah recommended that Heather and I cover our heads, the only occasion he ever requested that. The interview turned out to be a bland conversation wherein Rabbani denied he had ever been engaged in anything more than legitimate warfare. His only message was that the Americans didn't understand Afghanistan, which, under the circumstances, was an understatement.

Sher Shah knew it had not gone well for us. On our way back to the Mustafa Hotel, he told me he had arranged a meeting with someone who might prove to be more useful. Sher Shah had recently encountered a man who had a story to tell, a man who might be able to get us very close to Rashid Dostum. He described his contact as a fellow tribesman, a member of the Jaji clan of Paktia province, whose relatives were some of Sher Shah's closest friends. There was a strong bond of trust as a result of those connections and Sher Shah was certain his contact would come through. And sure enough, when we got back to the Mustafa, after hours spent snaking through heavy traffic and dragging all our kit up the four flights of stairs, there he was, sitting in our bureau.

It's almost impossible for me to now recall my first impressions of the man I met on that winter's day in 2002, a man whose face and demeanour I've come to know so well. At the time, he struck me as characteristic of most of the Pashtun men that I'd seen. Dressed in shalwar kameez, he sat in the sun-drenched room, legs crossed, his expression friendly but also watchful. There was nothing in the moment to suggest this man would one day shake the foundations of what I thought my role as a journalist should be.

Sher Shah introduced us to Asadullah Aryubwal. Most Afghans use only one name, but if Westerners insist, as we usually do, they offer their clan name as well, which refers to where they are from. Asadullah was a Jaji from Aryub, referring to a village or tribe in Paktia province. "Wal" means "people." So "Aryubwal" means "people from Aryub." As I came to know him better, I began to refer to him as his family does, simply as Asad.

In the detailed diaries I kept, I described a man who looked much older than his thirty-nine years. His complexion was leathery and deeply lined, probably from the harsh Afghan weather, I thought, but I later found out it was also from a lifetime of stress. His head was covered with a thicket of dark hair and he wore an equally dense brown beard flecked with grey. His eyes were difficult to read. There were flashes of mischief but they became flat black when he described the grim realities of life in Afghanistan. Just as quickly, he would break into an infectious grin.

What I also noted was a sudden revival of my spirits. Here we had a living, breathing Afghan who seemed prepared to talk—on the record—about the reality behind what was being projected by politicians here and in the West as the "new Afghanistan." Plus, if we understood him correctly, he personally knew the most notorious and well funded of the Afghan warlords, Rashid Dostum. He had served in Dostum's army—as a general, no less. And he was willing to be critical of Dostum and all the warlords. Publicly. This was what we in journalism call "a get." The man would also go with us right into the heart of Dostum territory. If all of this panned out, he could drive the narrative of our documentary.

Asad seemed reliable. He was willing to speak only about matters of which he was factually confident, which was a good sign with regard to his credibility—for instance, he could not corroborate a *New York Times* account of the alleged massacre by Dostum's people of Taliban prisoners of war. Asad had been living in Kabul when it happened and the atrocities took place in the north, near the city of Mazar-e-Sharif. But he said that the story was consistent with what he knew of Dostum's character. He was well aware of the warlord's capacity for cruelty and he'd had many opportunities to see him in action when Asad was living in Mazar-e-Sharif, near the Qala-i-Jangi Fort where some of the POWs had been incarcerated before they were killed.

Asad briefed us on life under the warlord: Dostum ran northern Afghanistan as his private fiefdom and he exerted a level of control over people's lives somewhere between that of a Mafia don and a medieval prince. In the years of Afghanistan's civil war he had allegedly tortured and murdered people, including his own soldiers when they defied him. His men had sexually assaulted women and, in some cases, Asad had heard that they mutilated the women's breasts. To challenge Dostum even over small matters was all but suicidal.

So we asked why he was willing to talk to us. Did he have a death wish? We had found no one else willing to say such things, never mind on the record.

He told us that he was deeply disturbed to see the United States collaborating with warlords and he hoped that, by speaking out, he would help to warn the foreign troops of their disastrous liaison with men who were, in his mind, war criminals. What good was it to rid his country of the Taliban only to empower those who had been robbing and murdering innocent Afghans for years? Asad could make no sense of it: Why would a country he admired, the United States, engage someone who shared none of its values? Dostum's mayhem had been documented by any number of international human rights agencies well before Washington engaged the Northern Alliance as its surrogate. The US could not be—or should not have been—ignorant of Dostum's past.

Asad wasn't naïve about politics. He had witnessed the self-serving nature of US policy when the Americans had abandoned Afghanistan after the Soviet withdrawal. And yet he wanted to believe that this time they would see things differently if only there was some way of demonstrating the dangers of empowering the likes of Dostum. He also thought the Westerners who were arriving by the day, including those from Canada, would give him the security to speak freely for the first time in decades. Asad had been thrilled to see Americans and NATO forces chase out the Taliban. He believed that his country would now experience a renaissance and become a modern society where he could raise his family, educate his children, live in peace and speak his mind, if only the foreigners could get it right.

Asad agreed to give us an interview. He would say it all on camera. And he would take us to the north, into Dostum's heartland, and show us what he considered to be a crime scene.

We sat for hours that afternoon, while fresh snow fell on Kabul, obscuring our view of the Hindu Kush, the mountain range we would need to cross in order to get to Mazar-e-Sharif. Someone from the hotel arrived with a barrel of sawdust to stoke our stove, providing enough warmth to get through the night. As the room filled with radiated heat, we sketched out a plan to investigate the relationship between Dostum's Northern Alliance and the United States government. Asad would be our guide and the main character of our documentary.

We knew about the legendary hospitality of Afghans, but it was still unusual for foreign reporters to be invited to someone's house, especially so soon after the Taliban had been running the country's affairs. Asad, however, insisted that we meet his wife and five children. He lived in one of the old Soviet-style cinderblock and cement apartment complexes near Airport Road, a district once occupied by Communist Party apparatchiks but now the home of what remained of Kabul's professional class. Brian wanted to film the former general walking in his neighbourhood and he also hoped to capture him at home with his family. We got our pictures and then Asad's wife, Mobina, along with his two older daughters, served up a feast of Afghan food.

Mobina was from the Persian north of Afghanistan. Her features were Tajik—high cheekbones, a broad forehead and coal-black eyes. She had been a teacher before the Taliban banished women from the profession. Her two sons had been permitted to attend classes under Sharia law but her daughters were prohibited from engaging in any studies. So Mobina started up her own clandestine school for girls, at home. It was risky but when neighbours heard what she was doing, they begged her to help their daughters as well. Soon Mobina was teaching about twenty girls and young women, including the children of some Taliban. Asad supported her completely, even though he knew that, if the school was detected, he would be severely punished; jailed and possibly executed.

To say the least, this family wasn't typical of Afghan households. Or perhaps we had been influenced by shallow stereotypes. They showed us how educated, middle-class Kabulis were living in post-Taliban Afghanistan and it provided us with a window on an aspect of this complicated country that we might never have discovered otherwise. It was clear that Asad and Mobina had a love marriage: they were equal partners in their union and they were raising their sons and daughters with little distinction between genders—all of which was unusual in the larger Afghan society. Their oldest child was Robina— Ruby—a fourteen-year-old girl who spoke English and French and was comfortable in conversation with strangers; she told animated stories of life under the Taliban. Everyone in the family was happy that this dark period of their history had passed.

It was a delightful visit and if there was a downside at all it was that in the back of my mind there was a tiny wedge of worry: What might happen to this man and to this family after we were gone? It was a question that my first visit to Pakistan had taught me to always consider. But we had work to do.

II

The Massacre at
Dasht-i-Leili

IT WAS A COLD BUT BRILLIANT BLUE DAY when we set out from Kabul traveling north in two vehicles to accommodate a team that now included Asad and our TV gear. We drove through the Shomali Plains, known as "Kabul's gardens" back in the day when it was the most fertile zone in the country and families would come here for walks and picnics. But the area had been a major battleground in the Soviet war of the 1980s; then again when civil war erupted in the 1990s. What we saw was a wasteland, littered with rusting artillery pieces and armoured personnel carriers; not a house or tree in sight and no evidence of life. The ground was punctuated with red-painted stones—warnings that this once-verdant farmland had since become one of the most lethal minefields in the world.

Asad pointed out locations where some of the decisive battles had taken place. The evidence was obvious—the abandoned machinery of war, the remnants of trenches and defensive bunkers. In the Panjshir Valley we crossed a pontoon bridge that was ingeniously supported by the twisted body of a Soviet tank. Various militias fought each other here for years, only to change allegiances and join forces to fight other militias. The valleys and hills were haunted by the souls of tens of thousands who died here having accomplished nothing.

We could save three days of travel over the Hindu Kush range by going through the newly reopened Salang Tunnel, a three-kilometre route that had been one of the Soviets' boldest engineering accomplishments during its occupation of the country. The tunnel was abandoned in the 1990s after Massoud triggered an avalanche to block his then-adversary, General Dostum, from advancing south to Kabul. It had become drivable again just three days before our trip. The passageway was narrow, still badly damaged and treacherous, but it was a shortcut to our destination—Dostum's northern stronghold, Mazar-e-Sharif.

Even the usually rock-steady Brian Kelly found driving through this dark and crumbling tunnel a nerve-wracking experience. The air was heavy with exhaust fumes and the only light came from holes blown through the walls by artillery shelling during past battles. It was a relief to be greeted by sunshine at the other end, even with the blast of icy wind and drifting snow that accompanied it. Asad pointed out a place in the mountains where Dostum's army had camped out for a year, trying to get through Massoud's blockade—a stalemate that was only resolved when the two joined forces to take on the Taliban.

The descent on almost sheer ice made driving treacherous and we soon pulled over onto the side of the road to wrap the wheels of our vehicles with chains. I'm not sure who started it, but we were soon all caught up in a snowball fight and carrying on like giddy children on the first day of winter. Asad warned us not to leave the hard-surfaced road—the fields and ditches were probably infested with landmines. But he was otherwise like a boy just let out of school and it was intriguing to see this other side of him. He had seemed troubled for most of the trip so far but now he and Sher Shah were frolicking in the snow.

Our drivers finished with the chains and joined the game but one of them took me by surprise when he hurled a chunk of ice. Asad told me later that our driver, like many Afghans, was unreceptive to the presence of foreigners in his country. Over the course of our travels in Afghanistan, we encountered more hostility—but just as often we were treated to hospitality that was almost excessive. Sher Shah explained it was part of a code of conduct known as *Pashtunwali*. Under its rubric, Afghans are expected to provide lavishly for any and all visitors, be they friend or foe. They are also required to offer sanctuary in their homes to any who require it—even if it's someone who has hurt them. But a Pashtun is also obliged to seek justice on behalf of one's clan and to inflict punishing revenge on those who harm kith or kin. The Pakistani superspy, the late General Hamid Gul, a former head of the ISI (Inter-Services Intelligence), once told a Canadian

A snowball fight during the trip to Mazar-e-Sharif. Asad and Sher Shah flank our driver.

colleague of mine that "the Afghan" will welcome you into his home, feed and entertain you with great warmth, "then shoot you in the back the moment you step off his property." I was confident we would not meet such a fate.

As we continued north and down the mountain, the valley softened to a pale green with an early wheat crop that appeared like a wash of colour on the landscape. The villages of Baghlan province were poor yet functional, with irrigation systems, brooks and rivers flowing clean and fast off the Hindu Kush. There was less destruction here than elsewhere in the country, where decades of war had decimated the infrastructure. By nightfall, we arrived at the halfway point in our journey, Pol-e-Khumry, a grim town distinguished from the surrounding emptiness by a looming grain elevator.

Brian, Heather and I shared a cramped, cold little room in a Swedish guesthouse. The others spent the night in the home of a local family that was distantly related to both Sher Shah and Asad. We joined them there the next day where we met their hosts, the Rahman family. The head of the household was a former police commander who had been wounded in a battle with the Taliban and had been held prisoner by them for three years. And yet Habib Rahman declared an opinion that we would hear frequently—that the Taliban, for all their faults, had been not as bad as the alternative. At least you knew where you stood with the Taliban, he said, unlike the uncertainty inherent in the corrupt inconsistencies of General Dostum and his henchmen.

The Rahmans are a conventional Muslim clan and, consequently, the unrelated men in our party were not invited to meet female members of the family. But as women, Heather and I are allowed entry into the cloistered parts of Afghan homes and as soon as the Rahman sisters, Nasreen and Zarina, learned we were among the foreign guests, they asked that we be escorted to their private quarters immediately.

The sitting room where the sisters could shed their head covers and relax was warm and light-filled with a pot-bellied stove, big cushions and a samovar. The women were in their early twenties, well educated, with a good command of the English language, which they had learned on their own. They were dressed very simply, in plain shalwar kameez, but the conversation was vibrant and lively, full of questions and observations. As we chatted over tea and snacks, I felt slightly guilty that Brian, Asad and Sher Shah were confined to the cold and less-interesting formal living room where the Rahman men held court.

Nasreen and Zarina wanted to reveal a secret. They led Heather and me into a back garden, through rose bushes and plum trees, to a doorway of what seemed to be a garage. Inside we saw a heap of blue burqas tossed into a corner near a jumble of women's shoes. We climbed a steep wooden stairway to a large room where we were greeted by a crowd of animated young women, dressed in bright dresses, their hair uncovered and faces on full display with kohl-lined eyes and bright shades of lipstick. It was a burst of colour and energy I had seen nowhere else on our journey and it was a welcome relief. These women were obviously the escapees from the burqas we had seen downstairs.

This was a school for young women, still operating in semi-secret since no one could be sure the Taliban—and their woeful influences— were really gone. The Rahman sisters had been teaching female students just as Mobina, Asad's wife, had done, during the years when they were officially banned from schools. The students were brimming with questions posed in halting English for two Canadian women who were travelling unaccompanied by male family members. We were thousands of kilometres from home, working on our own, and we were just as fascinating and exotic to them as they were to us.

Once we'd satisfied their curiosity about life in Canada, Heather asked them what they thought of women like us. They sought the word in English but finally reverted to their own language. Nasreen laughed as she translated. "It's a Pashto expression. It means 'lion-hearted.'" Then one student blurted out in English, "Women are going to the moon. Why can't they go to work in another country?" I didn't tell them that it wasn't so long ago when my own news agency would have refused to send me here.

To some extent, the sisters shared their father's view that the Taliban had not been all that bad, which surprised me considering how they had been forced to live. But their family was conservative and their rights and opportunities were limited even in the absence of the Taliban. Though the family abhorred the lack of schools for women, the Taliban had provided security. Dostum's private army, known to them as the Junbish militia—the military wing of the warlord's political party—had acted with impunity, looting, kidnapping, extorting ransom, sexually abusing women and executing people who got in their way. It's difficult to imagine but the Taliban had been regarded as an improvement.

The Rahman household encompassed many contradictions. Purdah, the practice of separating the sexes by keeping women veiled and behind walls and curtains, was enforced, and the women couldn't show their faces publicly. But Habib, their father, understood that he had bright and ambitious daughters who should not be stifled. He had allowed this school to function, undoubtedly risking punishment, so his daughters could provide instruction to their pupils. Yet his own wife remained almost invisible during our visit, a mere shadow lurking in the background even when there were no men around. The Rahmans had wealth and a sophisticated world view and yet Habib limited the women's freedom to the home, bound as he was to culture and tradition. Having seen the energy, curiosity and determination of the young women in the secret school, I wondered how much longer they could be repressed.

As Heather and I helped to load our vehicles to continue on the journey to Mazar, a side gate opened at the back of the Rahman house and a line of silent burqa-clad figures filed out. I recognized some of the shoes that I'd seen piled helter-skelter at the bottom of the stairway to their secret school, and as I watched the women go, I saw a hand escape the folds of stifling blue cloth to wave goodbye.

It's perhaps significant that Afghanistan's only female warlord, Bibi Ayesha, actually lives in this same province, not far from the Rahmans. She was considered to be as bloody-minded as any man, fiercely resisting the Soviets when they invaded Afghanistan and killing Dostum's men until she joined with him and the Northern Alliance to take on the Taliban. At the height of her power in the 1990s, Ayesha commanded 150 armed men, but she never went into battle unless accompanied by a male member of her family—to protect the honour of her clan, if not her life.

We drove through farmlands and then up snowy winding roads through villages populated mostly by ethnic Tajiks and Uzbeks, their Persian and Mongol features distinguishing them in subtle ways from the darker-skinned ethnic Pashtuns who make up Afghanistan's majority. Asad pointed out more locations where there had been vicious battles between Dostum and Massoud, and he also told us he harboured no feelings of reverence for the martyred Lion of Panjshir. He regarded Massoud as just another warlord, even if his crimes weren't as excessive as those of others. But in crucial ways Asad believed Massoud was worse than other commanders. He was charismatic and he could have used his considerable influence to negotiate a compromise; to end the war and spare the lives of Afghans. But Massoud was too determined to emerge from the civil war as the most powerful warrior in Afghanistan. To that end, he had once sanctioned an attack on Afghanistan's Shia Muslims and had attempted to rid the north of its Pashtun population. In Asad's assessment, the Lion of Panjshir had been driven by ego. This was not an assessment of Massoud I had heard elsewhere but we would learn that Asad had unconventional views on many subjects and was not afraid to make them known.

We carried on through Tangi Tashqurghan, a narrow mountain pass where American B-52s had carpet-bombed Taliban positions just months earlier. The powerful and sustained aerial assault had provided a tremendous advantage to the Northern Alliance, allowing it to rout the jihadists in the region. Abandoned ordnance littered the roadside while an unexploded bomb sat in the brook just below the gorge. A lone man with a shovel and wheelbarrow appeared to be trying to clear away the tons of rubble to let vehicles, including ours, pass more easily. It seemed an impossible job and we gave the wheelbarrow man some money, for which he seemed immensely grateful.

As we drove away, our driver glanced in his rear-view mirror and laughed, telling us that the man was now returning the rubble to the middle of the road to await the next carload of dupes who might come along and pity him. The driver had now added "stupid" to the growing list of reasons why he despised us.

After a barely edible lunch at a roadside diner, where taciturn men lounged on rugs watching Bollywood movies on TV, we made our final approach to Mazar-e-Sharif.

Massoud posters had been everywhere in Kabul, but in Mazar it was Rashid Dostum's image that was ubiquitous, testimony to his years as the reigning despot here. The general's moon-shaped face with its thick, arched eyebrows wasn't just on walls and billboards; it was also on the money. As far as I know, Dostum is the only warlord in Afghanistan who actually printed his own currency with his own likeness on all the bills. The dostum was the coin of the realm in the north and the legal tender in the region, along with American dollars. When we arrived in Mazar, the dostum was trading at 56,000 to the US dollar. The afghani, legal tender in the rest of the country, had been trading at 36,000 to the US dollar when we left Kabul, which was a better exchange rate, but the dostum was apparently more stable.

Mazar-e-Sharif is the capital of Balkh province and it would have been an uninspiring place if not for the stunning Shrine of Hazrat Ali with its luminous blue dome in the centre of the town. Mazar-e-Sharif means "noble shrine" and this dazzling structure was worthy of the title: the blue-tiled minarets and the vaulted roof seemed to glow as if from an internal light. The city itself was jittery, bustling with military traffic and reckless drivers who had scant regard for pedestrians or traffic signs. Most were US Army vehicles but there were also Japanese-made pickups full of smirking Afghan men brandishing Kalashnikovs and rocket-propelled grenade launchers. They made for an intimidating presence, armed to the teeth in spite of having undertaken to surrender their weapons to the American forces after the Taliban had been expelled.

We had been hoping for an encounter with Dostum but the Uzbek general was nowhere to be found in Mazar. There was speculation that he had fled the country, possibly because of the recently published news reports that his lieutenants had massacred Taliban prisoners of war. But there was no doubt in anyone's mind that Dostum would be back. He had ruled the north for decades, having consolidated his control over the region after he ingratiated himself with the all-powerful forces of the Red Army.

When the USSR invaded Afghanistan in 1979, Dostum had been employed as a member of an armed security detail for Afghanistan's state-owned gas refineries in the Mazar region. The Soviets needed men like Dostum to protect their supply routes into the interior of the country and Moscow liked the cut of his jib. Balkh province butts up against both Tajikistan and Uzbekistan, which at the time were republics of the USSR, and tight control of northern Afghanistan allowed the Soviets a deeper reach into Central Asia. Dostum was more than willing to protect those interests.

He amassed a semi-private army, drawing not only from his Uzbek ethnic group but also from the ranks of Tajiks and Hazaras. At the behest of the Kremlin, Dostum maintained control of northern Afghanistan and in exchange for his loyalty he was allowed to do as he pleased. Even after the Soviet withdrawal, and through years of civil war, the warlord continued to hold sway over eleven northern provinces, a third of Afghanistan, with the support of his mercenary fighters. Other than Asad, few people would publicly discuss the dark side of life under the man who was known locally as the Uzbek Pasha.

We went to the bustling Kifayat Market in downtown Mazar-e-Sharif where Asad had once owned a wholesale business selling tea, soap and cigarettes and where he had spent his days trying to stay off of Dostum's radar, even after he'd been recruited into the warlord's ranks. In the 1990s, when the Taliban took control of the south and began to fight its way north toward Mazar, Asad had also been among those who briefly entertained the thought that the Taliban might be an improvement. He freely admits now that he had been wrong, but his willingness to consider Mullah Omar as the supreme leader is testimony to how bad life was under the Uzbek Pasha.

The Taliban had roared into Mazar in 1997, launching an orgy of killing. Asad had closed his shop at that time and fled the region while Dostum and his army retreated—the first time they had ever been defeated on home turf. Dostum had not been able to reclaim his northern empire until November 2001, when US Special Forces arrived and American bombs flushed out the Taliban. This trip to Mazar-e-Sharif to help us investigate Dostum's alleged war crimes was Asad's first venture back in five years.

This is what we know of what's called the massacre at Dasht-i-Leili.

In November 2001, as Taliban fighters beat a hasty retreat before the advancing Northern Alliance, thousands of them became stranded and trapped in the province of Kunduz. Those men agreed to surrender to Dostum's forces with the understanding that they would turn over all their weapons and go home. The UN would take custody of the foreign fighters in their midst. Most of the Taliban were Afghans but a large number had come from other places including Pakistan, the Caucasus and the Middle East. Among their ranks was an American, John Walker Lindh. The US wanted to interrogate some of the POWs, especially those from other countries, and possibly transport high-value captives, such as Lindh, to their newly created prison facility in Guantanamo Bay, Cuba.

As many as five hundred selected prisoners were transported to Qala-i-Jangi, a fortress under General Dostum's control near Mazar-e-Sharif, where the CIA had unfettered access to them. Several Western journalists and TV crews had managed to get into the fort and were present for the prisoner hand-off. They filmed some very revealing scenes of the captives and how they were treated by the CIA.

From the videos, we can see the POWs had their arms tied behind their backs as they were brought out of a holding cell, then searched and made to kneel on the ground in an open area of the fort. CIA interrogators move through their ranks, badgering and threatening them with serious consequences if they fail to cooperate. Though it's not clear that the US agents knew at the time that Lindh is American, a CIA operative is on tape saying to him that he must decide whether he wants to live or die. Witnesses to the event said later that the captives regarded these death threats as a violation of the understanding they'd had when they'd surrendered. On film, you can see them become quite agitated as the CIA harasses them.

The interrogations continue but the Northern Alliance men appear incompetent. They try to maintain control over the POWs, who are becoming more difficult to manage as the CIA becomes more forceful. The next sequence of events is not entirely clear but it seems that some of the prisoners were able to overwhelm their captors and seize firearms. Other POWs, who had managed to conceal grenades in their clothing before they were captured, detonated their explosives, killing some of Dostum's people. Johnny Michael Spann, the CIA agent who had interrogated Lindh, was also slain, becoming the first US casualty of the war.

Prisoners then seized more weapons and engaged their captors in a fierce gunfight. POWs who were unable to escape died in the open field, their arms still securely tied behind their backs. Dozens of others managed to disappear into a rabbit's warren of underground tunnels known to those who had been in Qala-i-Jangi before. Through those passages, the POWs located weapons and ammunition depots with which they launched a full-scale revolt against the Northern Alliance and the foreign troops.

Spann's companions called for air support but they urged caution. There were American and British agents in the close confines of the compound in addition to Dostum's men. The US military response was anything but restrained. A barrage of bombs, including a guided device that weighed a ton, killed and wounded prisoners and Afghan allies with little distinction. Despite the overwhelming US aerial assault, the standoff lasted more than a week until all the POWs had been killed or recaptured.

When Heather, Brian and I arrived at Qala-i-Jangi, we couldn't get closer than the gate until Asad used his leverage to convince the guards to let us in. I doubt that the doors would have opened had Dostum been in town but in his absence, the man in charge of the fort trusted Asad and accepted whatever persuasive arguments our friend presented.

It had been less than two months since the prisoners had been in the fort, and the events were still clear in the minds of Dostum's men. Another senior commander, General Kayum, gave us a tour of the fort and explained the role he had personally played in quelling the uprising. He said that the US aerial attack had caused a lot of damage but had done little to restore control. Kayum claims that he managed to end the battle when he flooded the underground tunnels with ice-cold water that he had pumped in from nearby irrigation canals. He said that Dostum had ordered this tactic only after everything else had failed, including pouring oil into the underground and setting a match to it. While these manoeuvres forced the survivors out, an unknown number of them suffocated from the smoke or drowned in the irrigation water.

Of the five hundred men incarcerated at Qala-i-Jangi at the beginning of that week, only eighty-six came out alive. Many of those survivors later died of their injuries. Kayum seemed indifferent to the death count.

Everywhere in the fort we could see remnants of black turbans in the rubble, unwound and fashioned into tethers. In the film footage captured by the reporters, POWs had been forced to surrender their turbans; the cloth was then used to bind their arms. Witnesses claim that some of the prisoners were summarily executed; their corpses found still bound tightly with their turbans. We saw white embroidered skull caps with bullet holes through them and spent shell cartridges everywhere. There were claims that some of the less militant prisoners had begged for mediation in an effort to surrender but they were refused. International human rights agencies called for an investigation, arguing that the high death count at Qala-i-Jangi indicated that this was as much a massacre as it was an uprising. But the US government turned down the demands for an independent review of the events.

The remaining Taliban prisoners who had surrendered, numbering in the thousands, were to be transported to another prison under Dostum's command in a place called Sheberghan. Many of these militants were teenagers and young men who had little experience in war and had believed they were defending their homeland from an invader. They were loaded into shipping containers mounted on trucks, two or three hundred men in each cargo, squeezed in tightly with no food or water and, according to survivors, compelled to lick each other's sweat to quench their thirst. It took days to transport the captives a distance of only a few dozen miles and during that time many of the POWs suffocated.

The most complete account of the event comes from Irish documentary filmmaker Jamie Doran, who obtained interviews with survivors and truck drivers. The witnesses claim that many of the prisoners died when Northern Alliance soldiers shot through the walls of the containers after the captives demanded ventilation. All of the dead prisoners, including those from the fort, are believed to have been buried in mass graves at a place called Dasht-i-Leili. Dostum later admitted to logistical mistakes, acknowledging that perhaps a few hundred of the POWs were killed by accident. But Doran's film features a man in Kunduz province who claims to have negotiated the surrender of the prisoners. He insists that eight thousand militants had turned themselves over to Dostum's command, and most of them have never been accounted for since. In the absence of an investigation the precise number of dead remains unknown.

Afghan soldiers, truck drivers and surviving POWs told journalists and human rights investigators that US military and intelligence personnel were aware of the unnecessary deaths in the fort and those in the deadly shipping containers. Jamie Doran's documentary, *The Convoy of Death,* has images of what he believes to be American soldiers at the prison in Sheberghan where the trucks full of dead and near-dead POWs arrived. Given that the US had control over the region, in addition to satellite surveillance of Dasht-i-Leili, Doran maintains they could have intervened to prevent what was probably a war crime. But they didn't. The Americans were also warned in advance that there might be reprisal killings of the remaining Taliban fighters, since the Northern Alliance militias had suffered many casualties at the fort. In response, the Pentagon issued a statement to Doran, affirming that "no American had taken part or observed any atrocity at Dasht-i-Leili or Sheberghan."

The damage to Qala-i-Jangi when we saw it in January 2002 was considerable. General Kayum gave us surprising access to what was a potential crime scene and it was astonishing how much evidence was still around. It was as if the battle had happened the day before—the place was a garbage heap of spent munitions while every wall in the prison area had been riddled by the bullets. Bits of torn clothing littered the tunnels where the POWs had spent their final hours.

At all times during our visit we were surrounded by dozens of Northern Alliance men. They described for us the terrifying US air-strikes and they were eager to talk about the prisoner uprising even though they couldn't imagine why it was of concern to foreign reporters. Weren't the dead men also *our* enemies? And if we cared so much about massacres, where were we over the past twenty-two years, when hun-dreds of thousands of Afghans, most of them civilians, perished in war?

After filming at the fort, we went to the US base near the centre of town where an American army major, the official spokesman, agreed to be interviewed. But he had no comment on the killing other than to observe that the insurgency at Qala-i-Jangi had been successfully sup-pressed. As for the empowerment of local warlords and their militias, Major Martin Rose declared that they were "like children" and it was best to treat them that way. He said there were no plans to disarm them because the militias were on the same side as the Americans, though Rose said the warlords and their fighters had been warned that NATO would send in peacekeepers to replace the friendly Americans if they didn't behave.

"And then all their fun will be over," he said, with a chuckle. "But we've had no encounters with them being bad," he added. "They look out for us."

In the absence of General Dostum, the resident despot in Mazar-e-Sharif at the time was Atta Muhammad Noor, a Northern Alliance commander who had also fought alongside American Special Forces. The armed men in the pickup trucks around town were his—we had presumed they were

Dostum's—flaunting the entitlement, not to mention the immunity that comes from close association with the US military. Atta and Dostum were the only Afghan commanders who had been successful in the fight against the Taliban in this region; the Americans were impressed and grateful. General Atta was the man of the hour but there was no doubt in anyone's mind that Dostum would be back in Mazar soon, once again enjoying the largesse of the Americans—if the funds had ever ceased to flow to him.

Atta was at his compound, surrounded by a legion of armed men. The soldiers were not pleased to see us, but General Atta seemed delighted by the prospect of publicity. Brian filmed him meeting local people as they paid homage just as they had once been obliged to do for General Dostum. They were civil servants who hadn't seen their wages in months and they came because General Atta now had the money to meet the city's payroll. Atta's reception room was filled with school administrators and teachers, all of them women, the veils of their burqas

Me, Asad, Sher Shah and Mobina's nephew, Haris. There were many happy moments during the trip, which was otherwise bleak and often dangerous.

flipped up over their heads to show their faces as he doled out American dollars and beamed at the women who feigned gratitude. I thought of the old cliché: He who pays the piper calls the tune. Here was proof that the "pipers" here, the warlords, were being paid by Washington.

General Atta was keen to give an interview but it didn't go the way he had hoped—we asked too many questions about what the militia had done to win the favour of the US government. Sher Shah could understand the Persian chatter around us and after a time he quietly warned that we should pack and get out of there without lingering farewells. The militiamen followed our car for a while so we didn't immediately return to where we were staying. As it turns out, our caution was irrelevant. Atta's men knew exactly where we were at all times and they rarely let us out of their sight.

We were bunking at the rustic farmhouse where Asad's wife, Mobina, had grown up and where her brother, Sayeed, and her mother, Sarah, still lived. The family owned 1,120 hectares of land in the areas around

Me, Brian and Heather at Mobina's family farm in Dehdadi.

the village of Dehdadi, just outside
Mazar, where they grew vegetables,
herbs and wheat. They also owned
their own flour mill and local farmers brought their grain there for
processing.

The family gave us a large room
where we could sleep at night and
safely leave our baggage when we
were out. We shared a meal at the
end of each day, sitting cross-legged
around a plastic tablecloth spread
out on the floor of the same room

in which we slept. The evening meal
was always animated, though Asad
often seemed guarded. He had never
hidden the fact that part of the reason

*Asad engaged some men with guns to watch
over us while we were in Mazar-e-Sharif. I
would only learn much later the true reason
for the armed presence.*

he'd come with us to Mazar was for Mobina. She was obviously from an
important and well-established family and we learned that her father
had only recently died. According to Afghan law, Mobina was entitled to
a part of the inheritance, though as a daughter her claim was less than
that of her only brother. She wanted to make sure that her sibling was
looking after their joint interests and Asad was supposed to verify that.

I assumed that Asad's wariness stemmed from some family tension,
but I also noticed that he stayed up all night, playing cards and gambling
with some nasty-looking characters. Brian remarked that there were men
with weapons who seemed to be standing guard around the house. They
hadn't been there on the day we arrived. When you're in a dangerous

place, you usually know—or you think you know—what the threats are. But the most distressing form of anxiety is a result of not being able to perceive the danger around you; just a generalized feeling of dread. I felt there was something sinister in our midst but I couldn't identify its source.

We spent a week there and had dinner with Asad's in-laws every night while they regaled us with ghost stories including one about an evil spirit with cloven hooves lurking near the family outhouse—which gave me pause before making nocturnal toilet visits. I wondered if the absence of electricity contributes to belief in the occult, in ghosts and phantoms and mythology. Something about lamplight cultivates superstition. According to the stories, the entire region was haunted by dark and brooding spirits. And given what we'd learned about the recent history of Mazar-e-Sharif and Dasht-i-Leili, this theory was entirely plausible.

Whatever apprehension I felt during those days in the north, the one person I felt I could trust was Asad. He had a mysterious dark side, judging by the company he kept at night, but his honesty and decency prevailed. We were getting the visuals and the content for our story while enjoying many memorable moments during those days at the farm that had nothing to do with the story we were trying to tell: Sher Shah wrangling an angry rooster that seemed determined to sabotage our efforts to film Asad; Mobina's mother and her seemingly bottomless supply of steaming tea; her insistence on measuring us for clothing she would make for us as gifts to take away.

Asad's disclosures, many of them on camera, were deeply unsettling. He was painting a picture for us of life under dictators like the Soviets, the warlords and the Taliban that was larger than we needed and perhaps sometimes more than he should reveal. Off-camera he introduced us to people

Sher Shah Sarbaz helping me interview Asad Aryubwal in Dehdadi, Balkh province.

who might be useful to our story and he directed our attention to the places we needed to film, sometimes even turning up to negotiate access. Thanks to this man, who two weeks before had been a stranger, we had evidence that significant offences against human rights had occurred under General Dostum's authority. And we felt confident that we could report that the United States military might have been an accomplice to those atrocities.

Television storytelling requires simple labels and doesn't allow for much context so in our CBC documentary we always refer to Asad as a former general. But it was apparent in our interviews and conversations that Asad was a general in name only. He'd been a conscript and his contribution to Dostum's military campaigns had been benign. He'd acted as a glorified gofer—arranging for the acquisition and delivery of supplies to militiamen and supervising the construction of storage depots while keeping his day job in the market. It was important for me to know that, while he'd served under Dostum, Asad had kept his hands clean.

Asad went so far as to declare on camera that he was willing to testify against his former boss, if ever the warlord should be prosecuted for his crimes. It's not clear what value Asad would have to a war crimes prosecutor. He could provide testimony concerning Dostum's character but he didn't have any special inside knowledge or documented evidence. What Asad told us about Dostum's activities could have come from many other potential sources in Mazar-e-Sharif. But no one else would speak.

Asad's true value to our documentary flowed from his courage and his fundamental honesty, his passionate belief that Afghans were entitled to the same rights, the same quality of justice, that other people in the world, especially in Europe, America and Canada, take for granted. The West had created a multi-billion-dollar tribunal in the Netherlands to prosecute former Yugoslavians for ethnic cleansing. Surely Afghanistan deserved as much consideration. If justice and reconciliation are preconditions for a lasting peace, as the UN and the White House frequently declared, why not justice for Afghanistan, starting with accountability for the many warlords who had created so much misery?

I had heard this argument often as I covered stories elsewhere in the world: Why justice for them but not for us? Why Yugoslavia and not the Congo? Why Sarajevo and not Mogadishu? Yes, there was a war crimes tribunal for Rwanda, but only because the genocide in Rwanda coincided with a genocide in Bosnia. The United Nations added Rwanda to the agenda because it was indefensible to seek justice for 600,000 dead in Europe while ignoring 800,000 slaughtered in central Africa. So what about Afghanistan after twenty-two years of war, reams of documents, eyewitness accounts and evidence of mass graves? These were questions raised in our conversations and our recorded interviews by Asadullah

Aryubwal, and in our hearts we knew they were questions that would, in all likelihood, go unanswered.

The weather shifted and snow was in the forecast for the mountain areas. We put the chains back on our tires and hoped for a speedy return to Kabul through the Salang Tunnel. But when we got there, the entrance had been sealed shut by an avalanche. It would take at least a day for the wheezing old plow on the scene to clear the heavy snow. There was no option but to look for some place to stay and we found ourselves welcomed with open arms back at the Rahman house in Pol-e-Khumry. This time Brian Kelly was declared an honorary uncle, allowing him to join the women and relax with us on pillows before the woodstove.

In the evening, Heather and I were invited to dine with the men, who now included Habib Rahman's son, Aziz. He had been absent on our previous visit and he seemed a bit surprised to find foreign women seated next to him on the floor, but he was gracious. Aziz had many compelling stories, including one about an encounter with Ayman al-Zawahiri, the second in command to Osama bin Laden, who was believed to be hiding in the mountains with other members of al-Qaeda.

I had met a number of al-Zawahiri's family members when I was on assignment in Cairo just before coming to Afghanistan. I'd been with another crew, investigating how a well-educated surgeon from an established family had ended up in an Afghan cave with Osama bin Laden. I was fascinated to hear from Aziz that al-Zawahiri, the man considered to be an inspiration behind the World Trade Center attack, had actually been here in Pol-e-Khumry just a month before 9/11, gathering supplies and, possibly, intelligence. He'd bothered no one, but made many purchases and visited the very house where we were now being entertained. Aziz said that he sold al-Zawahiri a team of horses for which he'd paid US$10,000—in cash.

"What's in store for you?" Heather asked Nasreen and Zarina before we departed. "Will you get married soon?"

The women declared that they had made a pact with their father that they would take care of his household for life and avoid the servitude of marriage altogether. They would never have their own children but the sacrifice was one they were willing to make in order to enjoy an existence of relative independence.

I wanted to know more about this difficult choice but we learned that the snowplows had managed to clear the mouth of the Salang and the tunnel was open, at least for now. We said hasty farewells, hoping to reach the passageway before a forecast storm hit the region. I was sorry to leave these delightful women. I learned much later that Habib Rahman died not long after our visit. In the absence of their open-minded father, both his daughters had married. That's the last news I have from them.

We had a few more visits and meals at Asad's home before we left Afghanistan and I found there was something about the Aryubwal family and its openness that drew me in. Maybe it was true, as Asad wanted to believe, that Afghanistan was changing, catching up with history, and was becoming an open society. Perhaps his willingness to speak the truth wasn't unique but part of a growing sensibility that was infecting the country. I allowed myself to think that the Aryubwals might be a model of the future.

More and more foreigners arrived each day with large amounts of money and a mandate to deliver goods and services, to open classrooms, to support the Afghan police and the rule of law, to build modern institutions, reform government. Ruby and her sisters could go to school. Their mother, Mobina, could return to teaching. But I also had many doubts. The Americans were already reconsidering their commitment to Afghanistan, wondering aloud if rebuilding the shattered country wasn't a task for other NATO countries now that the US had broken the despotic grip of the Taliban. The Bush administration hawks were restless, musing about another enemy, another villain in the hunt for the perpetrators of 9/11—an unlikely culprit, an enemy of all jihadists, Saddam Hussein. The US was moving on again, just as Ronald Reagan had done after his Cold War triumph. War in Iraq now seemed inevitable. No matter how motivated its people were, Afghanistan could not recover or reinvent itself without ongoing and massive financial support from the outside and that seemed increasingly unlikely.

We heard that Rashid Dostum returned to Mazar-e-Sharif not long after we'd been there, though General Atta continued to rule the region and was eventually appointed governor of Balkh province. Dostum didn't care. He now had ambitions well beyond the northern backwater as he was destined for a senior role in national affairs. When Hamid Karzai officially became president, he appointed Dostum as his special envoy for the northern regions. Canada was among the many countries that acknowledged the selection. A new Canadian ambassador, Chris Alexander, would join senior diplomats who held their noses as they welcomed the warlord into the ranks of senior statesmen. Dostum was invited to the White House. Asad's dire predictions about the prospects of justice for the Afghan people weren't so far-fetched after all.

Our television documentary, *In the Company of Warlords,* ran on CBC's *The National* and won a Gemini Award, then the highest mark of achievement in Canadian television journalism. There's no doubt in my mind that Asad's role in the story made that possible and I was grateful to him. I was also sure that my connection to him and his family was over. That's the way it is. We move on to other people and their stories. But it wouldn't be that simple this time.

I learned on my first visit to Pakistan that journalists have their best moments when others are having their worst. My career evolved, thanks in part to the success of the Afghan coverage. But Asad would suffer consequences for his involvement in our project. I would later find myself drawn back into his life with an urgency I could not have imagined during those pleasant meals and conversations in their Kabul apartment, or the later celebration of our journalistic accomplishments.

In a society held back for centuries by religious and cultural conformity, Asad was a free thinker, a man who charted an independent course for himself. He defied conventions and had paid a price for it in the past. But now these qualities would bring him to the brink of disaster. With help from me.

III

Mauled by the Russian Bear

KABUL, AFGHANISTAN
DECEMBER 1978

ASAD WAS FIFTEEN YEARS OLD WHEN his childhood, and all its youthful pleasures, came to an abrupt end. Members of Afghanistan's Special Forces arrived at his family's house on a cold December morning. They surrounded the premises before police burst through the door and began searching for all the adult men of the household.

The look of helplessness on his father's face would forever haunt Asad's memory of the man who meant the world to him but who was now being escorted out of the house in handcuffs. He watched as soldiers shoved his father through the door and towards a waiting vehicle followed by his father's brother and his cousin. Police would return later to arrest the other men of the family who had escaped the first raid.

Asad would never see any of them again.

Because he was a teenager, Asad was spared arrest but he now had to face an enormous obligation. He wasn't the oldest of the boys in his family, but the women still turned to him for direction, just as his father had done. He was now regarded as "the man of the house." Asad did what he could to comfort the women and children, especially his mother, who was shattered by the sudden disappearance of her husband. Lal Bibi was a traditional Afghan wife with no formal education. She didn't leave the house unaccompanied or with her face exposed and she lived to care for her husband, children and extended family. Though they had servants, she insisted on doing the cooking and performing many of the household chores.

Asad grew up in an elite suburb of Kabul with members of the royal family and the Afghan president, Mohammed Daoud Khan, as neighbours. It had been a world of privilege until April 1978, when hardline Marxists, members of the People's Democratic Party of Afghanistan, seized power and ousted the government. President Daoud Khan and his brother were killed in an early morning gunfight outside the presidential palace while almost all other members of the royal family were later murdered. The assassinations set off a chain of events that would catapult Afghanistan into decades of war. A cable to Washington from the US embassy in Kabul at the time summed up the so-called Saur Revolution in one line: "The Russian bear has moved south of the Hindu Kush."

Leaders of the coup d'état immediately launched a radical remodelling of Afghan society from top to bottom. They confiscated private property and outlawed traditional social customs. They set out to reform marriage, compel women to join the workforce, and shatter the influence of imams and mosques. The country was in need of social change but this was sudden and brutal, welcomed by no class of Afghan society. The coup leader and now self-appointed president, Nur Muhammad Taraki, ordered sweeping arrests of anyone regarded as an enemy of the state. His Stalinist-style purging meant that thousands of

Afghans were crammed into the notorious Pol-e-Charkhi Prison, where they suffered torture and summary execution.

The men in Asad's extended family were high-profile property owners with wide-ranging assets and as such they were prime targets for the Communists. Among the family's best-known enterprises was the Aryub Cinema—the largest and most successful movie house in Kabul. Running a business that catered to the leisure class, in addition to their considerable wealth, plus their association with the elites of Kabul society, established the Aryubwals as bourgeoisie—enemies of the Saur Revolution.

Before he was taken away, Asad's father, Muhammad Omer, had been trying to shield his family from the excesses of the new regime, allowing his children to continue living as if nothing much had changed since the takeover. Perhaps he was naïve. Perhaps he was merely trying to prolong a sense of normalcy in the face of the inevitable. But the sudden arrests of the men was a turning point. Within days, Asad and his family were evicted from their home, thirty people in all, mostly women and children. They were told to leave; to take nothing with them, not even their coats. It was a cold snowy December day in Kabul and they had nowhere to go.

Regardless of their social status, Afghans were appalled by the regime's changes and there was an outpouring of support for Asad's

Muhammad Omer, Asad's father, was arrested in 1978 and never seen by the family again.

family. Taxi drivers loaded all of them into their cabs and moved them, free of charge, to a house belonging to a relative. It was one small counter-revolutionary gesture, a harbinger of the armed resistance that would soon consume the country.

The Kremlin had approved and supported the Saur Revolution but had warned the leaders of the coup to proceed with caution, to introduce reforms gradually, exercising common sense. Afghanistan was a complex place with a long history of resisting change and it was vital to Soviet strategic interests in Central Asia that the country remain relatively stable. Moscow didn't want to run the country, just exploit it. The Kremlin's orders were simple: make this work; don't blow this opportunity. But the Afghan revolutionaries weren't listening.

President Taraki continued his reign of terror, arresting and executing people all over the country. Instead of sparking a people's uprising against feudal landowners, the regime's tactics only made more enemies. And inevitably, as it is with dictators who fail to develop allies or a bedrock of support, Taraki became a victim of the anarchy he had promoted. He was in office for only five months when he was murdered by his former collaborator, the man who would succeed him, Hafizullah Amin.

From the point of view of Afghans, the new Amin administration wasn't much of an improvement. The mass detentions continued for some months until Amin was himself assassinated. But not before an estimated twelve thousand people had disappeared into Kabul's prison system, among them Asad's father, uncle and cousins. It's estimated that another fifty to a hundred thousand people vanished from the Afghan countryside.

Before Taraki and Amin were killed (at Moscow's behest), Soviet leader Leonid Brezhnev had counselled them, warning that they were making a mess of the situation and could face a counter-revolution.

Moscow's intelligence assets knew that Afghans in rural areas, where the reforms were anathema to their way of life, were turning against the Communist authorities and organizing themselves into armed militias. Moscow was desperate to get control of its client state.

On December 24, 1979, in a move that stunned the world and seriously escalated the Cold War, the Soviet Union invaded Afghanistan. Tanks rumbled through the streets of Kabul; the city suddenly went silent; all communications with the outside cut off. Afghans collectively held their breath, wondering what would follow. It was a stunning geopolitical moment in history but for Asad, it was also intensely personal. The family had a lot at stake. Would the Soviet invasion mean the end of anarchy and despotism? Would it lead to the release of political prisoners, including his father, uncle and cousins? Or would it seal their fates?

Radio bulletins issued by the Soviets declared that Afghanistan was being "liberated"—ignoring the inconvenient reality that the coup had been sponsored by Moscow. A new Soviet puppet dictator, Babrak Karmal, announced he would soon pardon any prisoners who had been arrested without cause, raising expectations among the country's anxious population. There was a near riot at the Pol-e-Charkhi Prison when people gathered there, responding to a rumour that there was to be an amnesty at any moment. The crowd pushed against the gates of the jail until police began shooting over their heads to disperse them. No prisoners were released.

Pol-e-Charkhi Prison is a dismal fortress, a place where death could quickly become preferable to prolonged incarceration. Asad's family joined hundreds assembled at its gate each Friday to bring fresh clothing for their loved ones. The soiled laundry of a prisoner would be their only reassurance that the family member was still alive inside. Each exchange of clothing gave them hope, until one Friday visit when the Aryubwals were told the laundry service would no longer be necessary. What did this mean? Were the men dead? Or had they been transferred somewhere else? Whatever the answer, their last small link with the lost men of their clan was broken.

President Karmal never did fulfill his pledge to release political prisoners, but he relaxed some of the more draconian property laws. Asad attempted to return to school if for no other reason than to have some respite from home where his grieving mother was slowly going mad. Lal Bibi's breakdown had begun the moment police arrested her husband and Asad found it painful to watch. But at school he soon discovered that children of political prisoners were considered pariahs; Soviet-hired administrators blamed students from well-established homes for all of society's problems. There were no longer private institutions for privileged Afghans and Asad found himself mixed in with a general, and often hostile, student population.

It's hard to comprehend when you consider how regressive Afghanistan is today, but Kabul was once quite permissive and liberal, well out ahead of most other urban centres on the subcontinent. Many Russians lived and worked in the capital and they had substantial influence, introducing a European lifestyle to the urban elites. But changes had been well in the works before the USSR arrived. Since the early part of the twentieth century, Afghanistan's monarchy had been trying to modernize the society, culminating in the efforts of Western-educated Mohammed Daoud Khan, the king's cousin and the prime minister. Daoud Khan attempted to reshape the constitution to reflect his secular ideals and he refused to support imams who imposed religious laws on the society. His own wife and daughters had been appearing in public without hijabs since the 1950s and he contended that the head covers Afghan women were expected to wear had nothing to do with Islam. Impatient with the pace of progress, Daoud Khan launched a soft coup in 1973, overthrowing his royal cousin, abolishing the monarchy and declaring himself president.

In the sixties and seventies, Afghanistan had one foot in the Middle Ages, where ancient customs prevailed, and the other in the contemporary world. In the city, young people held their own opinions on a range of subjects—something foreign to a traditional society—and many were in the thrall of Western notions of liberation. Afghan women joined the faculties of Kabul University. They took on Western customs, styling their hair in the latest fashion and dressing in short skirts with high heels. They read foreign literature and talked about travelling abroad. They were leaving home to study and work in cities where they had no relatives, and they were making friends with people who had nothing to do with their traditional clans. Among them was a bright, prosperous young Persian woman from Mazar-e-Sharif, who had arrived in Kabul as a teacher.

Mobina Ahmady was the most intriguing woman Asad had ever seen, and he knew from the moment he met her that she would share his life. There were complications: she was five years older than he was—twenty-three to his eighteen. And she was his teacher. For many reasons, she should have been well beyond his reach. But even though Mobina didn't seem to be aware of his existence, he was determined that one day he would catch her eye, and then her heart.

Asad can describe the exact moment he was smitten, when she arrived in class wearing what he describes as a cowgirl outfit: boots, a short blue jean skirt and a blouse of flimsy orange silk that revealed

Asad at 19, standing near the family business, the Aryub Cinema.

Mobina at the age of 17, at her childhood home in Dehdadi.

almost too much for a teenager to bear except that Mobina's final accessory was an embroidered vest that covered vital parts of her anatomy. For someone who grew up watching American Westerns in the family cinema, this was the most provocative outfit imaginable.

To break the ice, he did what any young man would do: he invited her to a movie. The hottest ticket in 1981 Kabul was a Hindi film called *Laawaris*, roughly translated as "Bastard." Notwithstanding the title, it was a romantic comedy set in India with the usual Bollywood buffoonery, salacious insinuation, improbable plot twists and two of the top songs on the subcontinent hit parade at the time. The movie was sold out but since the Aryubwals owned the theatre, Asad had access to scarce tickets.

Afghanistan had a fledgling movie production industry of its own in the sixties and seventies, mostly funded by the government and later with assistance from the Soviet Union for worthy propaganda films.

But what people really wanted to watch were American Westerns and Bollywood schlock, and the Aryub Cinema was more than willing to accommodate those tastes. Asad grew up at the movies. He loved foreign flicks, the improbable adventures and romances, the daring escapes and swashbuckling heroes. And he was sure Mobina did as well.

Asking for a date was out of the question. She was a teacher and he a student. So he offered her two passes so she and her brother could attend. How could she say no? He briefly considered that he might try slipping into a seat beside her when the lights went down but that would be too risky. What if she found him forward? Besides, Asad didn't really want to watch the movie—he could do that anytime. He wanted to watch Mobina watch the movie. He wanted to see her laugh; to look surprised; to react to the suggestive songs and dances that were an integral part of a Bollywood flick.

He used his influence to get the best seats for her. He arranged delivery of snacks. People seated near her wondered who these VIPs were. Asad's ploy worked and Mobina took note of him. She found him attractive, mature for his age, obviously comfortable in his skin with a head of thick black curly hair and dark brown eyes that had a glimmer of mischief. That his family was wealthy was less interesting to her.

But Mobina remained circumspect and it wasn't just because of the age difference or even the teacher-pupil relationship. Despite Asad's charm and progressive world view, she knew him to be from a family that was traditional, even backward, especially where women were concerned. She was modern, probably too much so for their standards. And she was Tajik: her ethnicity would be frowned upon by the old-fashioned Pashtuns who stayed within their clans. The Aryubwal household was governed by purdah, which means "veil," literally and figuratively. If a woman has to leave the house, she takes the cloister with her, covered head to foot. Someone who wears sheer blouses and cowboy boots is definitely moving to a different drumbeat. Mobina was influenced by Western values and she was passionate about education, a no-no for the women in Asad's family. The Aryubwals profited from the free movement of women—half of the audience for the movies at their cinema was female—but that didn't mean they approved of it.

Mobina finally agreed to date Asad. They went to parties where she sipped Fanta and he drank whiskey. They danced. They dined together in restaurants. They talked of raising a family in a world where anything was possible. But their plans to marry had to remain a secret from his relatives. He knew his relations would not accept her at first, but he persuaded Mobina that his family would come around in time—once they were living together, once his people got to know her. He was taking a long shot. And, as would happen frequently in Asad's life, he would miss the mark dramatically.

Asad decided to first consult the female members of the family. He took the Aryubwal women to the charming Babur's Gardens on the fringes of Kabul, where they could have a picnic and speak openly to one another. He told them what he planned to do. They were happy for him; they encouraged him to follow his heart. There was something appealingly courageous and romantic in his plan to marry someone from outside the clan—a Dari-speaking Tajik with a university degree and a career, a woman who wore short skirts, no less. They would accept her and maybe she would break new ground for them.

But their approval carried little weight. It was, after all, a male-dominated society and the attitudes of the men were deeply rooted in conservative traditions. They would believe that such a union would dishonour and disgrace the whole extended family. Someone like Mobina was a threat to the status of the Aryubwal clan, its prestige and social standing. She could even pose a hazard to the family business interests.

To make matters more difficult, the Aryubwal family was still trying to recover from the loss of the most important members of the household—father, uncle, cousins. The surviving family members needed solidarity, stability. They didn't want challenges to their assumptions or a scandal caused by an outsider. But Asad was in love and he was sure he could surmount any obstacle. Perhaps he had been blinded by the generous response of the women in the family. In any event, he was completely unprepared for the reaction he'd provoke among the men when, during a family dinner, he announced his marriage plan.

The guests consisted entirely of male cousins and Asad's brothers. There was a murmur of approval when he announced he planned to marry. But when he told them who the bride was going to be, there was pandemonium. His outraged relations warned him that this Tajik, this scandalous outsider with her indecent clothes and lifestyle, would bring ruin to them all. Had he no respect for the honour of Muhammad Omer, his father? And then the men beat him until his face was bloody. Their wedding gift to Asad was a broken front tooth.

In his heart Asad believed that his father, who made no secret of his own progressive views, would have backed him up. Muhammad Omer had close friends in Afghan households where women both spoke and acted freely. He shared his son's attraction to people outside the family circle. Asad says his dad had always encouraged him to seek out those who lived differently, to move out of his comfort zone and grow. "My father would have loved Mobina," he told me once.

Despite the opposition, Asad married Mobina. They began their life together as it would continue, passionately in love but isolated from kinfolk.

If Leonid Brezhnev and the powers in the Kremlin thought conquering Afghanistan was going to be easy, they hadn't read their history very closely. The Soviet Union had already poured billions of rubles into the country over many decades to keep Afghanistan onside. Military occupation would turn out to be a colossally bad idea.

Afghans seem genetically predisposed to repel invasions, as every imperial power from the Moguls to the British had learned. Resistance to the Soviet presence was intense, and it was aggravated by the excesses of the local puppet governments. The much-loathed Taraki/Amin administrations, with their ham-fisted efforts to fast-track radical reforms, set the stage for a general uprising against the Soviets and their Afghan representatives.

In villages and farmlands, Afghans assembled loose coalitions of tribal militias and armed themselves with whatever weapons were available, then set out to make the Russians sorry they'd ever crossed the Hindu Kush. When the USSR's modern war machine crushed the poorly armed and inexperienced insurgents but the mounting casualties only drew more Afghan fighters to the cause. The word "mujahidin" is Arabic, meaning "fighters who wage jihad." Afghan tribesmen calling themselves mujahidin had fought British occupation a century earlier and the guerrillas who emerged to battle the Soviets were from the same tradition. This was soon a religious campaign, waged with the inspiration of their warrior prophet, Mohammed, and championed by Allah.

Mujahidin commanders quickly became household names: Ahmad Shah Massoud, Burhanuddin Rabbani, Gulbuddin Hekmatyar and Abdul Rasul Sayyaf. They would later come to represent their own form of tyranny, but in the war against the Red Army, they were heroes, celebrated at home and, increasingly, abroad. They fought with the kind of doggedness that can only come from self-preservation; fighting from the heart for family and home and history. When President Reagan became their generous benefactor a few years into the war, the mujahidin also acquired the technology to back up their zealotry.

For its part, the Soviet military used its overwhelming air power against the Afghans, annihilating villages they suspected to be hideouts for insurgents, while Soviet ground forces conducted scorched-earth campaigns. Russian soldiers were in hostile territory, fighting desperate people, and they showed no mercy. They killed Afghans with unfathomable cruelty; crushing prisoners under their tank treads, firebombing houses before women and children could escape, poisoning water wells.

The Soviets had the tactical advantage of helicopter gunships and modern war machinery and they also had their own legendary Afghan allies. Chief among them was General Rashid Dostum, who commanded a personal army of thirty thousand and was hostile to this anarchic and, in his view, doomed jihad. But Dostum and a few collaborators like him weren't enough. The Soviets needed ground troops if they were to prevail. Private militias such as Dostum's were badly outnumbered throughout the country while the Afghan National Army, on the payroll of Moscow, was ill-trained, listless and reluctant to fight. Most Afghans dodged conscription for many reasons, not the least being that they didn't want to kill their own people, or to be killed by them. Even those who opposed the mujahidin knew that their destiny would be to become cannon fodder—quickly deployed for frontline combat against their fanatical fellow countrymen.

In 1983, just after he married Mobina, Asad was called up for military duty in the USSR-led Afghan army. The newlyweds decided their best response was flight. By leaving Afghanistan, Asad would not only duck the draft, but also escape the disapproval of his family. He and Mobina didn't have much money, but they had dreams of starting a new life far away from conflict—maybe even in that land of migrant fantasies, America. They would start the journey by setting out for Pakistan.

Asad rented a mule for Mobina to ride and also to carry their few possessions to the Pakistani border. It was a journey that would have taken hours by car but it was safer on foot. They spent four days and nights trudging through flat farmland, then clambering through the rocky foothills near the border. They had known it would be a hard journey but they weren't prepared for the intensity of the fighting they encountered along the way.

In one pass through the terrain, Asad and Mobina suddenly found themselves pinned down by crossfire with no idea who was shooting or what they were shooting at. They were caught in a no man's land and, as the battle raged around them, they lost sight of one another. Asad, desperate to find his wife, began searching madly while mujahidin fighters screamed at him to get his head down—before he lost it. He persisted until he had Mobina in his arms but then realized they were both exposed to the gunfire. In a bizarre moment, the newlyweds actually tussled, each trying to protect the other from the bullets that were whizzing by, until they realized the futility of what they were doing—that life apart would be unthinkable. They would survive together, or die together. A brief lull in the shooting allowed them to run for cover. They found their mule and the footpath and continued their perilous journey.

The closer they got to the Pakistani border, the more intense the fighting seemed to be. They were eyewitnesses to the beginning of what would become a full-out proxy war between superpowers, the USSR and the US. The scene was chaotic, fighters and military hardware flooding into Afghanistan, Afghan refugees in the thousands heading out, towards Peshawar, the closest city across the border in Pakistan.

Where there are desperate people there will also be the predators who will take advantage of them. Criminal gangs worked the border crossings running drugs and guns in both directions, and preying on the refugees. Asad and Mobina welcomed the offer of assistance from "guides" who promised to help them find a safe passage through the fighting but who stole all their money. Whatever hope they had for emigrating to the United States had evaporated by the time they crossed the border. They were safe now, at least for the moment. But their dreams were gone.

There also was no turning back. Their country had become the nexus for the decisive battle of the Cold War. Asad and Mobina were—as millions had been before them, and millions more would be after—stranded, minor casualties in a global struggle that would consume their country and their future. They settled in Peshawar, the intersection of international manoeuvring and war-profiteering. Afghans were flooding into camps around the city, and Asad and Mobina might have been compelled to join them in those shelters of canvas, cardboard and wire. But in addition to the billions being spent on war, there was money for relief. Western-based humanitarian agencies were hiring local people who were educated and spoke the local languages. Asad and Mobina soon found jobs with a Western aid agency, Save the Children, where they worked in a primary health-care program.

The income sustained them through their early years together in Pakistan, and allowed them to avoid living in the camps outside the city. But working with those refugees forced Asad and Mobina

Mobina and Asad in 1984, when they were living in Pakistan.

to confront the harsh reality of life for disadvantaged Afghans. Their efforts in the clinics and the hospitals gave them a deep understanding of the catastrophe their country had become.

Asad and Mobina had grown up in different social circumstances but they were both products of privileged families. The camps, on the other hand, were filled with poor people from the villages and farm country most directly affected by the war: people who had been carpet-bombed and burned out of their homes by the Soviets. Children had lost limbs to landmines; women had watched as their husbands were mutilated and murdered; the refugees had fled villages to which they could never return. What Asad and Mobina witnessed in the camps would have a lasting impact on them, as it did on anyone who visited.

By the mid-1980s, the Communist government in Afghanistan could no longer even pretend that it had a functioning national army. Casualties, desertions and draft dodgers like Asad had depleted the ranks. Afghanistan's puppet president, Babrak Karmal, was now completely dependent on the USSR. He knew the war was bleeding the Kremlin's treasury just as Washington had hoped. Soviet casualties were now so horrendous that exactly how many young soldiers were coming home in body bags became a state secret. But the mothers of the dead soldiers knew, and their friends knew. Soon there was an unprecedented protest movement in the USSR that even a dictatorship could not ignore. And the incoming leader, Mikhail Gorbachev, was a man who clearly saw the future, one where there was no place for lost causes like the imperial struggle in Afghanistan.

Gorbachev made it clear to President Karmal that the Soviet Union could no longer afford to drain its coffers and sacrifice the lives of its soldiers to prop up a failing regime. Karmal objected—he knew that without Moscow, he was finished. He soon lost his job but he didn't lose his life—at least not right away. Assassination wasn't Gorbachev's style.

Moscow replaced Karmal with another puppet, Mohammad Najibullah, who swiftly moved to win popular support among his people by declaring a general amnesty for Afghan men who had deserted or left the country to avoid conscription. It was a signal to Asad that he might now be free to come home and it felt timely. Peshawar was unstable, though not yet as volatile as the city I encountered when I arrived there, wildly ambitious and green as grass, about eighteen months later.

But Afghanistan itself was now a lawless and unpredictable place. Leaders of the mujahidin were morphing into warlords, consolidating their military successes into fiefdoms. They were corrupted by the American dollars and guns that were arriving daily, especially the Stinger missiles that would be the definitive technology of the Cold War. With those weapons, the Afghan resistance was finally able to shoot down Soviet helicopter gunships and deny the Communists their greatest military advantage. Washington was succeeding in its ambitions but with no regard for the effect its war effort was having on the fragile country.

Asad wasn't sure he should trust rumours that draft dodgers could now return to Afghanistan with impunity, so Mobina agreed to go back to Kabul and investigate. She was reluctant to do so, knowing she would have to move in with the Aryubwal family. But Asad, ever optimistic, was sure that everything would be fine. Tradition worked both ways—she was his wife. His family would accept her.

He was wrong. Asad had failed to understand just how deeply the family resented his marriage and the loathing had only grown deeper while the couple had been in Pakistan. Back in Kabul, Mobina was made to sleep in a shabby little room and sometimes forced to bed down on the kitchen floor. The men verbally abused her and beat her. The women were sympathetic, tried to offer kindness. But the men were consumed by rage over the scandal they believed she had brought to the clan. Even years later, as she told her story to me in a safe haven away from Kabul, she wept, recalling how unbearable her pain and isolation had been.

Mobina sent word to her husband in Peshawar that it was safe for him to return; that the draft had been cancelled. But she didn't tell him what she was going through and so he was oblivious to her suffering. Asad began to arrange his departure but he was confronted with a dilemma. He and Mobina had applied for visas at a number of foreign consulates and, at last, the German embassy offered documents. It would be an opportunity to reinvent their lives in Europe. But there was a catch. He'd have to go on ahead without Mobina, then, later, sponsor her. It could mean a two-year separation at the very least. And that was a deal-breaker. He turned down the visa and began the journey back to Kabul, aching to see his wife.

Asad arrived at his family's house in Kabul in the early morning hours and began to look for Mobina. He was told she wasn't there. She had gone to Mazar-e-Sharif to be with her own family and no one in the Aryubwal household would tell him why she had left.

Mobina's brother, Sayeed, was living in Kabul at the time, and Asad roused him first thing the next day. It turned out that Mobina hadn't even told her brother that she was leaving for the north. Asad and Sayeed set off immediately to find her. Neither of them had any idea of what she'd endured in Kabul, so they anticipated a happy reunion. When they got to the farmhouse, Sayeed went in first to distract her. Then Asad slipped in through a side door, rushing to passionately embrace his wife, breaking all the cultural taboos that instruct men and women to maintain a semblance of reserved decorum when other people are around.

It wasn't long before he realized something was wrong—there was something damaged, if not broken, in her spirit. She would only gradually explain what had happened. Years later, after having lived through many sorrowful experiences, Asad would still consider that day as the saddest in his life.

It was the worst kind of betrayal—a betrayal of fundamental values that placed such a high premium on family and loyalty, hospitality and generosity. His family had abused his wife, a woman who meant more to him than his own life. In doing so they had exposed their own hypocrisy, the shallowness of their supposed commitment to tradition.

His first reaction was to blame himself. "I never should have married her," he once told me. But it wasn't the marriage he regretted—it was the failure of something more important—the failure of two fundamental concepts, family and home.

IV

Wrath of the Taliban

THERE COULD HARDLY BE A WORSE TIME or place to raise a family than the Afghanistan of the late eighties and nineties. Each of Asad and Mobina's children was born into a different phase of the country's troubles.

The couple settled in Kabul where Asad got work with the Aryubwals' cinema business and where they hoped to build a life together. Robina—nicknamed Ruby—came into the world on January 5, 1988, just before the Soviet Union began its final withdrawal from Afghanistan. Asad and Mobina cared for their first-born as they watched the last Russian tanks rumble away from the city leaving a dark cloud of uncertainty over the country. The Soviet departure should have elicited a collective sigh of relief except that Afghans suspected, quite rightly, that the shaky peace agreement that paved the way for the withdrawal had failed to provide any realistic way to transfer power from Moscow to Kabul.

The Geneva Accords for Afghanistan had been crafted by the United Nations and approved by the US and the USSR with Afghans allowed little say in the matter. According to the plan, President Najibullah and his regime would be weaned off the Kremlin's support just as Washington was severing sustenance to the mujahidin. The US government didn't care that no one from its Afghan proxy army had been part of the negotiations or signed the Geneva Accords—the mujahidin hadn't even been invited to do so. Those who did participate knew that the rebels would never support Najibullah; he represented everything they loathed. The whole arrangement seemed set up for disaster.

For the previous ten years, billions of US dollars and USSR rubles had poured into Afghanistan to finance destruction but little else. By the end of the 1980s, half of all refugees in the world were Afghans, mostly exiled to Iran or Pakistan. A million and a half civilians had died because of war, while countless others were maimed and wounded; the International Red Cross estimated it would take 4,300 years to remove all the landmines that the contending armies had buried in the countryside. Afghanistan ranked third from the bottom in development of all countries in the world. Its children were severely malnourished. The place was swamped with Kalashnikovs, Stinger missiles, rocket launchers, armoured vehicles, bullets, bombs and angry disillusioned men. Fertile farmland went fallow and food was imported or donated. Orchards and nut farms that had produced some of the few exports generating cash for the Afghan economy were dug up to make way for poppies and the flourishing trade in opium. Afghanistan had become the source of most of the world's heroin, feeding an addiction crisis in the US of epidemic proportions but also providing Afghans with their own generation of drug addicts.

As Ruby stumbled through her first steps and welcomed her baby sister, Hossai, into the world on December 24, 1989, Afghanistan began its descent into vicious civil war. The warlords Hekmatyar and Massoud were locked in a ferocious contest for control of the east, near the Pakistani border where Asad and Mobina had once been caught in crossfire. Dostum was fending off attacks on his fiefdom from rival warlords in the north while, in the south, around Kandahar, a competing network of tribal leaders was coalescing into a formidable fighting force known as the Taliban.

The Geneva Accords entrusted Pakistan with the task of post-war reconstruction. This is exactly what Islamabad had wanted: to establish its neighbouring country as a client state and to install its own regime in Kabul. Pakistani generals struck up opportunistic alliances with the worst of the Afghan warlords (if they can be ranked) and secured their economic interests to the lucrative trade routes through Central Asia. No one had plans, or offered money, to rebuild the country, only to control it. The prize for all of them was the capital city, Kabul. All the players with ambitions for power over Afghanistan were waiting for the Najibullah regime to collapse. But the president was proving resilient.

Najibullah had the advantage of the largest arsenal of ballistic missiles held by any army since the Second World War. He had tanks, armour, heavy guns and warehouses full of munitions—all left behind by a retreating Red Army. He didn't have much of a standing army but he did have one other highly lethal weapon: his pro-Soviet warlords. Rashid Dostum in particular was still loyal to Moscow's last appointed president. Dostum was known as an enforcer, someone who would do anything to protect the political leaders he served. His militiamen were seasoned on the battlefield and a merciless horde of looters when they weren't killing people. Dostum was able to tenaciously hold onto his control of the northern provinces as Afghanistan entered a period of tremendous uncertainty.

In Kabul, life was growing more dangerous by the day. Asad was hearing of Kabulis who had been murdered in their homes, their throats slit, presumably by mujahidin. No one investigated the crimes. In the absence of a functioning police force, people turned to their clans for protection but Asad didn't feel that he had the backing of his own family. Asad decided to move his family north, to Mobina's childhood home in Dehdadi, hoping that Dostum territory was now safer than Kabul. Najibullah hung on and was beginning his fourth winter as president when Mobina gave birth to her first son, Muhammad.

The fall of the Berlin Wall in 1989 marked the beginning of the final disintegration of the USSR. People around the world, especially those such as Asad who had lived in its imperial shadow, had considered the Communist empire to be as indestructible as steel pillars. They now watched in confused amazement as it crumbled like rotten concrete. While satellite republics, previously under the sway of the Kremlin, cut their ties and became independent, the government of Afghanistan still relied on the former empire. Its economy was in ruins and its exports were now almost entirely opioids. Its own natural gas deposits were exhausted and, for some time, its citizens had been depending on Russia for the basic necessities of life—food, energy and security. But Moscow was facing increasing pressure from US sanctions and it was forced to withdraw support from former client states, including Afghanistan. The situation for the regime—and for Afghans—was bleak.

For Dostum, there was no longer an incentive for supporting President Najibullah. When the Uzbek general concluded he could do better on the other side of what was increasingly a civil war in Afghanistan, it was a final blow to the old Communist regime. The UN arranged for sanctuary for Najibullah and was helping him to leave the country when, for reasons that aren't clear, Rashid Dostum prevented his departure. Najibullah was forced to take sanctuary in the United Nations compound in Kabul where he lived for the next five years.

With Najibullah out of office, every warlord and militiaman in the country descended on Kabul. The battle for control of the capital raged through the spring of 1992, marking the city for decades to come. Even with a dozen years of war behind them, the onslaught of these militias was terrifying to people living in Kabul. Armed with the arsenals left behind by departing superpowers, the warlords fought each other mercilessly with no regard for the civilians who were trying to live in the middle of pitched battle. Journalists reported on the carnage while human rights advocates tried to raise the alarm, but the suffering of civilians was met largely with indifference from world leaders.

The international community, principally the United States, wanted to get out of the business of caring for Afghanistan. Though it had been the final battleground for the Cold War and the US had pushed its economy to the brink through sanctions, Washington felt little responsibility for the country. It urged the mujahidin factions to agree to a United Nations brokered power-sharing arrangement where warlords, who had been killing each other for some years now, would unite as one big happy family and form a government. Once the militia leaders signed a troubled power-sharing agreement known as the Peshawar Accord, the world was content to move on and let Afghanistan face the future on its own.

The years from 1992 until late 1996 were a period of absolute chaos and anarchy in Kabul, a *Mad Max* scene played out in the city core and its suburbs. Competing militias pummelled whole neighbourhoods into powder while they tortured and killed people in the streets.

Members of Dostum's militia joined the other mercenaries as they robbed people's homes, carting off everything from fridges and stoves to masonry and sometimes even people, while their commanders extracted protection money and demanded that men of fighting age join their ranks.

This is where the term "warlord" comes from: they are lords as a result of war, and behave as if they own everything and everybody in their jurisdiction. Hospitals filled up with the wounded while many died on the streets, lying there for days or weeks before anyone could bury them. Even years after the fighting, the neighbourhoods that had been under attack remained piles of rubble. I once saw the ruins of a school with its front wall sheared off; the classrooms still had lessons on the chalkboards, a pathetic testimony to how desperately people had attempted to carry on living in the midst of carnage.

Kabul had been a beautiful and vibrant city with a rich cultural life, where people listened to music, danced and dined out. Mobina and Asad had enjoyed life. The Soviet-Afghan war had been largely in the country-side and Kabulis were relatively untouched by the fighting.

But the warlords' battle for control of the capital changed all of that. Kabul was no longer functional or safe and anyone who had another place to live soon departed. Mobina's childhood hometown of Dehdadi was the rustic hub of a feudal farm region where people lived much as they had for centuries. She had left home years earlier, moving to Kabul first for university and then employment, while Asad had always lived in the capital. Life in the north was a big change for Asad and Mobina, but when you are in the middle of a war zone, boring is good. Dehdadi was dull, but it was safe.

I never met Mobina's father since he had died before my visit to the farm, but I know she had adored him. Ahmad Ahmady was a mostly self-educated man, renowned as an authority on the history of Balkh province. Foreign scholars who came to research the culture-soaked regions of northern Afghanistan—where Buddhism, Islam and Zoroastrianism had all flourished at some point—would seek Ahmad out and often stay in the Ahmady house for long periods of time.

Among the many visitors were two American professors who lived with Mobina's family for more than a month. The young couple worked at a nearby archaeological dig, the excavation of an ancient Greek city called Ai-Khanoum, and when they were not employed on the site they enjoyed the hospitality of the Ahmady farm. The Ahmadys owned archaeological treasures of their own, including priceless jewellery of gold and precious stones that had been in the family for centuries. The craftsmanship of the artifacts, along with the background stories and legends provided by Ahmad, fascinated the scholars who were trying to learn more about the Persian culture of the region that had long ago supplanted the Greek empire. Ahmad was a treasure in himself, a receptacle of knowledge, history and language of the region that few scholars possessed.

As a teenager, Mobina was very much attracted to the female professor whom she remembers only as Jacqueline. They would spend hours together, especially on cold nights, their feet tucked into an Afghan foot-warmer stove known as a *sandali*, conversing in Dari, a language that Jacqueline had learned for her work. The professor was exotic, worldly and, from Mobina's point of view, provocatively independent. She stirred in the girl a desire to escape the narrow confines of rural life. Few Afghans are encouraged to have experiences beyond the family, and

Mobina was blessed with parents who were open to the lives of others. She has this in common with Asad—they are both comfortable in the company of strangers. In fact, they are drawn to them.

Though Mobina's father had been wealthy, he was unpretentious, preferring to live simply while he channelled all his capital and energy into the production of food. He designed a farmhouse that was sprawling but basic, with limited electricity and no indoor plumbing. We enjoyed its charms when Heather, Brian and I bunked there, but admittedly it was primitive. To live at the farm, after years away, must have been a shock for Mobina. The trade-off was that she had her mother to help with the children and she was away from the reproachful eyes of her in-laws.

Asad helped manage and protect the lands of his in-laws but it hurt his pride to have to live off of them. He was a shrewd businessman after his years of helping to run the Aryubwal family's affairs and he soon launched his own enterprises, a wholesale-retail business selling car parts and a shop in the market. By the time their new baby son, Mujeeb, joined the family in April of 1993, the family had moved to Mazar-e-Sharif where Asad built a house for his family. It was luxurious compared with that of his in-laws, with multiple rooms, indoor plumbing, a garden and living quarters for hired help. But there was no getting away from the fact that the country was on the verge of breakdown and the veneer of normalcy in Balkh province came with a price. Like a Mafia don, Dostum expected everyone to do his bidding, and Asad was no exception.

Dostum collected taxes and demanded that the merchants in his territory use the dostum as their currency. He ran a number of businesses, including his own airline, and people were expected to patronize them. Asad complied with whatever the warlord demanded of him, paying for protection and supplying food to Dostum's army from the family farm.

But as the battle for Kabul raged, and Dostum's needs became larger, the warlord's reach began to extend deeper into Asad's life.

The Uzbek general had taken control of some crucial entry points into Kabul but he had not yet defeated his rival warlords. Since he no longer had his Moscow patrons, he acquired what he needed by any means, including extortion, theft, kidnappings and death threats. Some of Mobina's relatives had been drawn into Dostum's expanding sphere, in particular two cousins who became senior commanders in his army. The cousins took control of irrigation systems that were necessary for running the family farm and they threatened to shut off the water supply unless the other men in Mobina's family agreed to join Dostum's brigade. The threats escalated: if Asad and the others continued to resist, Dostum's men would take over the family property and possibly kidnap their children for ransom.

Under such duress, Asad joined the 74th Brigade of Dostum's army where he was immediately made a general. For someone with absolutely no military background and no interest in fighting, the title was meaningless. Asad accepted the rank grudgingly because it would allow him to cross checkpoints when Dostum needed him to do so. In fact, Dostum once appointed five thousand senior officers in a single afternoon, all of them noncombatants. Asad was instructed to purchase a uniform in the market where he could also buy the insignia to go with the rank. He did as he was told, but he also derived some benefit from the title by delegating as much responsibility as possible to subordinates. Asad wanted to keep a healthy distance from the warlord.

Dostum's army was the military wing of his political movement, Junbish-i-Milli, but there wasn't much actual structure to his organization. When Najibullah's regime collapsed, Dostum absorbed five divisions of the Afghan army into his private fighting force. He kept the names and brigade numbers of the former Soviet-Afghan units but in reality most of the warlord's army was made up of an assortment of loosely affiliated mercenaries, each with its own feudal commander. They wore a jumble of Afghan army and Soviet-style combat fatigues along with their regular street clothes; they drove around in Russian military vehicles and had access to the arsenal left over from the occupation.

Asad's only experience with firearms had been shooting pigeons when he was a boy and he was terrified that he would be expected to use weapons. But Dostum wasn't about to arm a reluctant civilian. He had limited weapons and he provided them exclusively to his seasoned soldiers of fortune who were inspired by the warlord's commitment that they could keep whatever they seized from those they killed. Dostum's logistics units were made up of citizen conscripts who kept their day jobs but were required to provide goods and services to the fighting forces and support its infrastructure as it was needed. Asad's job was to supervise construction sites while arranging for deliveries of supplies to storage depots and occasionally to the front lines. While Asad was never issued weapons he did have a few dozen armed men assigned to him who acted as security for the shipments of supplies. They allowed Asad to fulfill his obligations to the warlord without getting involved in the actual fighting, though on some occasions he was close enough to the action to witness the savagery of the Junbish forces. He prayed that he would never be ordered to do more.

Rashid Dostum is credited with having protected the northern provinces from the war though he did little to create a civil society within his fiefdom. Proper schools were a priority for Mobina but she found the education system appalling, compelling her to supplement the poor instruction by teaching her children at home. No one in the family can remember much about the Mazar school curriculum, though almost certainly it would have been based on propaganda of either Soviet or American design.

USAID, a State Department agency with CIA connections had, in previous decades, provided Afghan children with books and teaching materials that were heavily infused with anti-Communist instruction. *The Alphabet of Jihad Literacy*, published in the 1980s by the University of Nebraska, is just one example of what children were using to learn their ABCs: "T" is for *topak*, meaning gun, "that my uncle uses for jihad." (At the time, the word "jihad" was a synonym for heroism because the targets of the jihad then underway were Communists.) "K" is for Kabul, according to a lesson, the capital of a country that can only be ruled by Muslims. "J" is for jihad. Here's an example from another a math lesson: "If you have 10 atheists and 1 Moslem kills 5, how many atheists are left?" Other questions are designed to normalize the language of war: "15 Kalashnikovs – 5 Kalashnikovs = ?" The texts were illustrated with images of weapons, bombs and tanks. American taxpayers spent around $50 million to produce these teaching manuals.

The Communists had provided their own propaganda during the occupation and it's possible that the students in Mazar-e-Sharif were still using texts designed to bend little minds in the direction of Moscow. But the biggest blow to education in Afghanistan wasn't the paucity of good learning materials; it was that there were no teachers. The universities no longer produced graduates and many of the best instructors had fled the country.

Asad and Mobina managed to shield their family from war but they all remember the years in Mazar as depressing. The young ones stayed indoors when they weren't at school for fear of kidnapping and they never really had a childhood. Social occasions were rare and they were usually conducted within the walls of their own home. It became almost a prison.

A remarkable glimpse into their lives at this time comes from a video recording of a large party at Asad's house; an event to celebrate the circumcisions of his two sons, Muhammad and Mujeeb. The actual procedure had been performed when they were newly born but this was the first opportunity the family had to fulfill the Afghan custom of a gathering in the boys' honour. A young, solemn-looking Asad escorts Muhammad and Mujeeb through the crowd of well-wishers, who number in the hundreds, as they sit or stand within the walled garden of the sprawling house. The little boys are wearing oversized suits that they will eventually grow into and they both look petrified.

Mobina is radiant in a white dress and headscarf as she thanks each guest individually for their cash gifts to the boys. Later there's live music, dancing and a massive feast spread out on tables, enough to feed what appears to be the entire community. All the children are mesmerized by the highlight of the celebration, a multi-tiered cake smothered in thick icing. The scene would have been idyllic except for the arrival of special guests. Dostum is not among them, but they are senior commanders, thuggish-looking, with thick necks and broad shoulders. The men are treated with extreme deference by the other guests and it would have been inconceivable to hold such an event and fail to invite senior members of Dostum's Junbish-i-Milli. In one scene, the men are seated, enjoying the food, when the most senior commander suddenly looks up and stares coldly into the camera. The video captures a chilling insight into the true nature of the kind of "peace" the family enjoyed in Mazar-e-Sharif.

———

The rival militias of Dostum, Sayyaf, Massoud, Rabbani and Hekmatyar might have gone on fighting indefinitely, or at least until they wiped each other out, but in the mid-1990s they were confronted with a common existential threat.

The Taliban had been a fledgling organization, largely confined to the south, in an area around Kandahar. Mullah Omar had gained control of the region after claiming he could provide an alternative to years of war and exploitation. The mostly Pashtun population of the south had bought into that promise and the Taliban had largely fulfilled its commitment, bringing relief from the violence and corruption. But not without a cost. Mullah Omar demanded that, in return, people accept an extreme form of Islamic, or Sharia, law. It was a price that southern Afghans had agreed to pay. Now Mullah Omar turned his gaze northward, to Kabul.

The Taliban had not benefited from the foreign patronage that the warlords had and Mullah Omar lacked the arsenal that would allow him to take on the other militias. But in 1996, the Taliban's fortunes changed. Pakistan was the dominant foreign player in Afghanistan since the rest of the world had abandoned it. The international community, led by the US, was content to leave Islamabad in charge of the region's affairs. Pakistan's largest military intelligence unit, the ISI (Inter-Services Intelligence), had been backing the warlord Gulbuddin Hekmatyar, believing he could bring stability to the country while ensuring that like-minded Pashtuns controlled Afghanistan's affairs. But Hekmatyar's campaigns against civilians were proving to be the most vicious of all the warlords. He thwarted opportunities to bring the fighting to a halt and refused to compromise with his enemies. He was draining Pakistan's military resources while Afghan refugees continued to pour across the border. Islamabad decided to look for a new partner.

The ISI wasn't interested in sponsoring the Lion of Panjshir, even though Ahmad Massoud controlled the largest militia in the country and was regarded, rightly or wrongly, as the least corrupt of the warlords. The ISI wanted someone whose cultural values and ethnic makeup most closely matched those of the government in Islamabad. Massoud was an ethnic Tajik with secular ideas whereas Pakistan wanted a religiously conservative, Pashtun-dominated Afghanistan. Massoud claimed to believe in the equality of women, transparent institutions, and land reform, all abhorrent to the regime in Islamabad. Teaming up with Rashid Dostum was also out of the question. He was Uzbek and if he possessed anything like a doctrine it was far too liberal. His interests had nothing in common with those of the ISI. The best candidate? The Taliban.

With considerable backing from Pakistan's formidable military, the Taliban swept into Kabul in the fall of 1996 and forced all the warlords to retreat. Kabulis were pleased at first that these uncompromising, seemingly incorruptible religious warriors had driven out the murderous, thieving thugs who had run amok in the city for four years. But they got their first glimpse of what the Taliban would do with their new authority when its members captured former president Najibullah as he attempted to escape his UN redoubt. They beat him, cut off his genitals, tied him to the back of a truck, dragged him through the streets of the city and then shot him. Kabulis woke to the spectacle of the badly mutilated bodies of Najibullah and his brother hanging from a traffic tower in the centre of the city, with cigarettes stuck between their fingers and money stuffed into their pockets, symbols, to the Taliban, of Western decadence.

Had there been a shred of political sophistication within the Taliban, its leaders could have found loyal support for their cause in Kabul, given how Afghans longed for the arrival of anyone who might restore civil order. But the Taliban would have none of Kabul's multi-ethnic mix or its liberal mores and within days of victory it began a program of harsh Sharia law. Women and girls had to stay in the home or wear face-covering burqas if they needed to be outdoors. They could no longer work or go to school. Boys were to study and memorize Koranic texts that were carefully chosen to reflect only the orthodoxy of the Taliban. Men were obliged to grow beards and wear traditional clothes and turbans. Any violation of Taliban law would be punished without mercy.

Ahmad Massoud made one last effort to draft some kind of power-sharing arrangement with the Taliban, but Mullah Omar would have nothing to do with Massoud or Burhanuddin Rabbani, the nominal president of the moment. Rabbani fled and Massoud retreated to the Panjshir Valley, engineering a landslide at the Salang Tunnel to prevent the Taliban from following.

The Taliban called its military takeover a "student uprising," which, narrowly defined, it was—its warriors had once been students in madrassas before they joined the war. It's difficult to overstate the influence of these schools in the creation of the Taliban. Madrassas are male-only Koran-informed seminaries that became a substitute for educating boys from poor families in southern Afghanistan. They were generously funded through donations from both Pakistan and Saudi Arabia and were designed to indoctrinate young minds with little more than religious zealotry and an extreme interpretation of Islamic law.

I had first encountered the effect of madrassas in the Afghan refugee camps in Pakistan in the 1980s, where the instructors had an abundance of young idle minds to capture. Their students were overwhelmingly drawn from the ranks of Afghan orphans. The boys and their teachers often lived in the schools, separated from civil society and away from the influence of women or girls. The madrassa system offered disillusioned and aimless youths a cause and a purpose. By the mid-1990s, the refugee camps around Peshawar had produced tens of thousands of students and trainers, all of them steeped in Islamic doctrine and prepared for holy war against the infidels. As Kabul fell, Pakistan's ISI delivered truckloads of these brainwashed men to fight for the Taliban.

Mullah Omar himself is a product of an Afghan madrassa but we know few other facts about his life. He was born into extreme poverty in Kandahar province. When his father died, Omar's mother followed custom and married her husband's brother, so the boy was raised by his uncle. The family shared the attitudes of many in the Pashtun tribes of the south: they rejected any interference in their affairs from foreigners; they had no interest in relations with anyone outside their ethnicity; and they hated the warlords. Hekmatyar, Sayyaf, Rabbani, Dostum and Massoud were all the enemy.

According to legend, Omar started his own madrassa after a woman appeared to him in a dream and told him he had a mission to help Allah to end the chaos in Afghanistan. He soon had dozens of students at his mud-hut school. "Talib" is a word that means Islamic scholar; "Taliban" is simply the plural form. As mythical stories about Omar and his apparition spread through the south, he began to attract hundreds and then thousands of former mujahidin fighters who were disgusted with what their former commanders were doing to Afghanistan and wanted to be part of the Taliban. Mullah Omar didn't regard the Taliban as a militia but as a movement, and he was its guru. His official title became "Commander of the Faithful."

There are stories of Mullah Omar and his followers rescuing girls who had been taken as sex slaves by warlords. He attained hero status when it was widely reported that he had intervened to oppose two commanders who were fighting over which of them would sodomize a boy. (The practice of *bachi bazi*—an Afghan slang term for "boy play"—was apparently common among the warlords.) Testimony to how many children had experienced such abuse, Omar soon had dozens of families begging him to intervene with, or to punish, abusers. He promised those found abducting and raping children death by hanging from the gun of a tank, and he delivered on that promise.

Omar's nickname was One-Eyed Mullah, and from the very few photos that exist of the Taliban founder, it's clear how he got the moniker. But stories conflict as to which battle resulted in the loss of his right eye. Omar had fought alongside the mujahidin during the war against the Soviets and it's believed he was badly wounded in one of the skirmishes. Pakistani journalist Ahmed Rashid, a leading authority on the Taliban, described Mullah Omar as tall and well built, with a long beard, a black turban and a dry sense of humour. Others who had met him say that though he was shy he possessed extraordinary powers of persuasion. Threatening to hang people can make quite the impression.

In addition to Pakistan, Mullah Omar's foreign backers eventually included Saudi Arabia and, covertly, the United States, whose president, Bill Clinton, was hoping the Taliban would be a reasonable alternative to war. The US energy giant Unocal had ambitious plans for gas pipelines across Afghanistan and Washington believed that the Taliban might be open to negotiations with American business interests. All of Mullah Omar's foreign supporters were urging him to go slow, to win hearts and minds. But he and the Taliban refused. They had captured Kabul, the epicentre of power in Afghanistan, and now set their sights on conquering the north. Kabul and Kandahar were the most populous parts of the country, but the northern provinces, controlled by General Dostum, were resource rich, arable and provided a much-coveted trade route through the subcontinent.

It would be impossible to invent a character more unlike Mullah Omar than General Rashid Dostum. The Uzbek commander is physically imposing and bear-like, with a resemblance to renderings of the Mongol conqueror Genghis Khan. Dostum has a larger-than-life personality to match his girth and there are stories that he could scare men to death with his maniacal laugh alone. Ahmed Rashid says he once arrived for an interview with Dostum to find bits of human flesh around the courtyard—remnants, he was told, of a soldier who had been punished for stealing. Dostum had a reputation as a hard-drinking man who liked to party. His markets sold a vast range of Russian products and luxury goods, smuggled in over the Uzbek border, including vodka and perfume. Many people claim that his militias abducted and raped children and took part in *bachi bazi*, though Dostum denies that his men ever engaged in such abuses.

The Taliban hated everything Dostum represented even as they feared his strength. But if they were going to control the entire country, they had to confront him and the army he commanded, which in the mid-1990s was possibly as many as sixty thousand soldiers.

Dostum had retreated north after the fall of Kabul to the Taliban, where he had taken up residency in Qala-i-Jangi, his fort of war. When Heather, Brian and I visited this complex five years later, it had been largely destroyed by US bombs. But in the 1990s the garrison was a striking work of architecture, appearing mirage-like on the barren landscape just outside of Mazar-e-Sharif. Though it looks ancient, it was actually built in the nineteenth century by a man known as the Iron Emir, Abdur Rahman, whose men had slaughtered an unknown number of Uzbeks at the behest of Great Britain. As a reward, the British Empire gave Rahman title and deed to the region and the emir set about building a monument to himself. The pink-hued fort was designed to replicate the mogul citadels of medieval India, with parapets, ramparts and a moat. In addition to providing a garrison for the emir's forces, the impressive structure was also intended to be a symbol of Pashtun power in northern Afghanistan and a tribute to his colonial overlords.

Now Qala-i-Jangi was the Uzbek Pasha's headquarters. Dostum held his war councils in the fort while his personal guards braced themselves for the arrival of the Taliban. His troop numbers may have seemed impressive on paper but the ranks included many people like Asad who had been coerced into joining and were not going to help him to take on the Taliban. Dostum had a large cache of weapons, and he even had military aircraft, but he was up against a well-motivated Taliban backed up by the powerful Pakistani defence establishment. The deck was stacked against Dostum.

Asad and Mobina didn't know what to think about the possible arrival of the Taliban. They wanted to escape the Mafioso-style grip that Dostum had on their lives. But was it possible to live under the rule of Mullah Omar? Throughout eighteen years of war, fighting had never really come to Mazar, largely due to the intimidating presence of their local warlord. But most people in the region wanted to see him gone and Asad heard that Dostum's own men were plotting against him.

Trying to determine a safe path for his family, Asad sought advice from a senior commander in Dostum's army. General Abdul Malik was a member of the Pahlawan clan, one of the sub-militias that made up the Junbish forces, and he had a great deal of influence with Dostum's men.

Malik was respected as the first in his family to have received a high school education, a status that was in sharp contrast to most of the men in the ranks, including Dostum himself. There was a great deal of friction between the two commanders.

Asad's import business brought him into frequent contact with Malik's brother-in-law, a man who worked as an agent in the customs office. Through this connection, Asad learned that General Malik had broken ranks with Dostum and was having secret dialogues with the Taliban to allow for a peaceful takeover of the region. Pakistan was apparently facilitating these talks. Asad felt reassured after he was able to consult Malik, himself. If this senior commander was negotiating a power-sharing arrangement with the Taliban maybe the Taliban had learned a few lessons about diversity and tolerance since its invasion of Kabul. Many northern Afghans wanted to believe there could be an orderly succession of power.

With help from General Malik and his brothers, the Taliban faced little resistance as it rolled into Mazar-e-Sharif in the spring of 1997. Dostum quickly realized that he had been betrayed by one of his commanders and he bolted for the Uzbek border, bribing his own men to allow him passage (they had not been paid in six months). He found refuge in Turkey where he had a vantage point from which to watch what happened next.

During their earlier negotiations, the Taliban had told General Malik that he would become the governor of an independent northern principality and that Mullah Omar would respect his autonomy. But as soon as Malik had facilitated the Taliban's arrival in Mazar it was clear there would be no such arrangements. The Taliban commander who led the charge, the same man who had ordered Najibullah to be castrated, announced in the central square of the city that Taliban authority would reign supreme. There would be no more schools for girls, women would appear in public only if completely covered by the burqa, and all men would attend mosque. There would be no games, toys, kite-flying, dancing or music. Black-turbaned Taliban agents went door to door smashing television sets and destroying anything they regarded as an affront to Allah, and indiscriminately killing anyone who resisted.

Asad was a man of fighting age and a member of Dostum's militia, however reluctantly he had joined. If the Taliban discovered this fact, he might be killed. But Asad was also worried about Dostum. He knew that the warlord would soon return—this was his fiefdom after all—and he would demand that Asad join the Junbish forces against the Taliban. Asad had to leave quickly. It was too dangerous to take his wife and small children through the war zone that now surrounded Mazar, and so he reluctantly left them behind. Asad spent one night in Kabul—long enough to know that his native city was not safe either—and then joined the exodus of people heading to Pakistan. Mobina and her family decided to hunker down in Mazar-e-Sharif hoping the situation might improve.

The Taliban's grip on the region soon suffered a serious setback. Once General Malik realized he had been used, he rallied his personal militia to launch a fierce resistance and he recruited more than just his Pahlawan clan for the counter-offensive. The Taliban had been targeting Hazaras in a campaign of ethnic cleansing of Shia Muslims that began with the gruesome murder of the esteemed leader of the Hazaras, Abdul Ali Mazari, who had been tortured and, reportedly, thrown from a helicopter while he was still alive. Vengeful Hazaras eagerly joined Malik's forces and, with their help, the general recaptured Mazar-e-Sharif. It was the first time Mullah Omar had met such resistance; the Taliban suffered some of their greatest casualties since they'd launched the war to take over Afghanistan.

The Taliban also learned their enemies could be just as ruthless as they were. General Malik innovated a form of punishment that all sides in the conflict would eventually employ—death by shipping container. More than a thousand Taliban POWs suffocated in the holds of transport trucks, killed on Malik's orders. Thousands of other Taliban prisoners had been thrown down wells along with live grenades, or executed and buried in mass graves in the Dasht-i-Leili fields, the same place that Dostum's men would use a few years later to bury the prisoners captured with the Americans. The UN in Afghanistan was notified about the massacre of Taliban POWs, but the agency had little affection for the Taliban and in the midst of the fighting, no one would investigate.

After the Taliban was ousted from Mazar, Mobina and her family thought they might be safe. But Mullah Omar's men regrouped and launched a more organized and brutal assault a year later, determined not to repeat previous mistakes. Ahmed Rashid wrote a description of the scene when the Taliban returned to Mazar-e-Sharif in August 1998:

> Mullah Omar had given them permission to kill for two hours, but they had killed for two days. The Taliban went on a killing frenzy, driving their pickups up and down the narrow streets of Mazar shooting to the left and right and killing everything that moved—shop owners, cart pullers, women and children shoppers and even goats and donkeys. . . . Soon the streets were covered with dead bodies and blood. Dogs were eating human flesh and soon the smell became intolerable.

The Hazaras were targeted for a different punishment. Those who were captured were crammed into shipping containers to die as the Taliban captives had perished the previous year.

Mobina tried to shield her children from the carnage, but one day a young cousin came to the house and described what he had seen on the streets, where bloodied, bloated corpses were everywhere. It had become more dangerous to stay in Mazar than to flee, and Mobina, along with her mother, gathered up the children and headed southeast to join Asad in Pakistan.

Ruby, who was ten at the time, was old enough that she would not forget the absolute terror of their flight. The women and girls covered themselves from head to toe with burqas in case they met the Taliban as they joined a mass exodus of people, on foot, heading for the mountain pass that would lead them out of the country, a journey of fourteen hours. A cold rain soon soaked the impractical burqas and many families became separated in the gloom. Mobina and her sister-in-law were trying to shepherd their children along the route as best they could when a man whom they didn't know offered to carry little Mujeeb. Mobina was so desperate for help that she had to trust the stranger while he scooped up the little boy and carried on.

Ruby walked with her grandmother, holding on for dear life as they picked their way along the sodden route. But they fell behind the others, eventually losing sight of Mobina altogether and she feared they were lost for good. Strangers coaxed them on, providing direction, until they arrived at a checkpoint where travellers had some shelter and could reunite with those they had lost along the way. Robina searched frantically for her mother among all the other disoriented people until Mobina and the others were found. The good man who had carried Mujeeb had already delivered the boy safely into her arms and now that Robina was recovered, they could all carry on over the border.

Asad (with beard) and Mobina with relatives at a wedding party, Peshawar, 1998.

In Peshawar the family reunited with Asad at a pre-arranged location. He had been in Pakistan for months and had found a place for them to live near where he and Mobina had waited out the Soviet-US proxy war years earlier. But Peshawar was now, like Kabul and Mazar, under siege from religious zealots. Islamic extremists attacked schools, shot at buses carrying female students, and threatened teachers. Afghans who had any association with the Western agencies that were trying to help refugees were threatened and sometimes killed and so Asad and Mobina recognized it was now too dangerous for them to approach the NGOs that had provided employment in the 1980s.

Everything was more difficult for the Aryubwals in Peshawar this time around and, with four children, the problems were compounded. There was no work, no security and a palpable hostility towards the Afghan refugees. The family stayed for eighteen months until their money completely ran out and they had no other option but to return to Afghanistan. In Mazar, Asad knew he would face the double threat of the Taliban and Dostum so he decided the best course for them would be to go back to Kabul.

As restricted as their lives had been in Peshawar, nothing could have prepared the family for the limitations and dangers of life under Sharia law as interpreted by the Taliban's imams in Kabul. Men who had hailed from the poorest of villages, who had received only corrupted Koranic instruction, who had only known a harsh existence where women and girls were unseen, were now drafting laws and edicts for the entire population. Men who had been raised in madrassas had become ministers in a national government. They feared women as dangerous creatures who appealed to human weaknesses and wicked appetites. They believed men needed protection from women. Women needed protection from their own vanity.

Here is a sample from a decree posted to the citizens of Kabul, as translated from Dari:

> Women, you should not step outside of your residences. If you go outside of your house, you should not look like the women who used to go with fashionable clothes wearing much cosmetics and appearing in front of men before the coming of Islam.

One half of the city's population literally disappeared under a sea of bright blue burqas. Female faces vanished from all public places and were seen only within the security of their own homes and only by those who were closely related. The veil ruled the lives of women and girls, reducing their public personae to the anonymity of a piece of cloth.

Ruby rejected the burqa until she realized she could not leave the house again unless she wore it. She was a tiny girl for her age and the clumsy garment tangled with her feet. She fell down a flight of stairs the first time she tried to go outdoors and swore she would spend the rest of her days at home rather than don the offensive thing again. But Mobina needed the help of her oldest girl for shopping expeditions that had to be completed quickly, lest they run afoul of the religious police. The girl was forced to put the burqa on almost daily.

Ruby recalls returning from the shops one day with a bag of groceries in each hand. She couldn't see properly through the gauze that covered her eyes and she fell into an open sewer that was deep enough that she all but disappeared. Some shopkeepers came to help Mobina to get the little girl out of the muck and she was still holding the grocery bags in both hands when she surfaced. A stranger took her and Mobina into his shop and attempted to clean the foul water from her burqa as Ruby cried.

There was another memorable outing involving both girls and their mother. It was a warm summer day and the religious police didn't seem to be around, so they dared to stop for ice cream on the way home. Robina pulled her treat under her burqa to eat it but suddenly she saw people screaming and running. The authorities were chasing people and beating them as they ordered them to the mosque for prayer. The girls dropped the ice creams and ran as best they could for the safety of home, not even stopping to see which way their mother had gone. The plan was drilled into their heads—if they should become separated for whatever reason, they were to head for the apartment rather than run the risk of being alone on the street, looking for each other. Mobina arrived home shortly after the girls did.

That plan didn't work on another occasion when the sisters and their mother were out. Hossai was wearing only a chador, as the headscarf is called in Afghanistan. It covered her hair and neck but left her nine-year-old face exposed. That was enough to incite the rage of one of the morality officers who began to chase her. Hossai ran while the enforcer pursued the little girl through the streets. Hossai will never forget the shock of being repeatedly struck on her back with the short leather whip the religious police used to discipline miscreants. A stranger quickly pulled her off the street into a shop, away from the officer, and then stayed with Hossai until her mother and sister arrived.

The girls' existence in Kabul was without play, joy, or celebration of any kind. They were not permitted the kiss of the sun on their faces or the flutter of a breeze through their hair. They dared not look out a window without wearing a burqa for fear of being seen by the police who sometimes ordered windows to be whitewashed so passersby could not be tempted by even the glimpse of a female face. Dolls were considered idolatry; toys forbidden; TV and movies were the work of infidels; books other than the Koran were banned.

Life for the boys was not substantially better. Muhammad and Mujeeb, now eight and six, were compelled to attend the Taliban's version of Koranic school. Boys who failed to properly recite selected passages from the holy book had the soles of their feet beaten with sticks. The brothers were compelled to wear turbans; Mujeeb could never properly wrap it around his head and he lived in fear of being punished for his poor decorum. They didn't dare fly kites, once an obsession for children in Afghanistan. Only on rare occasions would they join other boys to kick a ball around while always on the lookout for the police. Sports arenas were used for public executions and

Afghans were expected to attend. They did so by the thousands though the Aryubwals were never among them.

Mobina home-schooled her daughters as best she could and soon the neighbours begged her to teach their daughters as well. Mobina soon found herself running an underground school for girls and young women where up to twenty pupils arrived each day, wanting instruction in the basic curriculum. Mobina taught reading and writing; Asad was the math instructor; Ruby taught them English. Mobina hired a male teacher, a former colleague, to conduct tutorials for her own children while she became preoccupied with lessons for the other pupils.

It's difficult to exaggerate how dangerous it was to run this school and also to bring a man who was not related into their home. Mobina taught the students in small groups and staggered their arrival throughout the day in order to avoid detection. When a local Taliban member learned of the school he inquired whether his three daughters could attend. Mobina could hardly say no. Asad knew that if they were caught they could be thrown in prison or even executed, but he and his wife viewed education as paramount, almost as important as life. And it wasn't enough to teach only their own children. Asad and Mobina believed in the power of universal education, the liberating quality of having a mind well developed. The Aryubwals were living under the authority of people who corrupted the idea of learning, who poisoned young minds with dogma. The Taliban had banished teachers from the schools and rejected the curriculum precisely because they knew how powerful it was. Asad and Mobina defied them in the only way possible, by secretly empowering girls and young women.

Thanks to her mother, Ruby had more book learning than most other girls in their pre-teens and she had taught herself to speak and read English. She was gratified to hear women twice her age call her "teacher." Her pupils would stay late, even as she was obliged to help prepare the evening meal for her family, in order to benefit from more instruction. Ruby put them to work, peeling, chopping, frying, while she recited the alphabet and provided the English words for common objects. There was one dangerous moment when the Talib father accused them of attempting to teach Christianity to his daughters, a charge that alarmed and confused the Aryubwals until they realized that the man had conflated the English language with the religion of the infidels. All was explained and the underground school continued.

The Talib was relieved, since he was happy to have his girls educated, testimony to the fact that there were many in the organization who were actually relatively moderate. A large number of Taliban members had only joined in order to help drive the warlords from their streets and they didn't really subscribe to the extremism. The Wahhabi-style government that had been imposed on Afghans was mostly the influence of Pakistan and the Arab clerics who had sway with the Taliban leadership. The Taliban was a complex and often misunderstood organization.

The Aryubwals found a rhythm to survive their troubled years in Kabul. Mobina gave birth to her fifth child, a little girl named Hossna. The entire family doted on the new baby even as they despaired for her future as a girl in the Taliban's Afghanistan. Asad was earning money working at a public call centre, a facility where Afghans had access to telephones. Mobina and Ruby ran their illegal school and the boys were learning how to circumvent the wrath of the mullahs. But outside forces were conspiring to roil the waters once again.

On a bright September afternoon in 2001, as Ruby lectured "A is for Apple, B is for Ball" to a dozen girls and women who dutifully recited back to her, nineteen young men on the other side of the world boarded passenger planes that would never arrive at their destinations. Instead, the aircraft would become weapons of mass murder, smashing into buildings in New York City and Washington, DC. A fourth plane crashed into a field outside Shanksville, Pennsylvania.

George W. Bush was in Sarasota, Florida, also in a classroom, reading a book that would have appealed to Mobina's young scholars—*The Pet Goat*. He was awkwardly hunkered down among the children when an aide interrupted and whispered the catastrophic news. The expression on his face was one of bewilderment as he learned that jumbo jets had just crashed into the twin towers of the World Trade Center.

At the same time, Osama bin Laden and his sidekick, Ayman al-Zawahiri, were on the move in Afghanistan, packing their wives and children into vehicles to be whisked to safety by Pakistan's ISI. The men would follow soon afterwards, suspecting that Taliban hospitality might now become a little strained.

For many people in the West, possibly including George W. Bush, the well-coordinated attack on a beautiful late-summer's day seemed to have come out of nowhere. But Asad remembers tensions and fears mounting in Kabul well before September 11.

Just a year earlier, al-Qaeda had ambushed the destroyer USS *Cole* as it was anchored off the coast of Yemen, killing seventeen US servicemen. Asad was among the many Afghans who suspected that such a brazen attack on a presumably secure American target would embolden al-Qaeda to try something bigger, and he was troubled that his country was playing host to the most dangerous terrorist organization in the world. If al-Qaeda attacked the United States, its leaders would be punished. But Afghanistan, where they'd found safe haven, would undoubtedly be punished too.

Asad says that an even louder alarm went off in his head when he learned that Ahmad Massoud had been assassinated. Though it merited hardly a mention in Western media, Massoud's murder was shocking news in Afghanistan. Two men, posing as journalists, had gained access to the carefully guarded inner sanctum of the Lion of Panjshir and detonated concealed explosives. It was an open secret in Kabul that al-Qaeda was behind it. Afghans knew that if Osama bin Laden was so determined to get rid of Massoud, it meant something major was possibly about to happen. And it did, just two days later, on September 11.

Access to news was difficult to get but people in Kabul had their clandestine sources—radio receivers and concealed televisions kept them up to date. Asad first learned about the attacks at the public call centre where he worked. A number of Arabs, thought to be related in some way to al-Qaeda, lived in Kabul. On September 11, the Arabs suddenly arrived at Asad's office eager to use the phones. Public calls could be monitored by the Taliban but Arabs were allowed to use a special line inside the office where they had privacy. Employees were curious about all the excitement and they listened in. Asad remembers how the Arabs seemed to be gloating as they relayed the news of the successful hit on the United States. He felt badly for the Americans but he feared what was coming next. Afghans braced themselves.

Even after twenty years of war, hundreds of bombardments and countless lethal attacks on the cities where he had lived, nothing could have prepared Asad for the intensity of the US-led attacks on his country after 9/11. The war did not come from the north, south, east or west as it had in the past: it came from 35,000 feet in the air, as the US and its British allies unleashed their lethal fury. Spirits, Lancers and B-52 Stratofortress bombers dropped their payloads on the densely populated cities of Afghanistan—wherever US intelligence told them the Taliban and al-Qaeda might be lurking. Supersonic fighter aircraft attacked multiple targets; Tomahawk cruise missiles screamed across the skies. There has never been an accurate count of the civilians killed in the course of Operation Enduring Freedom and it's hard to credit White House claims that they did whatever they could to reduce the "collateral damage." In its quest to avenge the deaths of so many innocent Americans, Washington believed it had righteous indignation on its side as well and political consent at home and abroad.

George Bush launched a war that would consume the remainder of his presidency, spill over into his successor's term of office and destabilize the world order for decades. He set the rhetorical tone in his address to the nation, on September 20, just over a week after the World Trade Center collapsed and after he had signed an authorization for the CIA to do whatever it thought necessary in Afghanistan to avenge the attacks on Americans. "I will not forget the wound to our country and those who inflicted it," he said. "I will not yield; I will not rest; I will not relent in waging this struggle for freedom and security for the American people." He told Americans to anticipate a military campaign "unlike any other we have ever seen."

Journalist Bob Woodward had access to the secret deliberations of the US National Security Council and he also interviewed the president for his book *Bush at War*. He wrote that while Bush was on television encouraging Americans "to live your lives and hug your children," Cofer Black, the director of the CIA's Counterterrorism Center, was telling the

Russians: "We're in a war . . . we're coming. . . . We're going to kill them. We're going to put their heads on sticks. We're going to rock their world."

Yet in all the communiqués and discussions to which Woodward was privy, it was unclear whom the White House regarded as the enemy. Obviously Osama bin Laden was a target, but what about the Taliban? Woodward's book reveals that the US was deeply confused as to who its adversary was, where the enemy resided, and how extensively the US should "rock their world." How was the US to give the American people what Bush believed they wanted—revenge delivered with shock and awe, death and destruction—and not consider the effect it would have on Afghanistan?

In the backrooms, Defense Secretary Donald Rumsfeld insisted that after the military operation, the US had no interest in nation-building. Secretary of State Colin Powell saw the future differently, and claimed that the US would have a moral obligation to repair the damage it inflicted on Afghanistan. Powell wanted the White House to reassure Afghans that there would be a cohesive plan following the US invasion of their country. For those State Department and CIA personnel who had been around when the US abandoned Afghanistan the first time, under Ronald Reagan, this was déjà vu.

While President Bush exhibited no reluctance to order aerial attacks on Afghanistan, he was squeamish at the prospect of putting American soldiers on the ground. And so the Pentagon cast about for likely collaborators among the various Afghan warlords who could follow up the aerial assault. The most promising ally would have been Ahmad Massoud, now lost to them. Only after 9/11 did the State Department acknowledge that Massoud had actually warned the US that a massive attack was coming. Al-Qaeda had had good reason to kill the Lion of Panjshir.

Washington was prepared to pour millions of dollars into the pockets of Northern Alliance commanders if it meant they could save the billions of dollars it would cost to put American soldiers into combat. And the word "quagmire" had emerged in White House circles. George Bush feared finding himself in an offensive that might later be compared to the failed American war in Vietnam. So the United States turned to the next most powerful warlord after Massoud. General Rashid Dostum didn't hesitate before he accepted the assignment.

Once on the US payroll, Dostum offered American dollars—already arriving by the truckload—to anyone who would join him. All his officers would be salaried and their expenses would be covered by American taxpayers. This was a departure from Dostum's previous recruitment drives. When Asad was compelled to sign up in the early 1990s, he was obliged to finance himself and supply the salaries of the few dozen men under his command. Dostum promised this time would be different. He got the message out to Asad, and anyone else who might have reservations about engagement, that there would be serious consequences for those who failed to do their duty.

Asad and Mobina realized that it was time, once again, to leave Afghanistan. Baby Hossna was only five months old and the entire country was under attack. They'd heard that the US had arranged for a cordon sanitaire—a safe passage through the fighting. And so the Aryubwal family joined tens of thousands of Afghans heading, once again, to Pakistan. US-issued leaflets dropped from the sky, warning that the Taliban was to be targeted in certain areas and that civilians should avoid those places. It was a treacherous journey.

US and British bombs whistled through the air while, on the ground, a posse of warlords and their men, under the banner of the Northern

Alliance, pursued the Taliban and al-Qaeda throughout the northern provinces. President Bush, National Security Advisor Condoleezza Rice, Donald Rumsfeld and Colin Powell followed developments from Washington and a record of their war-room chatter shows that they were in awe of the Afghan warriors, particularly Rashid Dostum.

The US backed him up with a fierce campaign of bombing, including several massive BLU-82s, or "daisy cutters," first used by the US in Laos, whose detonations could blow out the lungs and eardrums of people in the target zones. After defeating the Taliban in the north, General Dostum rode triumphantly back into his hometown with six hundred men on horseback. He was then preparing to lead the charge into Kabul, the final stronghold of the Taliban, but to the surprise of everyone, the Taliban simply fled the city before the US and the Northern Alliance could attack. Some thousands of Taliban stragglers got trapped in the neighbouring province of Kunduz where they surrendered to Dostum's men, with the negotiated understanding that they would turn in their weapons and go home. These are the men who ended up in the mass grave of Dasht-i-Leili.

Mobina, Asad and the children had made their way along the dangerous roads and over the now too-familiar mountain pass into Pakistan. Much of Asad's extended family had also fled Kabul and the Aryubwal clan secured a large house where five families could stay together. Robina found herself surrounded by cousins, most of them girls and women. Pakistan did not provide schools for the refugees, but many foreign countries sent aid for Afghan children, in particular for females. Horror stories of Taliban abuse, especially that of women and girls, were part of the daily fare of US, Canadian and European news. Ruby, along with her sisters and cousins, returned to classrooms supported by aid agencies.

Asad once told me that in the course of his marriage, he was the most proud of his wife during the time his extended family stayed together in the big house in Peshawar. Instead of being cowed by her in-laws, Mobina would get up early each morning to wake all the children and ensure that they got off to school on time. Ruby's girl cousins wanted to lounge around, waiting out the war, but Mobina wouldn't allow it. For whatever reason, the other parents tolerated her morning regimen. They were perhaps relieved that the children had something to do.

By December 2001, Kabul was in the hands of the Americans and Asad decided he would attempt a return to the city to see if it was safe for the family to come home. The worst of the fighting had ended, but the Afghan countryside was lawless and he had to choose his route carefully. He still ran into trouble. At one checkpoint, he and all the other people travelling with him were ordered out of the car. They were beaten, then forced to stand, waist deep, in frigid water for hours, while they bargained for their lives. Without explanation the renegades spared them but took everything of value, including the money Asad had hoped to use to rent a house for his family in Kabul. He was now broke, but he wasn't broken and he was, at least, alive.

Asad continued on foot through rough war-torn terrain, talking his way past skittish militiamen who no longer knew who ran the country, who was fighting whom, and what side they were on. When he finally arrived in Kabul, the scene shocked him. Yes, the Taliban were gone, but there was no one in charge, no authority of any kind. Even in the years of civil war there was always some faction in control of particular city sectors, but this was just anarchy. In Washington, Rumsfeld and Powell were feuding and they still hadn't resolved their difference of opinion about what role the Americans should play in a post-Taliban

Afghanistan. There was a power vacuum in Afghanistan that was, in military slang, FUBAR: Fucked Up Beyond All Recognition.

What that translated to on the ground in Kabul was bedlam. Afghan militiamen roamed the streets in Datsun pickups, wielding rocket-propelled grenade-launchers and submachine guns. Kabul had been a prize they'd been seeking for years. They had fought the Soviets, then each other, and finally the Taliban. Now they were over-armed by the Americans and overstimulated by victory but they were under-led and definitely under-disciplined. Asad also soon discovered that Kabul had been invaded by another force, this one unarmed, but also overstimulated and largely under-disciplined: a legion of foreign journalists. Television crews and news reporters had arrived on the scene to cover the US-led war within days of the first bombs. French journalists, who had employed his brother as a fixer, booked Asad for a TV interview when they learned that he could describe the mayhem of the countryside he had just crossed. Asad found the experience of being questioned by a journalist to be disorienting but liberating. Strangers seemed to care what he had been through and what he had to say about it.

News stories and pictures of Afghans like Asad were broadcast around the world, raising questions about Washington's lack of control. The reports finally forced the US to impose some kind of order. NATO countries, including Canada, agreed to take a role in nation-rebuilding following a donor's conference at which a number of countries pledged billions of dollars in aid. The US eventually decided to join the effort but at Rumsfeld's insistence, it would contract out the work to private American companies. Warlords soon reinvented themselves as politicians and entrepreneurs, lining up for contracts and jobs in government.

Mobina later followed Asad back to Kabul with the children. Even with the Taliban gone, most women were still wearing the blue burqas in the streets, but every day more of them ventured into public places without one, choosing a head scarf instead. The boys could safely go outside to kick a soccer ball or fly a kite without fear of punishment. Ruby and Hossai could once again feel the sunshine on their faces.

Senator Hillary Clinton and the former US secretary of state Madeleine Albright led an international outcry against the injustices suffered by Afghan women and girls under the Taliban regime. They raised international funding for education. Schools whose doors had been shuttered for years reopened. Eager young students crammed into shrapnel-scarred classrooms, happily doubling up at broken desks. Overflow classrooms were set up in the hallways while foreign aid agencies repaired the damaged buildings. The Afghan Ministry of Education put out a request for teachers to return to work and Asad urged Mobina to sign up. She feigned reluctance and then surprised the family by coming home one day with smart new clothes and a fashionably short haircut, announcing she was going back to work.

Asad happily agreed to become the house husband and the Aryubwals began to enjoy their lives. Predictably, Asad's kin condemned their lifestyle. It was too Western, a betrayal of traditional values, especially with a new baby in the family, but Asad and Mobina didn't care. To whatever degree it was possible, they were going to have the life they had dreamed of since the day Asad persuaded Mobina to marry him.

The future seemed secure and, for once, they thought they could look forward to a period of stability. But then they encountered a little team of journalists from Canada.

V

When Warlords Rule

BY THE TIME ASAD WAS IN HIS FORTIETH YEAR, he had been compelled to leave his country three times. The first was to escape being drafted into the Soviet-led Afghan army. The second was to elude the wrath of the Taliban after it invaded Mazar-e-Sharif. The third was to protect his family from the American bombing campaign and to avoid being conscripted into Dostum's Northern Alliance militia. After each escape, Asad returned. Afghanistan was his home.

But the fourth and last time he had to flee was because of me. And on that occasion, there was no going back.

He had survived Soviet despots, the Taliban theocracy and the tyranny of warlords. He had kept his wife and children safe through three wars. But he couldn't escape the consequences of speaking his mind to a journalist. The penalty for that was banishment.

Asad doesn't remember much about our first encounter at the Mustafa Hotel in January 2002. I told him what I recall: returning from the

Rabbani interview, feeling dispirited, meeting him in the big room of our makeshift CBC bureau and then having a lively conversation. Realizing that he could become the heart of our documentary.

What he remembers is his frame of mind during that encounter. Sher Shah, our fixer and his relative, had asked him to come to our hotel, possibly to do an interview about Rashid Dostum. He agreed, he says, because he felt burdened by his thoughts and feelings concerning the warlords. He needed to vent and he decided that he would do so with us.

It's surprising that he was willing to meet us at all, given his previous experience with foreign journalists. The French TV crew that had interviewed Asad when he returned from Pakistan had seemed decent enough at first. At the behest of his brother Akbar, who was the fixer for the Agence France-Presse reporters, Asad had told them about his horrifying journey back to Kabul. The interview became part of a news story about the anarchy that was sweeping Afghanistan since the US-led invasion. When the French reporters learned of Asad's association with the notorious Rashid Dostum—that he had actually been a general in the warlord's militia—they begged him to talk about it on camera. But the reporters wanted to script what he'd say. When he refused, they offered to pay him. "My words are not for sale," Asad told them. The last straw was when one member of the TV crew inquired whether Asad would agree to submit a phony invoice for a false expense claim—he even offered a kickback as an incentive. Asad was outraged.

The pool of fixers working with foreign reporters in Kabul was small and they kept in touch with each other. Sher Shah knew about this incident with Akbar's AFP clients—he had actually introduced Akbar to the French TV crew—and he wondered if Asad would be more willing talk to the CBC. The fact that we don't pay for interviews worked to our advantage; Sher Shah was able to persuade Asad that he would have a better experience with the Canadians.

What motivated Asad was that he wanted to be an active contributor to Afghanistan's recovery, not someone sitting on the sidelines, a passive spectator. After everything he had been through, he thought his experience and inside knowledge might be put to good use. Sher Shah assured him that we were attempting to do a serious examination of the role of warlords and their influence and that telling his version of events might make a difference.

Asad says he was pleased with our encounter at the Mustafa Hotel and that's why he had agreed to the interview. He decided to escort us to Mazar-e-Sharif because it would give him a chance to inspect his wife's property but he also wanted to be part of our field trip. He was curious as to what we would find. Afghans are usually cautious around strangers, a product of both culture and history, but Asad was different.

To me, he had seemed relaxed and even playful on the road trip to Mazar-e-Sharif, especially during our snowball fight, but in actual fact Asad had been quite tense. He was acutely aware of the perils along the northern highway, having travelled the route many times before, and he was on the lookout for a possible ambush. The NATO disarmament program, which obliged Afghans to hand over their firearms to the authorities, had yielded scant results. Asad knew there were a lot of people still in possession of a wide range of weapons, including Kalashnikovs, and he was on high alert throughout the trip.

At Mobina's family farm in Dehdadi, Asad spent his first day on the land while Heather, Brian and I went off to explore Dostum's fort. When we couldn't get past the gate, Asad offered to go back with us and provide an introduction. At the time, that's all I knew of his efforts to help. I've learned since that he actually went much further, persuading

Dostum's people to allow us in and telling the senior commanders of the fort that it was in their best interest to show us the scene of the uprising. Dostum's men knew that the vast majority of the Taliban POWs had been killed and they were aware that the deaths were controversial. But Asad told them we were only interested in the truth. Somehow, the commanders didn't see that as threatening to them. Without Asad's powers of persuasion, I doubt we would have gained access to the fort. But I think that it was that intervention, as much as it was the on-camera interviews, that ultimately sealed Asad's fate.

As we continued our filming around Mazar-e-Sharif, Asad would sometimes turn up to see how things were going and perhaps offer his assistance. He felt it was his responsibility to support us but he also wanted to help Sher Shah, his relation, who didn't have many contacts in the region. When Asad appeared bothered and distracted, especially at the end of the day, we assumed it was something to do with the estate. I've since learned the true reason for his apprehension—he was actually trying to thwart a plan to take us hostage.

Asad was on friendly terms with many people in Mazar, a prerequisite for surviving in that complex world. One night, a local gangster came by to tell Asad something he had heard from his criminal network: the militiamen who worked for General Atta were planning to abduct me and my colleagues. That's why the men in pickups had been following us around town since we had done our interview with Atta. Apparently, they thought we were Americans and assumed we were travelling with large amounts of money.

Since the kidnapping operation would be large, they were looking for recruits with weapons who might want a piece of the action, which was how Asad's gangster contact had learned about it. According to the plan, Asad would be killed because he would be able to identify the criminals. They would also have to murder Sher Shah and then hold the rest of us for ransom, after stealing whatever valuables we were carrying. Asad stressed to the man that we were Canadians, and probably had very little money. We'd be insignificant in terms of an exchange. But the informer said he was already risking his own life just talking to Asad. He certainly wasn't going to give himself away by trying to dissuade the would-be kidnappers from their idea.

Asad then hatched his own plot. He hired off-duty police to stand guard all night with their weapons at the ready. Then he invited local low-lifes to hang out and play cards with him hoping they would notice the security arrangements and get word back to the underworld—best to steer clear of Asad and his guests unless you're interested in a shoot-out. Evidently, the strategy worked.

This, when I found out about it, explained the mysterious men with guns we'd seen around the property and the unsavoury types we saw visiting Asad late at night. He told Sher Shah of the plot as soon as he learned of it but Asad could never adequately explain why he kept it a secret from Heather, Brian and me. I once asked Sher Shah why he'd never disclosed the plot to us either, and he said he had kept us in the dark at the behest of Asad who didn't want us to worry. Sher Shah had feared for his life at the time and yet he never abandoned us. They both confess to having been hugely relieved when we'd finished our work and headed back to Kabul.

Asad was pleased that I kept in touch with him and his family after my return to Canada but it was his daughter Ruby who really drew me into their orbit. She wrote charming emails and phoned me from time to time.

I usually persuaded her to hang up so I could call back and absorb the long-distance charges. The conversations invariably began with a dozen questions about everyone's wellbeing, including my own family members whose names Ruby was learning. At first I was uncomfortable with these exchanges, realizing that there was a kind of intimacy developing. I often maintained contact with subjects of past stories, but I was beginning to feel personally involved with this family, especially with Ruby.

I convinced myself that this relationship was a part of the job. Ruby provided me with a unique vantage point for observing what was happening inside Afghanistan at this crucial point in history. Canada was among the players who were deeply engaged in the post-war redevelopment of the country. International aid agencies were arriving in droves and NATO countries had pledged billions of dollars in support to keep Afghanistan from sliding once again into chaos. Ruby's teenaged chatter about her life in Kabul was illuminating.

All of the Aryubwal children had returned to school and they seemed to be thriving. One of the many institutions in Kabul that began offering instruction to girls was a school called Lycée Malalai, named after the woman known as Afghanistan's Joan of Arc. As legend goes, Malalai was responsible for a decisive Afghan victory against British forces in 1880, when she shamed her countrymen into having the courage to confront the foreign invaders. Many girls bear her name, including the Pakistani Nobel Peace Prize–winner Malala Yousafzai, author of *I Am Malala: The Girl Who Stood Up for Education and Was Shot by the Taliban*.

The streets of Kabul could still be dangerous, but Asad was pleased to see his daughters in their uniforms heading out to Lycée Malalai. Ruby passed her entry tests with perfect scores of 100 percent in all subjects. The foreign instructors found her and Hossai's level of competency to be quite unusual; they were among the few female pupils whose interrupted formal schooling hadn't left them almost hopelessly behind. Aid agencies were coaching Afghan girls and sometimes fudging their grades in order to get them through the high school curriculum. But this wasn't necessary with Ruby and her sister. The European NGOs running the schools began to engage Ruby to translate Afghan languages into English and French. "Finally, I can prove myself," she told me over the phone. Each day, she donned her black uniform and white chador and eagerly headed off to school.

Ruby was like someone who had just spent years crossing a desert and had now arrived at an oasis. She was drinking in every opportunity for education. When she wasn't attending classes at the Lycée, she was pursuing a diploma in computer sciences and furthering her English studies at a language centre run by Ustad Hamid, a childhood friend of Asad's. Hamid had given Robina one day to prepare for an oral and written test of her facility in English and she scored a perfect 100 percent. He offered to teach her free of charge and wrote a glowing letter to Asad about Ruby's intelligence. I felt proud of her.

In early 2006, Canada opted to take on a much larger role in post-war Afghanistan and I returned to the country in February, four years after my first visit. This time I was accompanied by a cameraman, Glen Kugelstadt, but no producer. The CBC was cutting back on the numbers of people who would be dispatched to cover hotspots like Afghanistan. These assignments were expensive—airfares, accommodations, fixers— but now there was the added cost of insurance. Excursions into war zones required special policy coverage and after 9/11 it seemed as though there was no safe place left on the planet. Security consultants were training journalists in basic conflict survival at the insistence of insurance companies, presumably to mitigate threat. But the companies were still charging exorbitant premiums on travel to what they determined were high-risk areas. And Afghanistan was top of the list.

I had never worked with Glen before—we actually met for the first time on the way into Kabul—and I was wary of going into a conflict zone with someone I didn't know. But he had come highly recommended and we actually hit it off from our first encounter. Glen is a big, affable man who has an ability to put people at ease. I knew we'd be okay.

At first blush it seemed that Kabul had made a lot of progress since I'd left in February of 2002. The city was bustling and lively; most women had abandoned the full burqa, opting simply for the chador head cover; there were goods in the stores and flocks of children in uniforms scampering to school each day. The effects of the foreign aid were visible, especially in Kabul. Streets that had been rubble on my last visit were paved and parks restored; families went out together and the chatter in tea shops turned to more ordinary matters than those of life or death.

Much was improving for the foreigners as well. Entrepreneurial Afghans had launched restaurants and snack bars where you could get a cup of coffee—or even a beer, if you knew where to look. Glen and I joined most of the other foreign reporters in Kabul who were staying at a luxury hotel called the Serena. It had working phones, Internet access, and claimed to have better security than guesthouses like the Mustafa, though that proved not to be the case a few years later when Taliban gunmen stormed into the hotel and massacred nine people. While we were in Kabul this time around, there was at least a veneer of normalcy, but appearances were deceptive.

Goods in the shops were prohibitively expensive. The Hamid Karzai government was barely functional; police were incompetent at best and often corrupt; and the economy of the country was based almost entirely on foreign aid. As money flowed into the country from donors, it was enough to paper over the cracks but never sufficient to reverse decades of war and neglect. Glen and I sensed the underlying tension in Kabul and felt it even more so when we travelled outside the capital. In 2002, I had rarely felt compelled to cover my head, but on this trip, it often felt necessary. I can't explain why; it was just a general feeling that there was something less predictable in the environment.

How long the international community would continue to prop up the country, given the war costs that George W. Bush was racking up as a result of his 2003 invasion of Iraq, was anyone's guess. The American presence in Afghanistan was much less visible than it had been just after the US invasion, and many Afghans thought that was a good thing. They were following developments in the Middle East, in particular the arrests and torture of Arabs in US prisons like Abu Ghraib and Guantanamo Bay, but learning that much of the same abuse was going on in Afghanistan. The US had established a detention facility at its Bagram military base where it held hundreds of people without laying charges or providing legal counsel.

Afghans had been hearing about excesses in the prison long before the *New York Times* got hold of a two-thousand-page report documenting the extent of the abuse. It revealed, among other things, that two detainees had been tortured to death, their legs so badly mangled, according to the investigation, they appeared to have been run over by a bus. And while US soldiers were actually put on trial for the deaths of the two prisoners, the Bagram facility continued to swell with detainees.

Those who were released spoke of torture and humiliation that continued unabated even after the abuse had been exposed.

Afghans had no control over whom the US considered an enemy combatant. And they were also painfully aware that the Americans had established a clique of warlords who seemed to have unfettered authority in the country. Many of the detainees held in Bagram, and at other "black sites" run by the US, were simply the enemies of former Northern Alliance commanders who had turned them in. Antipathy towards the Americans was even more intense outside of Kabul, where US and NATO troops conducted raids on villages, arresting or killing those who posed any perceived threat to their mission. Afghans were becoming convinced that the US-led mission had little to do with rebuilding their country and perhaps they would be better off if the foreigners simply departed.

There was the illusion of democracy in Afghanistan, reinforced by the election of President Karzai in 2004 and the establishment of an elected government. But many of the people who held positions of power or sat in the National Assembly had blood on their hands. We had a different fixer this time—I'll call him Karim for his own protection. He still lives in Afghanistan and it has since become quite perilous to be associated with foreigners. Karim shook his head in dismay when he took Glen and me to the Parliament, pointing out to us the former militia commanders in seats of government—men who had struck terror into the hearts of Afghans during their campaigns. Now they wore fine clothes and controlled the affairs of state.

There was Mohammad Qasim Fahim, a warlord who had supported the US Green Berets during the American invasion in the fall of 2001. He had been vice-president until the Americans suspected he was plotting to assassinate Karzai. Anywhere else, that might get you charged with a criminal offence or at the very least barred from office, but in Afghanistan you simply got another job. Fahim was now marshal of the Armed Forces, which allowed him to continue the family business of drug trafficking and bank swindling while benefiting from his associations with the government. Fahim was on friendly terms with Tommy Franks, the US general who led the US invasion into Afghanistan. American officials seemed able to turn blind eyes and deaf ears to Fahim's ugly history, though they surely were aware, or should have been aware, of his record.

Perhaps the most offensive presence in the chamber was that of Abdul Rasul Sayyaf, the former mujahidin commander, who now sat in the Wolesi Jirga, the lower house of the Afghan Parliament. Sayyaf and his men had committed numerous pogroms and massacres during the civil war and he was also deeply associated with the foreign fighters who had come to Afghanistan to join the jihad. Sayyaf had persuaded the Taliban to allow Osama bin Laden a safe haven and he helped al-Qaeda to establish its base in the Hindu Kush Mountains. It was no secret that he wholeheartedly supported the jihadist campaign against the United States. Yet, here he sat in the house of Parliament, enjoying pay and perks provided by American taxpayers.

Sayyaf was campaigning for a general amnesty for all former warriors and militiamen that would grant them immunity from prosecution. So far, he had been unsuccessful but it hardly mattered: the US had already declared there would be no trials for past war crimes in Afghanistan, arguing that such tribunals would destabilize the country. The Bush administration also didn't want to invite scrutiny of its own alleged involvement in the crimes.

A notable absence among the warlords sitting in the house of Parliament in Kabul was Rashid Dostum. President Karzai had appointed him deputy defence minister in December 2001, but allowed the warlord to run his office from the comfort of his personal quarters in both Mazar-e-Sharif and Sheberghan. *New York Times* reporter Carlotta Gall described the bizarre scene when Dostum announced his new post to a gathering of elders: "I told Karzai your government cannot work without me. I captured the whole of the north of the country from the Taliban and the whole world knows I am the winner in all of the north."

Gall reported that an elder in the audience called out, "Everyone is very proud of you!" Dostum answered: "I know everyone is very proud of me."

The announcement had taken place in the rose garden of Dostum's government guesthouse, one of the few venues with a swimming pool in northern Afghanistan. Gall noted that the pool was drained and badly needed repairs and the paintings in his office had been defiled by the Taliban, but the warlord insisted on his rightful place in history.

There were some good people in Parliament as well. A twenty-six-year-old spitfire named Malalai Joya (another Afghan named for the legendary nineteenth-century woman) had a seat in the Wolesi Jirga from which she fearlessly took on the warlords. One celebrated speech spun her onto the international stage when she stood in the house and denounced some of the new ministers and parliamentarians, demanding that they be prosecuted instead of seated in the assembly. The warlords were outraged; Sayyaf screamed at her and eventually someone shut the microphone at her desk. But she wouldn't stop speaking, her chador frequently falling from her head as she continued her passionate tirade against them. There's video of the event and you can see the fuming warlords yelling as they lurch forward menacingly, perhaps reaching for the weapons they apparently kept with them at their seats.

I later met Malalai Joya in Canada when she was touring the country in an effort to warn Canadians—as Asad had done—that they were funding and assisting mass murderers and drug dealers. Joya needed bodyguards even in North America since there had been a number of attempts on her life.

Another intrepid parliamentarian went even further than Joya. Ramazan Bashardost erected a large tent in a Kabul park and declared he was there to listen to any and all complaints about corruption and the behaviour of the warlords. Basherdost was a senior politician in the Loya Jirga, the upper house, and held a post with some authority in the Karzai government. But he was so outraged by events, he abandoned his government office and installed himself in Shar-i-Nau Gardens in central Kabul.

Glen and I went to see him there. He told us he would not return to government house until the international community recognized that thieves, murderers and drug dealers had taken positions of power throughout the Karzai government. He was surrounded by Afghans, mostly women, who came for help or just basic information, something they were not able to receive from government departments. The president routinely sent agents to try and talk to Basherdost out of his tent, which foreign news reporters routinely featured in their dispatches. But Basherdost stood in the park each day with a megaphone, denouncing corruption and savaging the foreign patrons of the warlords. Canada was a chief target for him, since Ottawa had become a major donor to Afghanistan. He'd considered Canada a principled country, a force for good on the world stage. Surely Canadians could see that there was something fundamentally wrong with this picture?

It was also obvious that rich and powerful warlords had special advantages at every turn. As the remains of shell-destroyed houses were plowed away in Kabul's suburbs, garish mansions replaced old Afghan dwellings, the construction financed with foreign currency. When they weren't building houses for themselves they were busily doing image makeovers. Dostum had hired people to sanitize his biography and a glowing version of his apparently distinguished life appeared on the website generaldostum.com, replete with information about his charitable works and his friendship with General Franks, who had reportedly given him a token of his esteem—a handgun. Dostum wouldn't make himself available for an interview with me but other militia leaders were now eager for the international exposure and Glen and I pursued them. We saw Sayyaf in Parliament one day and I slipped him a note requesting an interview. He sent a note back, agreeing to a 4:30 rendezvous.

We went to his house at the appointed hour. Our fixer was visibly shaken to be in the same room as the infamous and violent warlord. But I also knew that Karim expected me to ask hard questions, to be at least as forward as Malalai Joya, who fearlessly confronted Sayyaf time and time again in the Parliament. Sayyaf is a tall man with a long salt-and-pepper beard and a big turban. His eyes are his most striking feature; there's something cold and dead at their centre and those who meet him have a hard time making eye contact.

"People say you have blood on your hands, you should face justice," I said to Sayyaf, while Glen recorded his reaction. "Your men are accused of murder, rape and torture. How do you respond?" Sayyaf is fluent in English so my questions didn't have to be translated (to Karim's relief), but I realized how many of his aides—a dozen of whom sat in on the interview—also understood the language when they pitched forward in a reflexive reach-for-the-gun motion. Sayyaf raised a calming hand to indicate that this conversation was part of the new transparent society.

He answered that he had only been a brave mujahidin warrior, as had so many others. Death is a part of war and any killing was in the interest of liberating Afghanistan from its enemies. I didn't expect him to confess all that he had done, but I could tell from his demeanour that threats of war-crimes prosecution were the least of his worries. He was on the US payroll; he had friends in high places; no journalist was going to shake his confidence or shatter his immunity. The warlords ruled.

Before I'd left Canada I'd told Robina that I was coming to Afghanistan and we would certainly spend some time together. But I was also hoping to interview Asad again, to see if he had maintained his optimism about Afghanistan's future. Through my conversations with Ruby, I knew that her father had not given up hope that Afghanistan would reform but I heard that the day-to-day developments were discouraging. Asad had voiced his concerns about the influence of warlords long before many others had the courage to do so. His pluck had been the product of an

Mujeeb, Hossai, Robina, me, Asad, Mobina and Muhammad, at their home in 2006. I didn't know it at the time but Asad was already in grave danger.

expectation that, by speaking out, he could change things. Asad didn't want to accept that it had been in vain.

Our first visit to the Aryubwal apartment on this trip was somewhat awkward since the family had been expecting Brian Kelly and not Glen. In my haste to arrange this shoot I had neglected to tell Ruby that I was with a different camera operator and that Heather was not with us. I was also slowly beginning to understand that there was a lot of tension between Asad's immediate family and the larger Aryubwal clan. Years later, when I was more deeply involved with their lives, I learned the full extent of the strain between Mobina and her in-laws and the history of violence. But all I could perceive on this visit was that Asad's relatives were unhappy that he associated with foreigners and they were especially miffed that he exposed the women of the family to men who were not related. Mobina and the girls disappeared from the room when relatives dropped by and returned wearing traditional clothes. I have a photo of a stilted encounter with Aryubwal relatives, as we sat together in the parlour, no men in attendance. I'm not sure who took the photo but it surely wasn't Glen, who was savvy enough to know there were some difficulties with our visit and kept a low profile.

I asked Asad if we could return on another day and talk to him on camera about the developments since last we spoke. He agreed without hesitation. During that interview, Asad repeated his hope that the foreigners, including the Canadians, would come to their senses. But off-camera he told me how desperate the situation had become. The international community should have dealt with the warlords immediately after the invasion but at this point it was probably too late—they had become too powerful. Asad was not alone in speaking out, nor was he the most vocal of those who were clamouring for an end to warlord rule. Malalai Joya and Ramazan Bashardost had become the public faces for the message that Asad had been delivering for years. But there was no safety in numbers.

Asad didn't tell me on that visit that he was dealing with serious consequences from his first interview with the CBC in 2002. I doubt that General Dostum ever saw our program, but he'd heard about it and had issued a warning to Asad—he should shut up and avoid speaking with journalists. Asad had also been told never to return to Mazar-e-Sharif. Dostum's people controlled all the checkpoints into the city and they threatened to kill him the next time he set foot in Balkh province. I would not have asked for the second interview had I known about the threats from Dostum and his henchmen. I only became aware when it was too late to undo the damage.

Glen and I left Kabul and travelled south to join reporters covering the action at a coalition military base in Kandahar. That's where Canada was taking over command of the Multinational Brigade for the southern region, relieving the United States of the task. In agreeing to send troops to Kandahar, Ottawa accepted not only a larger role in NATO's Afghanistan mission but also a more dangerous one. Kandahar was the original base for Mullah Omar and it remained the Taliban's heartland. There was no doubt that the Taliban still had broad support in the region, with new recruits joining up every day. NATO leaders wouldn't or couldn't acknowledge that many Afghans were joining the jihad not only because they could actually get paid and support their families, but also because they didn't want non-Afghans running their affairs. As NATO soldiers raided people's homes and arrested people suspected of Taliban activity, they created an even greater incentive for men to join the insurgency.

The road from Kabul to Kandahar is fraught with security problems and travel on that highway is particularly perilous for foreigners. Glen and I were advised to fly rather than drive to Kandahar, and we were fortunate to quickly book passage with the United Nations Humanitarian Air Service. The UN and its agencies own a fleet of aircraft that they use to transport aid and staff and they sell seats on those planes when space is available. Our fixer Karim wasn't allowed to join us because UN policy doesn't allow locals to travel on its flights. I could never get a clear answer as to why that's the case.

Karim agreed to travel to Kandahar by road, carrying with him TV equipment that we couldn't transport with us on the plane. I told him to take two cars in case something happened to one of them along the way. Sure enough, Karim's driver had mechanical problems that would have stranded them on what's regarded as the most dangerous highway in the world. It took most of the day to travel the five hundred kilometres from Kabul to Kandahar but they arrived safely. Since Karim was also not allowed to stay on the base, he found a guesthouse in the city. Glen and I checked ourselves into the military compound of the Kandahar Airfield, where we were to be embedded with Canadian forces.

We were among the first journalists to join the Canadian mission in the south and we found the rules to be fairly loose. Chief among the restrictions was a ban on alcohol, but many of the Canadian journalists had their stash, which was one of the few ways of surviving close sleeping quarters with a bunch of fellow reporters. The media tent was also in the worst possible area of the airfield, adjacent to a busy helicopter landing pad. No amount of alcohol could completely dull the effects of a military chopper landing right next to your head in the wee hours of the morning, but it helped.

The chief of the Multinational Brigade for Kandahar when we arrived was Brigadier General David Fraser, a Canadian. He briefed us as to how he saw NATO's role in Afghanistan. "The three greatest empires have invaded this country," Fraser explained, referring to the Roman, the British and the Soviet armies. "They all left with their tails between their legs. I'm going to reverse that trend."

It was unwarranted bravado, but it was a common sentiment among NATO officers, and I had heard the same line from the US military leadership as well. But General Fraser went further: "In fact, we have already won them [the Afghan people] over." When Glen and I told Karim about this briefing later, he laughed. If Fraser had spent five minutes walking around Kandahar City without his protective armour he would probably have found out just how "won over" the population really was.

It was fascinating to observe the Canadian Forces on a combat mission. I had already covered a number of peacekeeping forays and I knew that the military had long felt constrained by a national mythology of what our soldiers should and shouldn't be doing. The Canadian ten-dollar bill once featured the image of a woman in a peacekeeping blue beret while standing next to the banner "In the service of peace." She's peering through a pair of binoculars, ever vigilant, but she carries no weapon. It summed up the public perception of the Canadian military while ignoring the fact that Canadian soldiers, both men and women, were trained to do what military forces do everywhere in the world—to fight. Soldiers I have encountered over the years struggle with the contradictions, knowing that the Canadian public want to see them as benign police officers walking the beat.

Following the events of September 11, 2001, Ottawa assumed that Canadians had become more hawkish—although clearly not hawkish enough to join the Bush coalition in Iraq. But soon after Paul Martin became head of the Liberal government in December 2003, Canada accepted a hybrid mission in Afghanistan: the troops would fight the Taliban and build civil institutions at the same time.

I believe the Canadian government—first a Liberal one and then the Conservative one that replaced it—genuinely thought this dual focus was possible and it did produce some successes. The government seemed to think it was also the only way it could sell a combat mission to Canadians: our soldiers would be building schools when they weren't shooting people. In other words, Canada wasn't here to kill bad guys unless it was in the interest of helping children to get an education. While the US measured its success by telling its public that X number of Taliban had been killed on a given day, Rick Hillier, the Canadian chief of the defence staff, would tell us how many girls got to go to school thanks to the Canadians (though General Hillier also made it clear that he believed the Taliban "scumbags" deserved to die).

The nation-building part of the mission was conducted through Provincial Reconstruction Teams (PRTs)—operations that paired civilians with soldiers to deliver the programs to which Canada had committed. The leader of the PRT in Kandahar had been a career diplomat named Glyn Berry. Just before we arrived, Berry was killed. The Taliban drove a truck packed with explosives into his convoy.

His murder had a devastating effect on morale in Kandahar. When Greg and I went to visit the PRT base, we found a dysfunctional shell of an operation with dispirited staff members. They had no idea when or if there would be another civilian head of mission. The ambassador's death also happened just as the Liberals were passing the mantle of power to Stephen Harper's first Conservative government. Canada's Foreign Affairs Department, now under Peter MacKay, seemed averse to replacing Glyn Berry and Canadians at the PRT in Kandahar were waiting to see what the new regime in Ottawa would want from them.

As we were embedded with the military, Glen and I were living with a battle group from Princess Patricia's Canadian Light Infantry (PPCLI), Canada's first military contingent for the operation in southern Afghanistan. The Canadian Forces personnel were relatively new to this type of mission but they still gave us fairly wide latitude to move in and out of the base whenever we wanted, much as I had experienced in the past with peacekeeping missions. I'm told that this privilege is something subsequent embedded reporters did not enjoy because later the rules changed. Future rotations of Canadian battle groups kept a tighter control over the comings and goings of the journalists who were embedded with them.

We were sitting outside our tent having a nightcap when a soldier told us the PPCLI's commander, Lieutenant-Colonel Ian Hope, wanted to see us and so we walked over to his office. Colonel Hope is a short wiry fellow with a sunny disposition but hard-assed when he needs to be. I suspected that our freedom to cross the wire or to have a wee dram on the base was latitude that flowed from him. I had spent a fair bit of time with soldiers from the PPCLI in the past. This was the regiment that decided to interrupt its peacekeeping Rules of Engagement in Croatia in order to confront the paramilitaries who were killing civilians in the Medak Pocket, the scene of a legendary battle between Canadian and Croat soldiers.

The reconstruction side of the Canadian mission was clearly in trouble, but Colonel Hope was trying to make sure the military commitment didn't go off the rails as well. He'd been assigned to push back the Taliban from a major construction project on a highway near the

Panjwaii area of Kandahar Province where NATO-supported road crews were attempting to lay asphalt. A good road with a hard surface was an improvement that everyone would benefit from, including NATO forces vulnerable to the improvised explosive devices the Taliban so easily planted in the middle of dirt roads. When we went to see him, the colonel told us we were welcome to come along.

The next morning, PPCLI officers loaded Glen and me into a Light Armoured Vehicle, or LAV, for an excursion into the Panjwaii district where we would survey security on the road construction and visit forward operating bases controlled by Canadians. We would be gone for a few days so we had to scramble to find the kit we needed. CBC provides bullet-proof vests for these assignments that are heavier than the modern (and more expensive) ones and ill-fitting, especially for a woman. The jacket was long in the torso, and made sitting in the LAV for long stretches on bumpy roads excruciating.

The soldiers with whom we travelled were initially unhappy to have a reporter and a cameraman tucked into their LAV but we soon found common ground when we swapped some of our cold rations—cookies for puddings. One corporal whom I won't name had much to say about the mission as we lumbered across the dusty plains of Kandahar. I knew he would never be allowed to speak so freely in front of a camera but what he said was interesting and so I wrote it down later in my diary.

"I don't want to talk unless I can say the truth," he told me. "But I can't. We have to fight here, and to kill. That's what we do. That's what we're trained to do. But I don't think they want Canadians to know that. Canada isn't ready."

He told us that he had received a training brief and a card describing what he should say to the media if he were interviewed. "Some stuff we can't say because it's classified. But lots we can't say because it's stuff they don't want us to say. So we have this faggy pussy line about the mission. 'We're here to make this a safe place for Afghan people and Afghan people are leading the way.' But we're fighting an enemy here for our own protection and for the mission."

He went quiet for a stretch and then spoke again. "You see how people live here? I could never live this way. This is bullshit." I'd often heard Americans make remarks like this and they usually followed with some unselfconsciously racist remarks about primitive people with bloodthirsty tendencies who were not worthy of our efforts. Just when I thought the corporal was going in the same direction he declared, "And they shouldn't have to live this way. They shouldn't have the Talibs attacking them." It occurred to me that if our government let soldiers speak their minds, tell "the truth," the public might find the honesty refreshing.

For the most part, I found the soldiers skittish and reluctant to talk with us; they were focused on what they had to do but they also knew the mission in Kandahar was controversial. We were just weeks into the Harper era and no one was sure what the change in government meant for Canada's armed forces. The young corporal in the LAV had told me how much he resented the lines they were expected to recite; generally soldiers detest lying. But even officers such as the aptly named Colonel Hope weren't sure of how to talk about Canada in combat, as if the fact that our soldiers are trained to fight and kill was one of Canada's best-kept secrets.

Colonel Hope and I had a private conversation that's too nuanced and vague to capture here, but I sensed he was struggling to articulate what he perceived to be a major shift in our role on the international stage. The mandate was drilled into their heads: they were fighting the Taliban in order to make Afghanistan a society of freedom and liberty for all. They were prepared to kill and be killed in the course of fulfilling that mandate. They were not acting unilaterally but with local Afghan forces at their side.

I found myself wishing the soldiers had more contact with ordinary Afghans. The image I held clearly in my head was that of Asad and Mobina's daughters heading to school each day, something they had been prohibited from doing for much of their young lives. Little Hossna was soon to join them and I had some hope that she would never have to go through what her sisters had suffered. Muhammad and Mujeeb were also able to attend and now they all relished the simple pleasures of childhood.

We camped out in the open that night in the deadly Panjwaii district, a hub of Taliban activity. Just above us in the barren hills, about a kilometre away, was a Canadian platoon house, a small, fortified base from which the soldiers could observe and attempt to hold this part of the region. They were up against a formidable foe. Mullah Omar had escaped to Pakistan in the weeks following 9/11 but he kept in close contact with his men and helped to channel support from Pakistan to those who were fighting NATO. Canada and the other foreign contingents were dealing with a surprising resurgence of the Taliban that was large enough to threaten the entire mission.

While Pakistan pledged loyalty to the US-led coalition and claimed to be an ally, everyone in NATO, from the highest commanders to the lowest foot soldiers, knew or suspected that the ISI, Pakistan's powerful intelligence department, was feeding information to the Taliban, as it had done for years. This was a sore spot for the soldiers and they often spoke of how frustrating it was to see that the enemy could quickly regroup and resupply after a defeat. But blaming the ISI also allowed coalition partners to pretend that their mission would be successful if only Pakistan stopped helping the insurgency. What the US and NATO did not want to think about was that an unknown percentage of the jihadists were actually just local villagers who didn't want the foreigners there and didn't entirely like what they were doing in Afghanistan. A part, maybe even most, of the Taliban members were simply fighting what appeared to them as an invading force. They had no desire to attack the United States. They hated al-Qaeda as much as they loathed the coalition forces. Afghans, especially in the south, just wanted all the foreigners to leave.

It was a cold February night with a heavy cloud cover. Glen and I had just huddled down on the ground in our sleeping bags when we heard shooting and explosions. The Taliban was attacking the platoon house with rocket-propelled grenades and the Canadians soldiers were answering with small arms fire. Illumination rounds lit up the thick clouds and the hills. The soldiers were clearly on the alert but none seemed terribly alarmed by the skirmish while some were pleased that they would get a chance to try out a new M777 howitzer they had brought along for just this sort of occasion. It was a huge chunk of weapon on trailer wheels that had lumbered along with our convoy and its hulking shape, parked in the field next to our camp, reminded me of Second World War movies.

Glen and I were instructed to stay in the area where we were camped and to sleep tight. All would be fine in the morning. Despite the gunfire, I could soon hear not only Glen snoring but also other soldiers who were sleeping nearby. A light rain started to fall and I wrapped myself in a groundsheet but found it impossible to sleep. The howitzer blasted the distant hills, firing about five rounds a minute. I was shivering from the cold wet ground and each detonation jolted me. How could anyone sleep? Water pooled in a little trough over my head and when I moved suddenly the rain ran down into my sleeping bag.

The firefight eventually stopped as suddenly as it began, though the illumination rounds continued to light up the sky. Members of the Afghan National Army, NATO's ally, were now chasing the last of the insurgents up into the hills. When all the action was finished, the remaining soldiers settled into their sleeping bags on the ground and everything went still. But I noticed that there was still some movement around one of the LAVs.

A group of sympathetic young soldiers allowed me to crawl into the dry space of their vehicle—I probably reminded them of their mothers. Ian Hope had told them that I was the author of *The Ghosts of Medak Pocket*, an account of the battle in Croatia that the Department of Defence would never fully acknowledge had actually happened. That gave me some credibility—enough to be invited in out of the rain for the night—and it gave us something to talk about till dawn.

The morning was bleak. The patch of land where we had camped was sodden sand that looked like fur on a wet brown dog. A section of soldiers was trying to push and pull the howitzer out of the wet sand where its wheels had become dug in. I knew that the previous night's events was a news story that I would be expected to report, but we weren't allowed to make any calls or establish satellite contact so there was nothing Glen and I could do. We had not been given permission to film the events of the previous night so we didn't have much in the way of pictures either. Glen had been right to just try and get a night's sleep. We didn't know what the day would bring.

I sought out Colonel Hope for a statement about the shootout that I could post when we got back to base. His aide instructed me to address my questions to a US officer who had been up half the night watching the scene. Hope was still in the process of taking over command of

Kandahar from the departing Americans and this foray into Panjwaii was part of the handover.

Lieutenant Colonel Bertrand Ges of the US 82nd Airborne Division was asleep in his armoured jeep, and I suspect the soldiers were using me as an alarm clock when they instructed me to go ahead and approach him. I tapped on the window. The officer whom I presumed to be Ges opened one eye, peering from under his helmet and trying to figure out why a bedraggled woman in an ill-fitting flak jacket was standing in the rain and grinning at him. Colonel Ges leaned forward, opened a compartment and pulled out a large bottle of Listerine. He took a swig, gargled and opened his door, delivering the swill onto the wet ground near my feet. The colonel was now ready for the camera.

We didn't learn much in the little interview except that the insurgents who had ambushed the platoon house had disappeared as mysteriously as they had arrived, according to Ges, scurrying up over the wet hills in flip flops. The colonel had little to say about the value of a howitzer in the mucky fields of Kandahar, except that its noise was probably more effective than its firepower. We both stopped to watch the gun's wheels dig more deeply into the sand the more they turned. A sergeant yelled "Everyone on the howitzer, now!" as the situation seemed to get more desperate. Hope agreed to be interviewed after I spoke with Ges and he gave a more dynamic description of the firefight, making sure to mention they were working closely with the Afghan National Army. We learned later that Ges was pronounced "Jes," but Glen and I decided that you couldn't have two better names for this mission than Colonel Hope and Colonel Guess. We were now expecting the arrival of Major Doubt.

———

The firefight we'd witnessed was small on the scale of what Canadians would encounter in the Panjwaii area later that spring when the hand-over from the US was complete. In May, Captain Nichola Goddard became the first female combat fatality in Canadian history. She was peering out of the top of her LAV, something the soldiers in our vehicle had allowed me to do as we drove along, when the Taliban attacked, hitting her LAV with two rocket-propelled grenades. Prime Minister Harper refused to allow any news coverage of her ramp ceremony—the memorial service usually held at the airport when the remains of a soldier are returned to Canada. Harper's ban was seen as an effort to avoid public scrutiny of a fact he wasn't sure Canadians would accept—our soldiers coming home dead. But it soon became impossible to keep the truth under wraps, especially when Captain Goddard's father pub-licly condemned the policy during the eulogy he gave for his daughter at her funeral in Calgary. Harper relented and televised ramp ceremo-nies thereafter became a staple of the nightly news.

The Kandahar summer turned hot, dry and dusty as NATO and the Afghan National Army launched a major campaign for control of Panjwaii. Hundreds of both Taliban and Afghan soldiers were killed and wounded along with a significant numbers of Canadians. In September, an American A-10 Warthog aircraft accidentally strafed a Canadian position, killing one Canadian and wounding thirty-six others. That was during Operation Medusa, led by the Royal Canadian Regiment, the battle group that replaced Ian Hope's PPCLI at the end of its rotation. Another twelve Canadians died during the multiple phases of that operation while thirteen British soldiers perished when their aircraft crashed. There's no accurate count of the number of Afghan civilians killed in those months, but NATO admitted that the death toll was probably high, given the intensity of the coalition fire-power. This gritty valley, which should have been growing grapevines and pomegranate trees, would be soaked with blood within months of our time there.

We stopped a few times along the way back so that Colonel Hope could hold a council, a *shura*, with local elders and tribal chiefs, dutifully telling them that the Canadians were there to help, not hinder. But Canada was inheriting a lot of headaches from the Americans. In 2006, the US was deeply dug into its war in Iraq and was withdrawing more of its troops from Afghanistan. Washington commissioned private contractors to take on tasks the government was unable or unwilling to do. An international security company based out of Houston—United States Protection and Investigations or USPI—had been subcontracted to provide the security on the roads that NATO was building and the firm was also to help with construction.

USPI was among the American companies that enjoyed a great deal of latitude to operate in Afghanistan. It farmed out the task of road security to local people, issuing much-coveted weapons permits, special ID cards and money. USPI had no obligation to be judicious about the effect of its hiring practices and the result was a lot of tension among the various tribes. President Karzai's own clan appeared to be benefiting more than others from US subcontracts, a perception that created a lot of resentment among his many adversaries in Kandahar. Local villagers and farmers regarded the privately hired security details with much suspicion especially when they saw their enemies, armed with rifles, manning checkpoints and deciding who could pass. Communities that survive on subsistence incomes, where authority is a delicate balancing act worked out over centuries, were badly disrupted. People didn't know whom to trust—including the NATO troops.

Just as US cash had empowered the warlords of George Bush's Operation Enduring Freedom, the hundreds of millions of dollars pouring into these private agreements was creating another network of mercenaries and spawning a new generation of warlord commanders. They were now called subcontractors, their gangs were referred to as security personnel, and they were licensed by Americans. Afghans had seen it all before and they knew what it meant to have these militia units, with their weapons and impunity, roaming the countryside, even if the United States declared them to be good guys.

At one of the *shuras* we attended with Colonel Hope, people made it clear that they were angry with the gangs, presumably hired by USPI, and they were especially disturbed by the behaviour of a commander by the name of Sher Agha. Colonel Ges addressed a crowd of local Afghans who had gathered in the hot sun and told them that they had to get along with security personnel. "We don't need you fighting with Sher Agha." The Afghans said nothing in return and Ges thought he had made his point. But we discovered at our next stop the real reason people at the meeting had gone quiet. Sher Agha was in hospital. He had set off a tripwire as he walked through his booby-trapped front door that morning and had barely survived the explosion. Everyone had already heard the news but just neglected to pass it on to Ges and Hope.

Glen and I later went to see Sher Agha to determine why he had been attacked. He lay in his hospital bed bandaged and broken. On the scale of Afghan warlords such as Sayyaf or Dostum, he was only a bit player with a militia of about two hundred men, but he had ambitions to take over a bigger share of the business. He looked fairly banged up but he told us he was anxious to get back on the road, literally. He said he wasn't sure who had ambushed him. It could have been the Taliban, or his security company competitors, or someone who didn't get enough of a bribe. But it was obviously individuals who had been able to get close enough to his front door to plant an explosive device.

A few days later, I had a chance to ask Colonel Ges if he had concerns about the locally hired security detail. He became agitated and by way of a reply he blurted, "We have control over Sher Agha. If we have to, we will shut him down." I said it was quite apparent that someone else was already trying to do that and then asked who was really in control of Panjwaii. Colonel Ges declared that it was the allies of the United States, including the Afghan National Army, but he was unconvincing. Now Ges and the Americans were leaving and the Canadians were inheriting the whole mess.

The ham-fisted US policy of contracting out had created abundant disagreements that Mullah Omar and his people were more than willing to exploit. In the 1990s, the Taliban had won hearts and minds in the south when they eliminated highway checkpoints that had been set up by mujahidin warlords in order to extort money and goods from people. Now the same system was returning. The parallels were lost on no one, except perhaps the coalition forces.

Just how much of a fiasco the Canadians were inheriting became more apparent about a year later when the FBI raided the offices of USPI and found that the private company had defrauded US taxpayers of millions of dollars. USPI had been a small, family-run shop, co-owned by a husband and wife team from Texas, when its owners heard about the lucrative contracts in Afghanistan. The company was actually nearly bankrupt and going under when it hit the jackpot, cashing in on the loose tendering practices of the US Defense Department. USPI probably could have continued to profit from the Bush bonanza had it not gotten a little too greedy.

Delmar and Barbara Spier, the company's owners, eventually pleaded guilty to charges of conspiracy to defraud the United States in connection with their alleged rebuilding efforts in Afghanistan. USPI had been padding out its invoices for a number of costs, including hiring people such as Sher Agha and his band of warriors. Since the Afghans on USPI's payroll were making about five dollars a day, there must have been a lot of padding. The FBI investigation revealed the hopelessly corrupt and dangerous network of warlords that the multi-million-dollar US contracts were generating. Former employees of USPI told *Mother Jones* magazine that the company's locally hired personnel were poorly trained as well as violent and unpredictable, compounding the problems that NATO soldiers encountered on the road.

The US-led mission had relied on the assumption that Afghans wanted to rid their country of the Taliban and that was probably true. The Taliban had become a disappointment to many people in the south as the movement evolved into a law unto itself and also when Mullah Omar allowed the Arabs to establish al-Qaeda in their midst. But the Taliban had been true to its word: it had ended the warlord system of corruption and thuggery that had plagued the country since the end of the Cold War. Afghans had been ready to put up with a lot of excesses from the Taliban if it meant their daughters would not be abducted or their boys raped and they could travel on the roads without being robbed. NATO and the Americans had failed to understand that they were re-establishing the very network of petty militias and warlord commanders that the Taliban had routed. Afghans aren't stupid. They knew the US would abandon them when Washington decided its objectives had been reached. They would be left with a criminal administration that was becoming more and more entrenched with every truckload of cash that arrived to pay private armies masquerading as security companies. To this day, I'm dismayed to hear Westerners lament that their efforts to help Afghanistan failed because the people are wedded to their medieval ways and simply aren't ready for democracy. Afghans have had their fill of what Western countries think they need.

Kandahar was a volatile place at the best of times, and now with so many competing interests—Taliban, warlords, NATO, US private companies—the violence had become more capricious. Journalists who were willing to go outside the wire of the military compound were particularly vulnerable to attack since we were both conspicuous and unprotected. In addition to conflict-zone training and high premiums, insurance companies urged reporters to employ bodyguards. The experts who provided our war-zone orientation were ex-military types, often from the British Special Air Service (SAS), and they had access to a stable of former warriors like themselves whom they made available for hire to hapless journalists like us.

Even though we had been unable to afford the services of a television producer or a sound technician, whenever we left the base we found ourselves accompanied by Nick, a short, stocky former SAS parachutist. It came as a shock to learn that Nick planned to be well armed when he escorted us. When Glen and I first met with him, I said that journalists might not be trusted if we arrived with people bearing semi-automatic weapons. Nick offered that no one would know he was packing and, indeed, he showed us the neat little travel case in which he carried his assault rifle. It was an AK-47 that he had accessorized to give the appearance of a US Special Forces firearm when it was assembled. He also had a concealed handgun. Nick assured us he would never take out his weapons unless it was necessary. But then, should he be obliged to reveal them, he would probably be shooting people.

In February 2006, the threat level in the southern provinces was deemed by NATO to be very high. Since the US-led war had begun, many journalists had covered stories in the Kandahar region but we were among the first reporters to venture into the region since the Taliban had returned. We had few colleagues who could provide an accurate picture of what we would confront in what was a changeable environment. A reporter from CBC Radio-Canada, Manon Globensky, was staying in Kandahar City, moving about the streets while wearing a large burqa. She could conceal her compact radio equipment under its folds and the garment also rendered her anonymous, giving her freedom to come and go. Manon was discovering that the burqa was a mixed blessing. It definitely improved her security, but only because she ceased to exist; she was often left behind in cars or someone would shut the door in her face, not noticing she was there. She was learning how the burqa could dematerialize a woman. I admired Manon's chutzpah and she was getting great stories from the Afghans she met undercover. I could have done the same, and in fact I always covered my head when we were outside the wire in Kandahar but it didn't make much difference. Our TV gear was more conspicuous. Glen and I decided to go along with Nick.

We needed to be accredited in order to have access to coalition forces and we had registered in Kabul before we travelled to Kandahar. Glen and I had decided it was expedient to present Nick as our producer, not our bodyguard. The US Army personnel who conducted the registration looked at Nick with suspicion. I think military people can sniff out one of their own and Nick's cover was ultimately blown when a Glock fell out of his pocket as he passed through the metal detector. The story followed us around like a bad smell—media handlers on the base in Kandahar had heard about the incident before we arrived and smirked when they asked after our "producer." They wouldn't allow Nick to join us on the airfield, but we didn't need him inside the wire where we had more than enough armour to protect us. Glen and I wanted to cover other stories than the military in southern Afghanistan and Nick would accompany us when we ventured out on our own.

Nick had come by road to Kandahar City and moved into the guesthouse with Karim. The two of them seemed to be getting along well enough and I hoped that this hired gun would be a comfort to Karim as we worked in Kandahar. I learned later that Karim actually considered our bodyguard to be a liability; Nick liked to dress and strut like the American bodyguards we had seen around President Karzai and Karim felt that he attracted more attention than was necessary. But at the time, it was Nick's presence that probably gave Glen and me the courage to venture into an area considered even more unstable than Kandahar.

In 2006, an estimated 80 percent of the world's opium was coming out of Afghanistan and almost all of it was sourced from the fertile, well-irrigated farmlands of Helmand, the province next door to Kandahar. Afghan warlords, both the old guard and the newly minted, were profiting immensely from the sales of narcotics. The Taliban had once rid the country of the scourge of drug dealers but its members were now also in the business, pulling in healthy revenues from the poppy farmers under their control.

Nick made it clear to us that he was not going to pussyfoot around if we were going to Helmand. He claimed to be well informed about the perils facing us—his girlfriend at the time worked with an NGO there and the Brits were in charge of military operations. So when it was time to escort us into the poppy fields he didn't just arm himself but hired two carloads of gunmen. When I protested, he reminded me that he was the security advisor. If I wanted the story I had to let him do his job. And I did want the story, badly; few reporters had documented the level of opium production in the south and this was a opportunity for a little scoop. So I agreed.

We drove west into Helmand along roads that were often sabotaged with improvised explosive devices. An insurgent could plant an IED on the highway in a matter of minutes. One vehicle of a convoy could pass without incident while the next would presume the road ahead was safe and then get blown up. It was a warm late February day, early spring in southern Afghanistan, and the acrid odour of asphalt tanged the air. Highway construction crews, financed by foreign countries and guarded by local security companies, were installing hard-top on the highways where the British forces operated. Soon we were travelling through lush farm fields already planted with crops; sugar beets, tobacco, sunflowers, grapes and, of course, poppies. Through Karim's efforts, we connected with the people who would take us to a poppy farm where we would be able to interview the landowner.

When we arrived, Nick assessed the landscape and reckoned we had about a half-hour before our security situation would start to get dicey. His armed men fanned out to guard our position. With Karim translating, I began to interview the farmer as we stood at the side of his field. Glen filmed our conversation with impatience, wanting as much of the available time as possible to take pictures of the farm. The man explained that he had once cultivated orchards and nut trees but was making much more money growing poppies. When we got to the delicate subject of who his clients might be, the farmer became cagey and Karim remarked, in an aside to me, that the man was lying.

It made perfect sense that the farmer would obfuscate on the subject of whom he was supplying and I knew it would be possible, with the right questions, to get him to reveal his buyers. But I started to feel queasy. The heat, the leaden CBC-issue armoured vest, the day without food—maybe all of the above. I also had the sense we were being watched. A black SUV appeared on the horizon; someone was observing us from a distance. All the while Karim was pushing me to continue with my questions, since we were finally getting what we wanted.

I'll never be entirely certain why, but I decided to terminate the interview. I suddenly saw in front of me a vulnerable man, a needy man, who seemed to feel an instinctive need to be helpful, to tell me things that would definitely endanger him. I saw a tiny cog in a machine of incalculable complexity. Was this story, this interview, really worth the price that he might pay when we were gone?

Glen knew that the whole shoot would be lost if he didn't at least get visuals on the fields and the poppy plants and as I was making our farewells he was rolling on the scene around us. The black SUV moved slowly in our direction. When it stopped, a tall, heavy-set man in a black turban climbed out and spoke to us in English phrases, asking with a broad smile what we were doing. He appeared to be unarmed and we were surrounded by our security detail. We had, I presumed, superiority in numbers and in guns. Nick seemed unperturbed.

But I couldn't see everything. My instincts may have been completely wrong but I had a bad feeling about the situation. I decided we had to shut the whole shoot down and leave immediately. I ordered Glen and everyone in our team into our cars. Absent a real producer, I was the boss, and it was my assessment that there was something menacing here, and not just for us. I'm sure Nick would have protected Glen, Karim and me if something did happen, but who else was potentially going to get hurt? And what would be the fate of the farmer after we left? The hapless man had already said too much.

Glen was furious as he loaded his kit into the car because he didn't get his pictures. I didn't get the interview. We had paid a lot of money to undertake a dangerous trip for nothing. It wasn't Nick, the expert, who had called it down. Why did we hire him if I was going to overrule his judgement? Even Karim was angry with me. He had worked diligently to set up this interview with the farmer. What was the point of stopping now?

All good questions. I have wondered about my decision for years. The ride back to Kandahar was miserable. Glen pointed out that he could have hidden the identity of the farmer by pixilating his face. But my sense was that the Afghan man was not a good liar and he would have admitted to his indiscretions after we were gone. Plus we had been watched. I couldn't take the risk.

It was an impulsive decision and possibly I was losing my nerve, but more than anything, I was losing faith in the prerogatives of the profession, the entitlement, the assumed value of what we do that allows and even obliges us at times to pursue people without enough regard for the consequences. I tried to explain on the long ride home that I still believed in the importance of getting people to tell their stories but we had responsibilities. I didn't tell the others but I was hearing echoes of that trip to Pakistan years before when I concluded that journalists often have their best moments when other people are having their worst. What was the price of a story, and who would have to pay it?

I didn't get a last chance to see Asad and his family before I left Afghanistan, but I felt that things were going well for them. Things weren't exactly perfect but they had busy lives. Mobina was teaching and Asad had returned to the family business at the Aryub Cinema. The kids were in school and Ruby in particular was thriving. But they were on my mind as I returned to work in Canada. Ruby would send an email when she got access to the Internet, keeping me up with their progress. She finished her school year with some of the best marks in all Afghanistan and she was offered a scholarship to study for one month in Paris, an extraordinary opportunity.

This news was delivered by phone, because the family wanted to seek my advice. The problem, as they explained, was that the organization offering the scholarship would pay to bring only Robina to France and not a male member of the family to act as a chaperone. Ruby was eighteen now and very capable of handling herself, but it wasn't the welfare of his daughter that worried Asad—it was the reaction of his kinfolk. He was worried and, as I would subsequently learn, he had good reason.

"You have to let her go, Asad," I said. And I suspect that he knew that's what I'd say even before he asked. He and Mobina were looking for an ally, someone who shared their values about the modern world. In the years since then, Asad has consulted me often even though he was usually seeking my assent for what he had already decided to do.

I should have understood that Ruby's adventures in higher education might be causing trouble when I received a photo from her, posing in front of the Eiffel Tower. She was with a new girlfriend. She was smiling, but there was something dark and tentative in her expression, so different from the mischievous Ruby I knew. I kept that photo on my desk for years, its full meaning dawning on me only slowly, as the family crisis deepened.

Paris had been a jumble of sensations for Robina. She stayed with other international students at Cité Universitaire and was in awe of the

Ruby in Paris, in 2007. A jumble of sensations and emotions for her.

buildings, the avenues and parks, the people. She wanted everyone in her family to be there with her. She munched on buttery croissants for breakfast, sipped champagne and sang French songs with the other students. They toured the Champs-Élysées, the Château de Versailles, the Arc de Triomphe and the Left Bank. But Ruby also picked up on the thinly veiled racism of Parisians, the chauvinism that outsiders encounter there.

For the final party to celebrate the conclusion of their courses, Ruby wore her native Afghan clothing, a decorative shalwar kameez in a riot of colours—pink, yellow and green with gold trim—after having attended school each day in blue jeans. The outfit must have taken up half of her suitcase and she'd obviously planned the drama of this moment. It was just the sort of statement Ruby would make: "Yes, you have an amazing culture, but so do I."

On the flight home Robina allowed herself to think about what she would face back in Kabul. She was returning from the most memorable experience of her young life, an adventure that had the full blessing of her father. But she suspected that her Aryubwal relations were outraged by her actions. Robina had done something that everyone should have been proud of. She had completed high school with top marks and was the only woman among four hundred men to speak at her graduation. She excelled in her courses in Paris and, instead of abandoning her culture, Ruby had been an ambassador for Afghans. She wanted to tell her relatives all of this, to share the sheer joy of her accomplishment, to describe the sensational moment when she walked into her graduation ceremony wearing traditional dress. But when she got home, Ruby learned that there would be no celebration with the extended family. They quickly let her know that, in their eyes, she was little better than a tramp.

I can understand, but not accept this view, when I encounter it among the very poor where even the suggestion of independence in a girl or woman can ruin an entire family. But the Aryubwals were affluent, cultured people. The men were educated. That a teenaged girl had spent a month in Paris was not about to destroy a family as deeply rooted as was theirs. But to them, Asad had always been an outlier, and Robina's trip was just more evidence of his apostasy. The full strength of the family's censure came to bear on all of them, but Ruby describes one painful moment that summed up the level of disapproval. Sitting beside an aunt at a women's party not long after she was home, Ruby was smiling broadly as she turned to speak to her relative only to be met with a hostile glare. Then the woman pursed her lips and spat directly into the girl's face.

Robina's siblings watched their relatives' reactions with dread. They all had felt scorn from their father's kin before, harsh treatment or cutting comments. But this level of opprobrium was something completely new. And Robina's sister Hossai concealed a personal reason for her dread of the extended family. She had graduated from high school with the same high marks as her older sister and she, too, had been granted a scholarship to study abroad for a semester—in Japan. But in the months her sister was away, Hossai had watched her parents being ground down with constant criticism for what Asad had done. Hossai had forms to fill out and permission slips to be signed by her parents for her journey to Japan, but she'd locked them in a drawer and kept it a secret. Her father only learned of the missed opportunity when it had already passed. Hossai couldn't bear to put them through more grief.

As Asad lost the support of his family, a more menacing crisis was looming. General Rashid Dostum was moving up the political ladder, his sphere of influence growing. When I was in Kabul I saw the large mansion he was building for himself, and now Dostum was enjoying a series of promotions in the capital, putting him in a position of power and authority in President Karzai's inner circle. There were any number of people who were willing to help with the warlord's reinvention from maniacal killer to misunderstood Uzbek general. His sons were graduating from prestigious universities abroad and with foreign assistance he had established the Dostum Foundation, a charity that allegedly provided emergency assistance and offered educational programs, which helped remake his image.

Dostum would have known that being charged with crimes against humanity is a career ender. I learned this of the warlords and thugs whose activities I had reported in Bosnia: any suggestion that they should face justice at the war crimes tribunal in The Hague sets them off like nothing else. I saw it happen with Serbian president Slobodan Milošević, when the chief prosecutor of the day, Louise Arbour, indicted him just as he was launching his war in Kosovo. Suddenly, US secretary of state Madeleine Albright wouldn't return his calls. Sudan's president, Omar al-Bashir, faced the same problem after he was indicted for his war crimes. One day, you're a senior statesman and the next you're a pariah. Western diplomats will leave the party when you arrive and money ceases to flow in your direction. Maybe one day you get swept off the street by a cop or prosecutor and whisked to the Netherlands. Dostum surely feared such consequences as his ambitions for legitimate political power grew.

Asad first learned he was in big trouble with Dostum in 2002, just after our first warlords documentary went to air. The family had gone north to Mazar-e-Sharif for a little summer holiday, escaping the heat and dust of Kabul for the open spaces of Balkh province. They had spent a day picking fruit in the Ahmady family orchard and then went on a picnic near Chashma-e-Shafa where they could frolic in a cool river. It was the most fun any of them had had in a long time. As the children played and Mobina prepared lunch, one of Dostum's commanders drove into the picnic area and then approached Asad. The commander said they needed to have a little private talk and the two men moved out of earshot.

"Why did you discuss Dostum and Qala-i-Jangi with those foreign reporters?" the commander asked. "That was a very dangerous thing to do."

Asad attempted to brush the man off: "Dostum can't hurt me anymore. The Americans are here now. I'll contact the US ambassador to say you're threatening me." Zalmay Khalilzad was the US envoy to Afghanistan in 2002, a man who had been born in Mazar-e-Sharif and schooled stateside. "You can't get away with this intimidation anymore," Asad told the commander.

Asad believed the US ambassador had more authority in the country than Dostum, and he probably did. But the commander must have found the threat of a letter to the ambassador amusing. He would have known what Asad obviously didn't: that Khalilzad was very tight with the Northern Alliance and was instrumental in the promotion of warlords like Dostum. "Your whole family will be destroyed if you keep this up," the commander warned.

Asad left the conversation and rejoined his family but he immediately began to feel anxious. He sat for a moment, reflecting on what the commander had said, and then abruptly declared the picnic over. They packed quickly and the family drove back to Kabul. At first, Asad wondered if he had over-reacted. But once home, someone called to tell him that a car full of gunmen had arrived in the park just after his departure. It was a death squad and it was looking for Asadullah Aryubwal.

Asad tested his luck once again some months later when the family attended the engagement party of a relative in Mazar-e-Sharif. One of the most respected mullahs in the region was at the event and he approached Asad with genuine fear in his eyes. "You shouldn't be here. They'll kill you." The mullah was a good friend of Mobina's family and he offered to use his connections to help get Asad out of the city, through the checkpoints, and back to Kabul as quickly as possible. The mullah even went with them, making calls from time to time to assess if they were being followed. Once in Kabul, he advised Mobina that her husband should not come back to Balkh province. Ever.

Asad can't or won't explain why he didn't tell me about these threats before we did our second interview in 2006. Perhaps he realized I would never have aired more of his remarks if I had known what happened after our first broadcast. He remembers that he still harboured a belief that it was possible to turn things around and wanted to make a last-ditch effort to get the message out before the warlord menace became entrenched in the "new" Afghanistan. I think Asad was also drawn to the seductive power of free speech. He felt elated whenever he was able to speak his mind in interviews and he wanted more. Surely he should be allowed to indulge such a fundamental impulse in NATO-controlled Afghanistan?

Following the broadcast of the updated warlords documentary in 2006, Asad received an even more ominous threat when one of Dostum's most senior commanders paid him a visit at his home in Kabul. "Why are you still doing this?" the man asked. "Dostum doesn't like these programs about him."

I can actually imagine this chilling scene because I've seen the commander who made the visit. He was featured in the home video of the party in Mazar-e-Sharif for little Muhammad and Mujeeb; he was the man with the thick neck staring coldly into the camera while chowing down on the feast that Asad had provided. The purpose of that visit had been to present the warlord's blessing to the boys—the benevolent gesture of a Mafia don. The commander's visit to Asad's home in Kabul was also at the behest of Dostum, but it came with an entirely different message.

"If Dostum told me to kill you, I would," the man said. But he was prepared to be reasonable. Instead of execution, Asad's punishment would be banishment. Asad pleaded with the man for some understanding. "This is my life. This is where I live. Can't I go somewhere else in Afghanistan? Do I really have to go into exile?" The man replied, "If you want to commit suicide, then stay. If you want to live, then you must go." The man also suggested that the threat extended to Asad's sons, the boys whose party the commander had once attended. It was a well-known Dostum policy that if he couldn't destroy an enemy, he would go after the man's children. When Asad finally told me about the death threats, he said he was actually grateful to the commander for giving him an opportunity to leave. Dostum didn't usually provide a menu of options.

In Afghanistan, there are no police or courts to appeal to, no authorities who will protect you against one of the most powerful warlords in the country. Your kinfolk are usually your security and Asad was a member of a prominent family. But he'd defied them when he married Mobina and again when Ruby went to Paris. He felt that he'd lost his relatives' support and the situation was beyond saving. Asad immediately left for Pakistan. Mobina decided to stay in Kabul to plan their departure but also in the futile hope that circumstances might change. The children were thriving in their schools and she hoped they could continue their studies.

But Ruby was in her own bad situation. She wouldn't tell her father since he was already suffering so much stress, but her studies at university were fraught with problems. In the fall of 2007, she had finally entered law school in Kabul, the brass ring she had been reaching for during years of struggle. Nothing was more thrilling to her than to take a seat in a university class. Unfortunately, the very qualities that make Ruby so successful had a disturbing effect on one of her professors.

At first, he singled her out by asking her awkward questions, requiring her to stand to answer in front of the hundreds of other first-year students. Then he began to summon her to his office for meetings that he wanted to conduct behind closed doors. Ruby refused to go. He sent her warning letters and then he got hold of her cellphone number. The professor called day and night, leaving harassing messages. Muhammad once answered his sister's phone when Ruby had left it at home and warned the man to back off. But the professor was obsessed with Ruby and he wouldn't let up. There was no authority for her to appeal to either. She was a woman in a man's world and men—this one in particular—had a need to subjugate her.

Since Asad was unaware of what Ruby was encountering at university, he told her that if she wanted to stay in Kabul to finish her law degree, he would do anything possible to make that happen. But without her father for support Robina knew it wasn't safe to stay on alone. Another one of her dreams was evaporating. She would come with the family.

After months of living alone in Pakistan, hoping that the death threat was empty, Asad finally gave up any shred of optimism that he would be able to return. All his contacts confirmed what the commander had said—Dostum would have him killed if he came back to Afghanistan. He told Mobina he wasn't coming home. She had no choice but to pack up the children and set off on the well-travelled route to Peshawar. This time she rented a car in order to bring some of their worldly goods. But she knew they wouldn't be back.

As Mobina and the children crossed the border into Pakistan, the situation in Afghanistan was deteriorating rapidly. In the south, Canada was embroiled in a military and political situation that was becoming more complex every day. Ottawa was paying the salaries of warlords commissioned to watch over multi-million-dollar Canadian-funded projects. The Canadian government had granted Montreal-based engineering giant SNC-Lavalin a fifty-million-dollar contract to rebuild the Dahla Dam, a project that was to be Canada's signature contribution to Afghanistan. The Canadian company then subcontracted the project's security to Watan Risk Management, an outfit with strong ties to President Karzai's relations. The professional-sounding name gave a veneer of legitimacy to a militia that operated under the control of Commander Ruhullah, an infamous Kandahar-based warlord known as The Butcher. Even after the US government blacklisted Watan, having discovered the company was running an extortion racket on the Kabul-Kandahar highway that allowed for the safe passage of opium, SNC-Lavalin, and Canada, continued a relationship with the corrupt outfit.

Canadian soldiers were also working hand in hand with warlords, these ones appointed as law enforcers. Many Afghan police units were little more than armed gangs. Invested with authority from the US-led coalition, they extorted cash, raided homes, stole people's possessions and incarcerated prisoners. As part of an agreement, Canadians dutifully delivered Afghan detainees into the hands of policemen and prison guards who sometimes killed their captives.

In his memoir about Afghanistan, *The Dogs Are Eating Them Now*, *Globe and Mail* journalist Graeme Smith wrote that it "broke my heart" to see what the mission in Kandahar became. He wasn't the only reporter who had privately cheered the arrival of Canadian troops, believing they would make a difference and that the soldiers were fighting what President Barack Obama had once called "a just war." The intentions of the foreign armies may have been admirable, but the outcome was deplorable. Canadian soldiers were coming home dead or seriously damaged by post-traumatic stress disorder from a military operation that increasingly made no sense.

Warlords, both old and new, were prospering all over Afghanistan, moving up the social ladder, taking what they wanted and killing those who opposed them—all with the support of Western countries, including Canada. The Taliban was growing stronger, recruiting new members faster than NATO soldiers could kill them. Canadians were spending tens of millions of dollars on the mission and watching their sons and daughters return wounded or dead.

Asad, Mobina and their children were a model Afghan family, the ideal of what we claimed we were in Afghanistan to foster and protect. It was for people like them that Captain Nichola Goddard was in her grave. And yet Asad was forced into exile because he had spoken out against tyranny. He had exercised his right to use his voice—the voice he didn't have when his father was dragged away by the secret police; when his brothers assaulted him; when his wife was abused by his relatives; when the Taliban denied his daughters the education they craved; when he stood waist-deep in a pond and begged for his life; when Dostum tried to own him. He had found his voice when he spoke through us—Heather, Brian, Glen and me—to Canadians and to the world.

In good faith, he had pronounced the truth. He was now paying a terrible price.

VI

No Place to Call Home

Once we had a country and we thought it fair,
Look in the atlas and you'll find it there:
We cannot go there now, my dear, we cannot go there now.

—FROM "REFUGEE BLUES," BY W.H. AUDEN

MY FIRST INKLING THAT ASAD WAS in some kind of peril came in the fall of 2007 when I received a phone call at work from a man I didn't know, Mohammad Fahim, who claimed to know Asad. He asked if we could meet. He wouldn't say what it was about, except that Asad had asked him to look me up when he arrived in Toronto. Our rendezvous point was a strip mall in a down-at-heel part of Scarborough, at an Afghan restaurant I had never heard of. I was dubious about this encounter—it felt a bit cloak-and-dagger—but I went.

Fahim said he had located me through the operator at CBC, which seemed odd, since I thought the family had my contact information. He said that Asad needed my help but he was sketchy with the details. I learned that Fahim had never actually met Asad—he was only the nephew of a friend—and was simply following instructions that came from his uncle: "When you get to Canada, find this woman—Carol Off. Tell her that Asad needs her help." I didn't know what to make of it.

Ruby hadn't been sending emails of late but I thought it was simply because she was busy with school. And since my return from the last trip to Afghanistan, I had been too distracted by my own career to worry about the family in Kabul. After spending more than twenty years in the trenches of field reporting, both in Canada and abroad, I had thought it was in my blood. But my most recent assignments, particularly in Afghanistan, had left me in a state of doubt about my place in TV journalism.

There were the usual indignities of being a woman on television where we're often targets for gratuitous feedback about our appearance. I admit I was thin-skinned about it and perhaps too vain to want to age in the public eye. But what bothered me more than anything else was a feeling of futility. What was the point of what we did on these assignments? We risked lives to tell the stories about often desperate people in strange places, yet it seemed to me that most of the audience watching TV news was only vaguely interested in foreign reports. Senior editors at CBC encouraged correspondents such as myself to get in front of the camera, to become part of the story. The thinking was that the public would be more engaged in our reporting if they saw familiar and not foreign faces on the nightly news. The editors were probably right but it struck me as a dubious way to get people to care about the lives of others.

When I was offered the position of co-host of the national weeknight radio show *As It Happens*, it seemed like a welcome change. I wanted to be home more. My son, Joel, was grown up and I'd already missed many of his important milestones. But there were more to come and I might be better able to share them if I wasn't always on the road. My husband was travelling less for his own work, and taking the radio job would allow me to come home every night to have something like a normal existence. The meeting with Fahim came just as I was beginning to forget much of my previous life and settle into the new job. Now the past was returning with a nagging sense of unfinished business.

At the time of my encounter in the restaurant with Fahim, Asad was living alone in Peshawar and Mobina was still in Kabul with the children. He was broke, confused and fearing for his life. He had chanced to meet an Afghan man whose nephew was about to leave for Toronto and he requested a favour. "Can you ask your nephew to find this woman, Carol Off, and tell her I need to speak with her?" Asad could provide no phone number, only the information that I worked for the CBC. When we had met, Fahim conveyed no sense of urgency to me. He didn't tell me, and probably didn't know, that the reason Asad was living in Pakistan was because he couldn't go home; that the most powerful warlord in Afghanistan had issued his death warrant. And I might never have learned any of this if not for Benazir Bhutto.

A few months before the meeting with Fahim I had been on summer vacation in Cape Breton, attempting to avoid the news cycle and to indulge in a holiday without a work interruption for the first time in years. Someone had told me about an efficient, relatively effortless method for breaking sod for new flowerbeds. It involved old newspapers and manure—creating new life from waste products, in my mind, an appropriate distraction from the commotion of world events. For the previous year, my mother-in-law had been saving her *Halifax Chronicle-Heralds* for this very purpose. I was trying to resist reading the old copy as I spread it and the manure on what I hoped would one day become a bed of roses. Then the phone rang.

A CBC TV producer in Toronto, Sujata Berry, was looking for a reporter who would go with her to New York City in order interview Benazir Bhutto. For several years, Benazir had been living in self-imposed exile in London and Dubai as she avoided facing politically motivated charges of fraud levelled against her by the Pakistani government of Pervez Musharraf. In spite of a serious risk of prosecution and imprisonment, Bhutto had decided to return to Pakistan and run in the upcoming elections. She was in the United States for a few weeks, looking for support and publicity, hoping the Americans would help her if she ran into trouble back home.

Since I was no longer working in television, the opportunity to do the interview should have gone to someone in that medium. But Sujata wasn't finding much enthusiasm for the assignment in Toronto and she knew I would crawl over broken glass for the chance to meet Benazir again—it had been twenty-one years since I had first interviewed her. I dropped everything and flew to New York to join Sujata.

Bhutto arrived at our filming location in a Manhattan hotel looking as elegant as the first time I'd met her—she claimed to remember that encounter. I doubt it. She told me her plans were to run for the office of prime minister in the 2008 election, but President Musharraf was doing everything in his power to prevent it, just as President Zia had done in 1986. If Musharraf could, he would put Benazir in a jail cell just as Zia had. It was more difficult for him to pull that off, now that Benazir was older and wilier, with an international profile to protect her. But she also had more enemies than in 1986; if she were to return to Pakistan the risks were considerable. I posed the question my collaborator had asked twenty-one years earlier: Did she really want this life of politics? She told me that no matter what she sacrificed, she had to fulfill her destiny. It seemed to me that she was resigned to the reality that, if she went home, there was a real possibility she would be killed.

As Benazir was getting into a taxi after the interview, she suggested that I accompany her to Pakistan when she travelled there in the fall. She promised me access to her campaign and said I would get an inside story. An earlier version of myself would have jumped at the chance but I was now committed to a life closer to home. Thanks, but no thanks.

If I had accepted the invitation, I would have been among those in her convoy in Karachi in October of that year, when suicide bombers attacked, killing 136 people and injuring 450 others. While Benazir escaped the ambush unharmed, she wasn't so fortunate the next time. Ten weeks later, on December 27, 2007, as she stood, exposed, waving at a crowd through the sunroof of her bullet-proof limousine, a gunman opened fire while another assailant attacked the vehicle with a bomb. The combined attacks killed her.

Whatever faults Benazir Bhutto had as a politician, I mourned the passing of someone who had inspired women, especially those in Muslim Asian countries, to believe it was possible to participate in politics and to aspire to lead at the highest levels. As tributes to Bhutto poured in, they portrayed an ambitious woman who was able to turn her grace and toughness into a formidable political alloy. But I knew her as someone who secretly would have been happy to wander anonymously through the souks and marketplaces of Karachi, living the life of an ordinary woman. She had, instead, fulfilled the destiny her father had devised for her and now she was dead.

I emailed Ruby throughout the fall of 2007 but she didn't respond. I decided that everyone was just busy at work and school. Whatever message Fahim had been sent to deliver, I had to conclude that nothing was seriously wrong. But in reality, Mobina and the children were restricting their movements in Kabul for security reasons and Ruby wasn't going to the Internet café to check her emails. They were also clinging to a faint hope that their dilemma would solve itself, or that they would wake up and find it had all been a bad dream. That's the only way I can understand why Robina didn't call to tell me their problems—they had decided that there was no need to. Everything would work out.

Following Bhutto's assassination, the CBC agreed to send me to Pakistan to report on the election that she had hoped to be a part of before her death. *As It Happens* is not a show that travels and it was unusual to dispatch its host to cover an event. But I lobbied strenuously to go; I felt drawn to the story of Bhutto and had a special attachment to the region. Perhaps fate was also intervening, pulling me back to the subcontinent; the stars were merely lining up to allow it to happen. I again emailed Ruby, telling her I would be in Islamabad but not able to make it to Kabul on this trip. This time, she wrote back.

She told me that her father had left Afghanistan and the rest of the family would soon depart to join him in Pakistan. Could they meet me there? Since the Internet café was a public place where others might access your messages, Ruby didn't want to say much more than that. But I understood from the email that something was seriously wrong. There could be no other reason for the family to leave their home and go to another country.

I arrived in Pakistan in January 2008, along with Dara McLeod, a producer from *As It Happens*. The atmosphere was extremely tense as a result of the Bhutto assassination and the election campaign was being closely watched, both at home and abroad. Musharraf was desperate to control the outcome of the vote. He put strict limits on where foreign reporters could travel, confining Dara and me to Islamabad for the duration of our visit. In order to meet Asad in Peshawar, I would need a special visa that was almost impossible for journalists to get on short notice. But the Aryubwals could travel more freely and so we arranged to meet in Islamabad.

I had to ask our fixer to get me to Hotel Greenland, the place where they were staying in Islamabad. I didn't really want to share a private matter with an outsider and had my doubts about the man's reliability, but I needed his help to find the place. The doorway of the hotel was obscured with advertising, the steps were crumbling and the room was dismal, but it was apparently safe and cheap enough for the Aryubwals to stay a few nights.

Asad was there with his wife and daughters while the boys were still in Kabul. There were a few chairs in the cramped room and we all gathered as best we could on or around the bed. There were no laughs, no gleeful hugs, as there had been when I'd seen them in 2006—just a feeling of quiet desperation. I was distracted by my fixer who had taken an immediate fancy to Ruby, who was vivacious even in this gloomy room. But since he was more irritating than menacing, the girl seemed not to notice.

We sipped warm orange pop as I tried to absorb what Asad was telling me. At first he was vague on the subject of what had brought them to Pakistan and I thought his reticence was because of my fixer's presence. But I realized that he was actually just doing his best to avoid casting blame on me. I told him not to spare my feelings. As he spoke, Asad's predicament became clear. Rashid Dostum's people had threatened to murder him because of the interviews we had done with him. He had been compelled to get out of Afghanistan to avoid being killed, possibly along with his sons.

My head was spinning and the sugary soft drink was sticking to the back of my throat. I was remembering our times together in Kabul: the lively dinners, the feasts of chicken biryani and lamb, Ruby's stories as she spoke perfect English to strangers from Canada, Asad's laughter as we recalled road stories of our adventure in Mazar-e-Sharif. All of that was now gone, as was their home.

At some point I asked Asad point blank why he had risked so much to grant interviews to strangers, for consumption in a world he could barely imagine. "Why did you agree to talk about Dostum? To criticize him? You must have known there would be consequences."

He answered in Pashto, so at first I didn't know what he was saying, but his wife and children all broke into tears at the same moment. Ruby translated: "Because if I had not spoken up, if I had not told you the truth of what was happening, I would never be able to look into the eyes of my children again." I then saw Asad for what he was: a man who lived by a moral compass of his own design, assembled from his own ideals. In a society of conformity, he charted his own course with that compass as his guide.

It's true that he had agreed to the interviews of his own free will. But no matter how much he tried to diminish it, my role in his predicament was large. As I glanced at the anxious faces, I knew that, despite whatever code of conduct existed for journalists, whatever imperatives there were in our business to be disinterested and keep a distance from the subjects of our stories, I was about to cross the line that artificially separates a reporter from the story. I was about to get very involved in the lives that were now jammed around me in that hotel room.

———

Though he had been in Pakistan for months, Asad had not yet formally sought status as a refugee. But it was an important first step if we were going to get him out of danger. The future, I tried to reassure him, wasn't as bleak as he feared—the United Nations High Commission for Refugees (UNHCR) was an institution founded on ideals of compassion and generosity and it had a responsibility to help families such as Asad's. Refugee status could at least protect him while he applied for sanctuary in another country.

One of the conditions for making a refugee claim was evidence that you were being persecuted because of what you believed or for views you had stated publicly. Asad met that threshold easily. He was unable to live in his own country because he had openly expressed his personal opinions. He had been threatened by one of the most powerful men in Afghanistan and his security was further compromised by the fact that his relatives despised him for having granted too much freedom to his daughters. The authorities in Afghanistan would not or could not protect him nor would his kinfolk. It seemed to me that Asad had an open-and-shut case for UNHCR certification as a refugee.

I told Asad that formal registration with the UNHCR would also lay the path for the family to become Canadians, if that's what they wanted. And I would begin the process of helping make that happen. How could they not be qualified under my country's asylum program? Asad had risked his life when he spoke to the Canadian public broadcaster in an effort to warn our government that Canadians were unwittingly getting involved with the wrong people. I couldn't conceive of a better argument—Canada had an obligation to help. We talked it through and everyone brightened. They would be out of this mess soon and living in Canada. That's what they wanted. I genuinely—and foolishly—believed we could make it happen, and reasonably quickly.

The next day, I picked up Ruby and Asad at their hotel and we headed to the UNHCR building in Islamabad. It was in such a remote location that at first I thought we had the wrong directions. The route took us past embassies and the offices of assorted foreign agencies and then through slums on the outskirts of the city. I had called ahead to ask about the entrance to the compound and was told we would have to take a shuttle bus for the last stretch of the journey since unauthorized cars were not allowed near the place. The bus dropped us off at a gate where two Pakistani guards reluctantly allowed us in after searching our bags.

This was the door through which some of the world's most needy people had to pass in the first stage of their path to asylum. I'm not a Pollyanna. I wasn't expecting an orchestra and a tea party reception, but if they had purposely designed it to be inaccessible and unwelcoming it could not have been more so. The UN often sites its facilities in areas that are easy to secure in order to protect their people. But this isolation was surely an impediment to those who were in need of its services.

At the wicket inside, an official slid an application form under the bars and Asad sat down on a bench to fill it out. A tiny box asked for the reasons he believed he should be granted asylum. With so little space to explain a lifetime, I urged Asad to be blunt. He didn't want to mention the CBC or me but I insisted that he do so. I assured him it was not going to get me into any trouble. He filled in his information and then slid the form back through the wicket.

The waiting area was outside—a series of benches under a roof to protect petitioners from the sun and rain. There was only a handful of people sitting there and I had the impression that they had been there for a long time. Among them was an elderly woman, missing most of the pigment in her skin; a younger woman with penetrating green eyes who seemed disconsolate; a mother—or perhaps she was the grandmother—with a baby; and two men, maybe Hazaras, who looked bewildered, as though they had no idea how they came to be there, which summed up the mood for all of us.

Only the two men seemed to know each other and they spoke occasionally. The others stared into space. After sitting for a while, I returned to the wicket and politely but firmly asked to see someone in a position of authority. A man came out to meet us but only to say, politely but firmly, that Asad was in the wrong place. Since he was residing in Peshawar that was where he should register. He would have to apply for refugee status there, not in Islamabad. Our trip had been a waste of time. On the drive back to Hotel Greenland I tried to be encouraging, though I was feeling as hopeless as the others. I told Asad I would make some phone calls to the UNHCR right away—that we were now in motion and it would all work out if we were resolute and patient. That seemed to reassure him, mostly because he had no other options.

That night I called a friend in Hamilton, Ontario. Eno Causevic was originally from Bosnia and was well acquainted with the refugee system. In 1995, not long after the Canadian government had announced a special asylum program for people fleeing the breakup of the former Yugoslavia, Eno had allowed us to set up a camera in his Toronto office where he was counselling refugees who had just arrived in Canada. We had permission from those we recorded and we kept the camera mostly trained on Eno, but during a week of filming we heard every kind of horror story imaginable. Women who had been incarcerated in camps where they were raped almost daily; families with children who hid in basements and barns for entire winters to escape death squads; men who had been held in improvised prisons where they were tortured and where they watched their friends perish from cold or lack of food. As many as fifteen thousand people came through Eno's door during the course of the Canadian program, and he helped all of them to settle.

Eno was now an independent refugee and immigration consultant and he told me that we were on the right path. The Aryubwals needed to be accepted as asylum seekers under the United Nations Convention relating to refugees before they could qualify for resettlement in Canada. The Canadian consulate wouldn't even look at their files until they were referred by the agency. But Eno was willing to start the next step—finding a group of citizens who could sponsor the Aryubwals once they were approved by the UNHCR and were granted visas by the Canadian government.

Eno didn't take long to deliver. While I was still in Pakistan he found a church group in Hamilton, Ontario, that was willing to sponsor and settle the family in their community. I took the news back to Hotel Greenland. The procedure would be time consuming, I told Asad, but he and the family were on their way to Canada. People in Hamilton were already filling out the paperwork.

When I review diary pages I wrote during those first weeks of 2008, I'm amused by my optimism. We would soon learn that mobilizing the good will of ordinary Canadians was easy compared to surmounting the bureaucratic walls put in place, by accident and design, to test the mettle, patience and the honesty of applicants. All my efforts to get more information about how to register, or about wait times or short cuts came to nothing. At the time, I wanted to believe that this was an aberration; I just didn't know the drill. But who did?

The deputy representative for the UNHCR in Islamabad was a man named Michael Zwack. I wanted to arrange a meeting before I left

Pakistan but managed only to get through to him on the phone. I asked politely and, I thought, reasonably: "Could the Aryubwals register right now in Islamabad instead of returning to Peshawar?" And I told him bluntly, "Asad is in danger of being killed by a warlord."

"Well, that's the story he's telling you," Zwack responded. The man's indifferent tone was bad enough, but to suggest so flippantly that Asad was lying was vexing. It was Asad's need to tell the truth that got them into this mess in the first place. I told Zwack that I was convinced the story was true but the deputy wasn't buying it. I kept trying to strike the right chord in our conversation, trying to be assertive without aggravating him. Rules were rules, he said. Asad would have to try his luck with the Peshawar office.

I was in a bit of a moral quandary, introducing myself as a journalist from Canada while I sought information for Asad. On the one hand, I had an obligation to let Zwack, or others with whom I spoke, know that I was a reporter. I also felt that my inquiries were appropriate since Asad's predicament was the product of my work. But I was also advocating on Asad's behalf. Personally, my motives were legitimate. Professionally, I was in uncharted and thorny terrain.

Asad and Dostum are two sides of the same story. No one would argue they were equal, but to show partiality in favour of Asad was equivalent to putting my thumb on the scale. Asad didn't need any assistance from me to emerge as the good guy in this story, but journalists are supposed to avoid even the appearance of bias, even if the antagonist is a likely criminal.

I've struggled many times in my career with the tension between personal impulses and professional codes—how not to be emotionally affected by the misfortune I encountered; how to avoid getting involved.

A flood of images come to mind: children in Sudan kicking around a soccer ball made out of used bandages while trying to avoid airstrikes from helicopter gunships; the families huddled in the woods in Kosovo while Serb police combed the area, looking for Albanians to kill; the boys picking cocoa pods in Ivory Coast who were paid nothing for their work and locked up at night. So many times I'd wanted to bundle people into a car and whisk them to safety but then drove away alone to the comfort of a hotel or airport lounge, feeling impotent and remorseful.

Most, but not all, of my colleagues maintain that you don't look back. If you've reported responsibly, you have no obligation to those you leave behind. But on this occasion I had looked back and had caught sight of a man and his family in crisis. Would Asad be in exile if he had never met me? *In the Company of Warlords* was a prize-winning documentary that had been shown in Canada and abroad. The CBC had gained from it. I had gained from it. I couldn't ignore or dismiss what I had learned in Hotel Greenland. We had a duty to help the man who had made that story possible.

Asad is not given to overstatement so I was taken aback, the last time I saw him, when he told me that I was his only hope. There was no one else in the world to whom he could now turn. I told him I would do everything that I could. I finished my assignment in Islamabad and flew back to Toronto; Asad went back to Peshawar to start the refugee application process; the others returned to Kabul to close the apartment and terminate their life in Afghanistan. Mobina knew to be cautious and not draw attention to her movements as she departed her home. She said few goodbyes, gathered precious possessions and rented a single car with a driver for their departure. She tried to leave the impression that they were on a short excursion and would be back, though she knew that was not the case. She joined her husband in exile, throwing her own fate and that of her five children into the hands of strangers.

Once back in Canada, Eno Causevic invited me to Hamilton to meet a man and his committee from the West Highland Baptist Church, the group that had offered to sponsor the Aryubwals.

Alan Beech is one of those rare individuals who gets involved in the lives of others without hesitation. Eno had met him several years earlier when Alan had heard about some boys in Bosnia who wanted to play competitive hockey but couldn't find facilities in their own country. Alan had no connection to Bosnia nor experience with the Balkans, but someone put him together with Eno and soon the Bosnian boys were in Canada playing in a hockey tournament. Eno had figured that Alan was the right person to contact about the Afghans.

Alan and his committee members, Judy Wilcox and Jay Keddy, met me at Eno's house on a Saturday afternoon in the early spring of 2008. They were new to the business of sponsoring refugees and Eno explained to them that if they took on the obligation, they would form what's called in Canadian immigration law a Group of Five, and they would be responsible for the family for one year. Eno ran through what their duties would be and also crunched some numbers for them. For five kids, seven people all together, they might have to provide as much as $50,000, or at least pledge that they had those funds available.

Eno and I watched them closely as they considered the sum but no one even blinked. I didn't get the impression that these people were rolling in dough; more likely they had done their homework and had anticipated this was going to cost real money. I showed them pictures of the family, along with a few shots of Ruby in Paris. It felt a bit manipulative. But it was important for them to connect to the Aryubwals since they would have to sell this proposal to their church community. At the end of the meeting, it caught me by surprise when Alan asked that we say a prayer. Everyone held hands in a circle that included me, and Alan made a plea to the Lord to help us to help them. I had one of those out-of-body experiences when you watch yourself doing something uncharacteristic and I exchanged a quick look with Eno, a Bosnian Muslim, who was trying not to smile.

I'm sure Alan knew this was not how Eno and I usually ended meetings but I got the sense that he needed to know we were all in this together. My own petitions to celestial forces in the past have produced uneven results but Alan genuinely believes in the power of prayer. As we said amen—all of us with conviction—I knew I was now in too deeply to step back. I wasn't going to fob the burden of this family off on the West Highland Baptists or anybody else. I was the one who had to get them to safety, though I was thankful to now have allies.

At the time that Asad applied for asylum, there were ten million UN convention refugees adrift in the world, two million Afghans among them, most of them in Pakistan. Asad and Mobina knew the camps that ring the city of Peshawar and they had always managed not to end up living there. But even outside those settlements, life in Peshawar was more difficult for Afghans than on the previous occasions when Asad and Mobina had arrived, looking for sanctuary. The Pakistani authorities severely limited opportunities for Afghans to earn a living and made existence as miserable as possible for them, presumably to encourage them to leave. I began to send Asad money each month to make sure they would not end up destitute.

The UNHCR attempts to keep most refugees close to the country they have fled, the theory being that they will go home one day. That rarely happens. A majority of the two million Afghans in Pakistan at the time were actually born there, the children and grandchildren of refugees whom Asad, Mobina and I had encountered in Peshawar thirty years earlier. And yet they had no legal status in Pakistan, nor could they return to a country where they had no connections and had never set foot. Adding to the ranks of Pakistan-born refugees were more Afghans who arrived each year, fleeing renewed conflict and deprivation. It's understandable that Pakistan, a country with so much poverty of its own, would be unwelcoming; its own resources were stretched to the limit. But the Afghans didn't have many options.

Only 1 percent of all refugees who register with the UNHCR are deemed to be in need of resettlement in another country. The agency has a special program for those who are chosen to join this exclusive club. In theory, priority is given to the most vulnerable people in the asylum system, no matter their circumstances. But over the years, selection has evolved to favour refugees who would most easily settle elsewhere. That's an unfortunate development for the world's most desperate people, but it gave Asad and his educated, English-speaking family some advantages.

Canada is one of a dozen countries that accepts refugees from the UNHCR's resettlement program, with the assumption that those candidates have been thoroughly vetted by the agency even before their files landed on the desk of a consular official. I contacted the Canadian High Commission in Islamabad to alert them to Asad's plight, explaining that he was in danger because of his participation in a CBC documentary. But they confirmed what Eno had already told me: Canada would only consider the Aryubwals after the UNHCR had given its seal of approval.

Asad went to the Peshawar office of the UNHCR to apply for asylum as soon as Mobina and the children arrived. He found a place for the family to live for what they hoped, and we all believed, would be a year, or two at the most. The advantage of staying in Peshawar was that accommodations were substantially cheaper than in Islamabad. The downside was that the animosity towards Afghan refugees in Peshawar was even more palpable given the large numbers of them in the city. Asad also worried that his family was still too close to the source of his trouble; Afghanistan was only a short drive away. I thought he was being paranoid—until the day his son was hit by a car.

It was about six o'clock in the evening. Muhammad, now seventeen, was walking home when he noticed a vehicle coming towards him. It seemed to accelerate as it approached. He darted out of its path but in a split second he saw the driver jerk the steering wheel to follow him. The car struck Muhammad and then sped away. The driver could have killed him but the boy only suffered slight injuries to his legs.

Asad didn't report the hit-and-run to the authorities. Other Afghan refugees had warned him to do everything possible to stay off the radar of local police since he would get no justice from reporting crimes and quite likely would end up in even hotter water. He didn't tell me about the incident either (I learned of it later, when I asked why they had changed address) but, coincidentally, I had sent him extra money that month to cover any emergencies and he used it to pay the costs of relocating to another apartment. Everyone in the family now knew they had to keep a very low profile until they were able to leave for Canada.

We were launched on a process whose nature and outcome were a mystery to all of us. We were getting widely conflicting advice and we tended to believe the best version of what we learned, or at least I encouraged everyone to do so. Whatever doubts any of us had, we kept them to ourselves. Ruby wrote me cheerily, "I don't know what will happen now. OK dear, have a nice time! Bye."

Whenever Asad contacted the Peshawar office of UNHCR he could never get a straight answer as to how long the application process would take, though on one visit he was told it might be five years before the UNHCR completed its paperwork. And then the Canadian consulate would take more time to investigate the file. We tossed aside such information. Crazy. Implausible. It had to be part of the strategy to discourage people and persuade them to go back home.

In a diary entry from June 2008, I record a phone conversation with Michael Zwack at Islamabad UNHCR (a difficult man to reach) who assured me in his weary tone that everything was going according to schedule. I told him that I had a church group waiting to receive the family, but Zwack still wouldn't give me any sense of timing, and in all fairness to him, he probably didn't know.

I had presumed that the UNHCR head office in Islamabad carried some authority over its branch plant in Peshawar, and that the best place to push in order to get results was with the most senior people such as Zwack. I hadn't yet fully realized that the Islamabad office of the UNHCR and the one in Peshawar were often worlds apart and contact between them was often spotty and occasionally misleading. The only similarity in their operations was that with alarming frequency both facilities would shut down without much warning citing security issues. UN buildings had become targets for extremists, which was one of the main reasons why the UN offices in Pakistan were situated in such remote locations.

The Peshawar office of the UNHCR was, itself, a dangerous place for Asad or any refugee to be. Applicants were allowed to come to the office each Thursday to inquire about the status of their cases. Asad describes how the refugees were obliged to remain on the street in front of the building, awaiting their turn to go inside. UNHCR guards with walkie-talkies would get messages from time to time, then shout out people's names, demanding to know, on the spot, what the reasons were for their visit. Everyone within earshot could hear these conversations.

Asad was alarmingly aware that other refugees took note when they heard his name called. The Aryubwals were one of the best-known families in Kabul and people would probably want to know why a man of Asad's stature was standing on the street with the rest of them. He knew that such information would be valuable to his adversaries and he feared that someone might try to profit from the knowledge that Asadullah Aryubwal was at the Peshawar refugee centre every Thursday. Asad says he refused to disclose information to the guards, insisting that it was none of their business, and in so doing he probably gained himself a reputation as a troublemaker. He would wrap his head and face in a large shawl and try to keep to himself. Whenever he felt too vulnerable, Mobina would take over the Thursday ritual, covering herself in a big black burqa of the style that Pakistani women wear, and try to remain anonymous.

The refugees in the queue could also be seen by anyone on the street. Asad heard that some Afghans had been attacked while waiting, including a woman who was shot and another who was abducted. "People who are at the UNHCR have enemies—that's why they're there," Asad told me. "They need protection." Women were especially vulnerable to so-called honour killings since many of them were at the UNHCR seeking refuge from domestic violence or forced marriages.

Eventually, the UNHCR installed a kind of tunnel outside of its office which Asad said was only a marginal improvement. Once a name was called, the refugee would join other applicants sitting inside on chairs. The tunnel was narrow and stiflingly hot especially in the summer. Asad and the others would wait there for hours and sometimes for an entire day. When it was his turn, he was directed to a window where he was again asked to state his business. Everything he said could be heard by people in the passageway. He wanted to tell the UNHCR agent that he faced a clear and present danger and that he needed his case to be expedited. But he was reluctant to give details and he didn't tell them about the hit-and-run attack on Muhammad, information that might have made a difference to his status. Asad hadn't yet been called for a full interview at UNHCR, so all the agency had on file was his preliminary application and some very basic information about his case. Staff asked him pointedly why he felt threatened, but Asad was circumspect; he didn't dare name the source of his fear, Rashid Dostum. One of the most powerful men in Afghanistan wanted him dead. This was not something you wanted to broadcast to strangers in an environment where you have no protection.

Asad saw many of the same Afghans at the UNHCR office in Peshawar each time he visited and he began to speak with some of them, exchanging gossip and comparing experiences with the UN bureaucracy. They'd all heard stories about backdoor approaches for getting around the system. These shady methods required a lot of money. There were no specifics—just the hint that anyone who had the cash wouldn't have to wait around. Asad didn't ask too many questions; he wasn't interested in the back door.

In August 2008, a man who appeared to be just another refugee took Asad aside and told him he would soon be approached for money and an opportunity to accelerate his case. A short while later, when Asad was making one of his Thursday visits, a stranger sidled up for a chat. He said his name was Mirza and he was a refugee from Afghanistan. He said he knew who Asad was, which wasn't surprising since anyone with ears would have heard Asad's name called out each week. But Mirza claimed to have history with the Aryubwal clan, going back to their home village in Paktia. Mirza said, for a fee, he could arrange a satisfactory solution for Asad's dilemma. He said that he had handled other "cases" and had a good track record with influencing decisions within the Peshawar UNHCR office. When Asad looked puzzled, Mirza became more blunt: "If you want help, I will tell the UNHCR that we have an arrangement."

Mirza told Asad that he would have to wire US currency to an account in Moscow. Following that cash transfer, a Pakistani lawyer in Islamabad would get all the needed information about Asad's case from his contacts inside the UNHCR and they would collaborate to fix the file in Asad's favour. "Then your refugee documents will arrive in three months," Mirza told him. His tone was business-like as if this was all part of the normal procedure for refugees.

When Asad told me about it, I urged him to find out how much it would cost, something he hadn't bothered to ask because he had no intention of going along with the scheme. When I insisted, he asked Mirza and learned that the "fee" for his family of seven would be in the $50,000 range. It struck me as bizarre that the amount demanded by a crime ring in Moscow was the same as the fee for a Canadian private sponsorship of seven people. Why did everything cost $50,000?

I mostly wanted the details of the scam because my reporter-nose was twitching, but I'll admit I briefly thought about the possibility. If the worst-case scenario was true, the legitimate process could take five or even ten years. Since the hit-and-run attack on Muhammad it seemed the longer the family stayed in Peshawar, the more likely it was that something bad could happen to them. Working around the system was tempting. But I knew that winning an asylum claim based on phony papers would mean Asad would be looking over his shoulder for the rest of his life. It simply wasn't worth it. And in the end it wasn't my call; it was my luck to be trying to help the most honest man on the subcontinent.

Asad ignored Mirza's pitch but he learned of other cons that Afghan refugees said they had encountered. One scam sounded like a form of identity theft. A person's asylum claim might be quite legitimate but it would be turned down. In frustration, the individual would abandon his efforts, thinking they were futile. Then the entire file would be sold to someone else who required a compelling personal narrative and was prepared to buy one. The names, places and some details would be changed but the story, being true, would have the ring of authenticity. Asad had no way of verifying this information about cons. He didn't know if these crooks were people who worked inside or outside of the UNHCR, and there was no way to check the success rate of those who bought these services. Maybe people managed to get to other countries through these scams, but maybe they didn't.

While Asad learned more of the murky underworld of the refugee business I was trying to get answers from senior people in Islamabad. Michael Zwack eventually passed me over to a protection officer named Laura Almirall, a nice woman who answered my emails promptly. This was a welcome development, but I was alarmed when she told me that her Islamabad office could find no record of Asad's asylum claim. It was September and Asad had been dutifully going to the Peshawar office every Thursday since February and he was told on each occasion that the application was in progress. By now his asylum request should have been on tap. Where was Asad's file?

The next time he visited the Peshawar UNHCR building an official told Asad that they were "getting calls from Islamabad" about him. He wasn't sure if it was good or bad to be singled out this way but soon after, Almirall confirmed with me that they now had a record of the Aryubwals' case. She suggested that different spellings of the same name could sometimes create bureaucratic errors. I didn't remind her that one of the reasons why they hired local people was to help elimi-nate such mix-ups. But I did let her know that we were encountering irregularities in the Peshawar office, hoping that might have some effect.

I told Almirall—as I had informed Zwack—that the Aryubwals were in danger. She responded that Asad had given no indication to the office in Peshawar that his case was dire and I couldn't argue with that, since Asad was afraid to tell them. But the situation was critical. Rashid Dostum was now chief of staff for the Afghan Armed Forces and he had a wide sphere of influence that included Pakistan. And it appeared that the Uzbek general was often out of control. On one occasion, Dostum and about fifty of his militia friends showed up at the house of Akbar Bai, a former election campaign manager in Afghanistan, where they beat the man unconscious. The local police chief reported that Dostum had been in a drunken rage and had attacked his former manager because he thought the man was trying to undermine his authority in the north.

Dostum did little to conceal or deny his own role in the affair. Police surrounded Dostum's house and were about to arrest him when the attorney general of Afghanistan, Abdul Jabar Sabit, told them to stand down. He gave a startling interview to Radio Free Europe in which he affirmed that no one *should* be above the law, that Dostum *should* be put on trial for kidnapping, breaking and entering and assault. But it wasn't going to happen. The chief upholder of the law in Afghanistan essentially stated in the interview that the warlord was immune to prosecution. Dostum's spokesman had declared there would be civil war "if anyone touches even one of Dostum's hairs." It was a warning to everyone, including Asad, that the warlord could and would do anything he wanted.

One day, with little prior notice, the Pakistan government announced that it was planning to close its refugee camps and send all the Afghans home. The authorities had hinted on previous occasions that they might start to deport people, but this time there was evidence that they were actually following through on the threat. Afghans living in Peshawar were disappearing off the streets and being dumped at the border without their belongings and with no way to tell relatives where they were. The uncertainty filled Asad with dread and he feared what might happen if any of his family members should be deported.

I encouraged him with news from the home front where Alan Beech and the West Highland Baptist Church were still interested in sponsoring the family. But he wanted to know what the odds were that Asad and his family would be granted the necessary refugee status. Since Alan and I were both new to the business of sponsorship, we sought advice widely from those who had been involved with refugees for a number of years.

One of those we consulted was Rose Dekker from the Canadian chapter of the Christian Reformed World Relief Committee, an organization that helps to resettle asylum seekers. She had depressing news.

Groups who wanted to privately sponsor refugees to Canada were being discouraged from looking at Afghan refugees coming through Pakistan. Rose's contacts inside the Canadian immigration department told her the Harper government wasn't interested in Afghans. Only two Afghan families had arrived in Canada as privately sponsored refugees during all of 2007 and 2008, whereas in previous years, there had been hundreds. Dekker had no idea why only these two cases had been accepted and no one else. But she understood that these were directions coming from Ottawa. Though I didn't tell Asad, the situation appeared to offer little hope for him and his family.

The Aryubwals were finally booked for an interview with UNHCR officials in October 2008. We began to gather documentation to support the case which was this: Asad had been a civilian conscript into Rashid Dostum's militia for a few years in the 1990s and had held the rank of general. In interviews with the media, he had denounced Dostum and called for his prosecution as a war criminal. This led to threats on his life. Since no one in authority in Afghanistan was going to protect him (the attorney general of Afghanistan had just declared that Dostum was above the law), he could not return home.

The other Aryubwal family members had cases of their own. The girls and women were in danger because their extended family disapproved of their efforts to be educated; Robina in particular was at risk because of her recent studies in Paris. And Mobina fit the bill of a UN convention refugee by virtue of having married into a clan that rejected her ethnicity, not to mention her education.

Asad's health was deteriorating. He wasn't able to get any exercise or even go for walks because he feared both deportation and his enemies. He was having stomach cramps and chest pains from anxiety and he was unable to sleep. We needed this interview to be successful and he called me immediately after the session to say he had done exactly what we had discussed: he simply told the truth and handed over all available evidence. But the session did not go well.

The family went to the UNHCR office in Islamabad for the interview. They were led into a room where a Pakistani woman told them that she would conduct the meeting in English with the assistance of a Pashto interpreter. She peppered Asad with questions, sharply challenging all his answers. He had been told to expect this, especially around the issue of his military record, but he was unprepared when she suddenly accused him of lying. She didn't just contest details of his story—she put to him that his entire narrative was false. The woman insisted that Asad was really somebody else, a professional two-star general with Dostum's militia and a former battlefield commander. Asad presented documents to support his story but she dismissed them. The interview was surreal. Asad went on the defensive while she fired back that his entire refugee claim was bogus. The family sat dumbfounded.

The woman then turned to Mobina and the children for what should have been thorough interviews pertaining to their specific cases. But Ruby says she spoke with each of them only for only a minute or two. No one remembers what she asked except that the line of inquiry was so aggressive, and their father appeared so distraught, that the girls began to cry. The UNHCR interpreter intervened at one point and told the woman to back off—reminding her that they were only children. Robina remembers that the woman laughed. And then she declared the interview terminated.

We could make no sense of the encounter except to conclude, hopefully, that the hostile interrogation was designed to trip up applicants who weren't telling the truth—to throw them off their guard. The fact that Asad stuck to his story throughout and never contradicted any earlier statements would work in his favour. The UNHCR woman was simply playing bad cop.

I sent the UNHCR a copy of the CBC documentary along with a long letter outlining Asad's part in the story and how I believed his participation had put him in grave danger. I also told them that I had played a role in persuading Asad to allow Ruby to go to Paris and that that trip had caused her considerable grief. I informed them that the Canadian consulate in Islamabad was aware of this family and of the backstory involving the CBC. A church group in Canada was ready to sponsor the family as soon as the paperwork was done. With the interview completed and all the supporting documents filed, there seemed nothing more we could do.

We waited.

Every passing month was wretched. Mobina's health also began to suffer. We exchanged birthday greetings, then wishes for a cheerful Eid al-Adha and Christmas and then hope for a happier 2009. We vowed that we would celebrate the next year's holidays in Canada together. Occasionally, the UNHCR contacted Asad to clarify some statements and Laura Almirall told me they were seeking more data about Asad from Afghanistan. She told us to be patient. We took this to be a good sign. The UNHCR was obviously trying to get its facts straight.

Asad routinely went to the UNHCR office in Peshawar to find out if there had been a decision. On one of his visits, he encountered a refugee with whom he had become friends (I won't name him since Asad has asked me not to). The man said he wanted to offer some help. He told Asad that his narrative wasn't very convincing and his case might be in trouble. He needed to purchase a better one. It would cost money, but he knew people who could do it. Asad wanted to believe that his friend was genuinely trying to be helpful by offering his connections. But the encounter was unsettling since the man seemed to know something about the status of his case. Asad braced himself for bad news.

Robina wrote me one day to say that they had learned a decision had been made and the written response was on its way to the Peshawar office. The same day, I heard from the West Highland Baptists that the church was still interested in the sponsorship and wanted news of the progress of the Aryubwal file at UNHCR. This felt promising. I actually allowed myself to think we were going to be successful. During one long phone conversation with Ruby, I told her I was sure they would get good news. While we chatted, I watched from the upstairs front room of my house as Toronto city workers removed a diseased ash tree from our front yard. Another good omen and I told Robina that I was feeling confident.

Ruby sent me an email the next day to say how happy everyone had been with that phone conversation. The hour in Peshawar had been late when I called and the family was already asleep. But they all woke up to share my optimism. "All of them were crying with happiness," she wrote. "Honestly, I have not seen happiness on their faces in so long, this was so pleasant." Such is the power of hope, even when you have no logical support for it.

On one of his next visits to the UNHCR someone handed Asad a sealed envelope and told him it contained the response to his refugee application. He opened the letter as soon as he left the building, feeling his entire life hanging by a thread, and then called Robina to read the contents to her over the phone. It simply stated: "There is no merit to your case." Asad was in shock. Ruby told him to come home immediately.

Asad was making his way down the street, trembling and dazed, when his mobile phone suddenly rang. The phone displayed no number and the caller was someone he didn't know, a man who claimed to be inside the Peshawar office that Asad had just left. The man said he knew the contents of the rejection letter (a document that was supposed to be highly confidential) and he was terribly sorry. But help was on its way. He told Asad to expect a second call in just a few minutes. "That man will do your appeal for a fee. But he needs a guarantee of safety."

Asad disconnected and his cellphone rang again. Again no number was in the display box. Caller number two also knew that Asad had just picked up the rejection letter. "Who is this?" Asad demanded. The stranger had even more details of Asad's case—his file number along with a PIN code that was supposed to be a secret. The information could only have been provided by someone inside the UNHCR. "I can help you," the caller claimed. "I can do your appeal."

Then finally he had a text message from his friend, the refugee who had told him he needed a better narrative. "Asad jan. Go to Islamabad and call this number. 03335162727. The name of the person is Adnan. You tell him that Nazanen sent you and say I want to see you. The address is F,6 Ali Hospital."

Asad's head was spinning. He had just received some of the worst news of his entire life. All hope had been destroyed, he was unable to help his family and his life was still in danger. And now his misfortune had become a business opportunity for criminals. "These are very strange people," Asad told me that night. "Now you tell me what I should do. I've lost my way. I'm confused by these dirty people. This is a place of liars and cheaters that are more dangerous than Dostum."

Everyone in the family was shattered. Muhammad said that it was the first time he had ever seen his father cry.

Asad never called the number.

When her father had read the letter to her over the phone, Ruby felt her life falling apart. She asked Muhammad to tell me the news because she was too shaken to write. The rejection letter stated that the family had one month to appeal, providing reasons why the decision should be re-evaluated. Nothing more. I was perplexed, angry and determined not to give up. I wanted to discuss the appeal with Asad as soon as he recovered. But he asked me what would be the point. He had nothing to add to his story and he would give the same answers again if they asked him. I couldn't argue with him, but perhaps his story needed more context.

The next day I called the Islamabad UNHCR office but was told it was closed until further notice. Staff members were working from outside the building and no numbers would be provided. My emails also went unanswered as the clock ticked. Laura Almirall eventually wrote back. She apologized for the tardy response and told me the Islamabad office was not fully operational for security reasons. I didn't tell her about the extraordinary phone calls and text message that Asad had received because we had no idea from whom they were coming. Also, there was the very real possibility that these shadowy figures could have some influence on the outcome of Asad's asylum claim. We felt entirely at their mercy.

In her email, Almirall stated that the information Asad had provided was "not reliable on points that are material to the claim." She said there were "substantial inconsistencies between the information provided by the applicant and *information we obtained from Afghanistan* [my italics]."

Asad's statements in "the CBS [sic] documentary triggered more in-depth research into the applicant's activities as a commander."

In the CBC documentary, Asad doesn't hide the fact that he had once been a general in the warlord's militia. And he also never concealed his two-year stint in Dostum's army; he had provided every detail of his activities to the UNHCR. But the agency was saying that it had reliable information from Afghanistan that contradicted these statements. No one would tell us what that information was or where it came from.

Dostum's battlefield commanders—men who had been on the front-lines with him during the wars—were all thriving and enjoying positions of wealth and authority. At least the ones who weren't dead. Why would Asad be in Peshawar, surviving on money sent by a foreigner, if he had been an important soldier on the payroll of the most powerful warlord in Afghanistan? But Almirall was saying that the "CBS" documentary didn't jibe with what they had learned on the ground. Asad knew he had a lot of enemies back home, and he had warned the UNHCR of that when he was interviewed. But if someone was attempting to sabotage Asad's application, it seemed that the UNHCR was possibly listening. The agency's policy was to err on the side of caution. If it found a contradiction in a candidate's story, that was enough for a rejection.

I had to inform the West Highland Baptists that we were now caught in a legal process of unknown duration. Alan reluctantly told me that the church might move on to another project. The Baptists and the Aryubwals had always seemed an eccentric fit, but I had dared to picture Asad sitting on a nice patio in Hamilton with Alan Beech. Now it seemed impossible.

This was a time for all hands to be on deck. I told Brian and Heather that the application for asylum was in trouble and the three of us launched a call for help. Our campaign had the structure of a pyramid scheme: everybody we contacted sent out pleas to other people, eventually entreating a vast network of journalists, NGOs and people inside the UN to send us advice or write letters of support.

I also asked executives at CBC to provide a letter since Asad was in all of this trouble because he had appeared in a documentary on *The National*. But news management was willing to offer only a very limited endorsement, so watered down in its wording that I thought it might hinder more than help. The CBC's argument was that we couldn't be perceived to be taking a side in a story. My immediate supervisors in CBC Radio knew that I was engaged in Asad's case and trusted me to find my own balance. I knew they were also scanning my work on *As It Happens* for any possible conflict of interest, especially as we began to cover the steady flow of stories about the plight of UN refugees. For my part, I viewed my efforts on behalf of the Aryubwal family as a part of the job. If we had not interviewed him, twice, he would not be in Peshawar. But I was performing a juggling act and I didn't know if I would get much support if I started to drop the balls.

I needed more details from Asad in order to get others to corroborate his story. I never had any doubt that he was telling the truth but I sensed he felt that I had misgivings, especially when I pushed him on his facts. It was hard to help from a distance and sometimes there were misunderstandings. He carefully dictated a letter to Ruby which she sent to me as we launched the appeal: "I must convince you that I was never in touch with weapons and I never transferred any weapons. . . . Be confident that I was never on a battlefield. Whether I come to Canada or not I will never make you ashamed of me."

Asad was entering a kind of Kafkaesque haze of semi-reality, scanning all of his statements and responses to questions, wondering what he could possibly add or clarify that would convince people he was who he said he was and that his story was true. The problem was that we didn't know why he had been rejected or what sources in Afghanistan the UNHCR was relying on.

I turned to a friend in Belgium, a retired lieutenant-colonel who had helped me on a number of occasions when covering stories involving complex military matters. Joris Bladel had a doctorate in military history and was an expert on just about anything to do with mercenaries and militias, but he had specific knowledge of the Russian army and its engagement in Afghanistan. I was looking for arguments to support Asad's claim that, even as a general, he was just a logistics guy who never handled weapons—that such a designation was possible. Joris fell to work on the project as if it was a graduate thesis and he soon provided a concise and detailed analysis of the Soviet military hierarchy. Since General Dostum styled his army on the Soviet system, he argued they were comparable models. The Soviets employed civilians to work in the military and gave them officer ranks. It was quite plausible that Asad's job was to provide nonmilitary goods and services while not playing a combat role. Joris argued that this was also something that paramilitary groups did all around the world, investing civilians with senior military status in order to give them a veneer of authority. In reality, the ranks were meaningless. Militias had limited weaponry so they distributed firearms and munitions only to those capable and willing to deliver lethal force. Asad would certainly not fit the bill.

I shipped Joris's report to Islamabad, along with whatever else Heather, Brian and I could find to reassure the UNHCR that Asad was the man he claimed to be without any sense of what man they thought he was. Asad submitted his written appeal to the Peshawar office, continuing to ignore offers from those who would do it for him for a fee. I often wondered how things might have been different if Asad had opted at the outset for the Russian mafia to make his case. The fee of $50,000 was starting to look like a bargain. During the many years he spent within the Peshawar refugee system, Asad watched other claimants come and go, receiving their documents and moving on, including the friend who had offered to help him purchase a better narrative. It's possible their cases were simply more straightforward than his, not hobbled by unidentified contradictions from undisclosed sources. It's also possible that other refugees were playing the game.

UN operations around the world are plagued by corruption. In many other conflicts and war zones, people have told me stories of bribes and fees paid in order to get on official lists as refugees. When I was working in the Balkans, I was told the price for resettlement outside of Bosnia or Kosovo was US$5,000 a person, though whether any of these people safely made it to other countries or avoided legal challenges I can't say. It wasn't just the UNHCR that was beset with such problems; UN food supplies often disappeared and one official in an African outpost told me that it was assumed that a percentage of supplies would be syphoned off by militia leaders as a "commission" for allowing the provisions safe passage.

I had never before been so intimate with an actual asylum claim and what I was observing was disturbing. Western countries were in the midst of a heated debate as to how open their societies should be to refugees and whether migrants were being screened enough. I was wondering how anyone actually made it to another country. But while the Moscow crime-ring involvement was a new wrinkle, the sleaze Asad encountered was really not all that surprising. I occasionally alluded to the corruption in my emails with UNHCR staff in Islamabad but I was careful, not wanting to upset the apple cart while Asad was sitting in it.

As he prepared his appeal, Asad was again approached by someone who offered to help with the application. On this occasion, the man was brazen enough to give his full name, and he told Asad he had previously worked for the UN. "I know about your case," he said, "and you're wasting your time. If you want to get refugee status you'll need to pay someone for it." By this point, Asad was convinced this was an organized business as the man also told him the money would be paid to someone in Russia. He worried about how many of these crooks had access to his personal files.

Asad decided to lay it all out one day when he was visiting the Islamabad UNHCR. He told a caseworker that he had been approached for bribes and that he believed the UNHCR office in Peshawar was part of it. He also questioned the honesty of the appeals process. If the same story was found acceptable under appeal, after it was examined by people at a higher level, what did that tell you about the initial rejection? The caseworker was someone Asad believed was honest and trustworthy. But the man had no advice to offer except that Asad should continue his efforts. We don't know if the caseworker ever took the information about the corruption to anyone higher up. But Asad's file was eventually transferred from the Peshawar office to Islamabad. In part it was because of the amount of noise we were all making, though the security situation had a lot to do with it as well.

Peshawar was becoming engulfed in war. Homegrown jihadists now plagued the country, attacking even the heart of Islamabad. In the fall of 2008, terrorists drove a truck bomb into the Marriott Hotel, killing fifty-four people and wounding hundreds more, including many US service personnel. The popular tourist area known as the Swat Valley, just a hundred kilometres from the capital, was under siege from Taliban militias who had imposed Sharia law. The Pakistani military was battling Islamic insurgencies all across the Federally Administered Tribal Areas that bordered the province where the Aryubwals lived.

By the time Asad launched his appeal, violence was widespread. Suicide bombers blew themselves up in public places, gunfights erupted regularly and a full-blown war was breaking out with the Pakistani Taliban in nearby Waziristan. There were also the constant and destabilizing US efforts to locate Osama bin Laden, who was believed to be living somewhere in northern Pakistan. The CIA's Special Activities Division often lobbed weaponized drones into civilian areas that the US deemed legitimate targets. Whatever Washington believed it accomplished with such attacks, the blowback was always another wave of eager recruits who wanted to join the jihad. For his entire life, Asad seemed to find himself in the midst of international conflict, and again he was in the most dangerous part of a dangerous country in a very bad time.

While Asad's case had been transferred to Islamabad, the Aryubwals were told they had to continue living in Peshawar where the Pakistani authorities had first registered them. And Asad still had to put up with the Peshawar office's questionable practices. It took a month before his formal appeal request finally arrived in Islamabad. There's possibly an innocent explanation for his papers going missing once again, but Asad believed it was a form of harassment or, perhaps, a punishment for insisting that he would play by the rules. When he spoke with people at the Peshawar UNHCR, he often heard reference to his "Islamabad connections," which Asad was now sure was not a good thing. More often than not, I was able to get news and updates from my sources long before he did.

In early October 2009, the UNHCR asked Asad to bring the whole family for a meeting in their Islamabad offices. Robina phoned me after the session to say she didn't know what to make of it. It was unlike anything they had ever experienced at the agency.

Two Europeans met with them along with Asad's regular Pakistani caseworker, the man whom Asad had earlier told about the corruption at the UNHCR in Peshawar. Ruby failed to catch the foreigners' names, and she couldn't make out their nationalities, but she said they seemed very professional, if somewhat awkward. The man appeared to be in charge while the woman was possibly a legal advisor. The meeting began with an explanation that this was "a consultation" and not the interview concerning Asad's appeal. They wanted to explain that they had identified "some technical issues" with Asad's file and that their information was a bit . . . muddled. The man repeated the earlier allegation that Asad's interviews had not matched material they had collected elsewhere. And Asad repeated his assertion that it was probably because whatever material they had collected themselves was wrong.

This time, the UNHCR people didn't disagree and insisted that they had never actually accused Asad of misrepresenting his story. There were only these technical issues concerning his record in Afghanistan and, well, perhaps they didn't have accurate data. The headline coming out of the meeting was that all would be cleared up before the appeals interview. Ruby said the Europeans were actually friendly, agreeing with everything Asad said even before he finished his sentences. We all found it very odd.

A series of bomb blasts in Islamabad delayed another meeting, but Asad had a long telephone interview where they asked him questions about his activities during the 1980s. He told them he had been in Pakistan for much of that time, working for Save the Children as was also the case with his wife, Mobina. Their employment with the agency, Asad told them, was a matter of record and easy to verify. They asked if he had served as an officer with Afghan's Cold War leader Babrak Karmal or his successor, Mohammad Najibullah. The answer was no. Had he been a member of their Communist Party? No, never! He loathed the Communists, regarding them as worse than the Taliban. The Communists had taken his father away. The questions continued along this line and Asad grew more and more perplexed.

The official appeals interview was scheduled for October 16, 2009. The family travelled to Islamabad, trying not to heed reports of bomb blasts from every direction. The session was very polite and formal as the UNHCR officials admitted to . . . a misunderstanding. In earlier emails, Laura Almirall had told me that there were "substantial inconsistencies between the information provided by the applicant and information we obtained from Afghanistan." But it appears that the information they had gathered from Afghanistan was actually about another man—an Uzbek commander and a member of the Gilam Jam Brigade, a notorious gang of Afghan robbers that was active during the nineties. "Gilam jam" translates roughly as "carpet thieves," but its true meaning goes beyond the theft of rugs; it refers to looting so thorough that the militiamen would strip a house of everything of value, right down to its floorboards. The brigade was violent and cruel; its members are known to be very wealthy people. Upon a closer examination of Asad's documents, it was clear that he could not be the man with whom they had confused him. Both men were Asadullah (a common Pashtun name) but the UNHCR discovered that no other family names between the two men matched up. They belonged to different clans, their father's names were not the same, and they had completely different histories. In short, Asad was not the man they had thought he was.

What they were now admitting was that they had rejected Asad's application, possibly endangering his life and certainly plunging it into uncertainty, based on completely erroneous information. Yes, they had discovered the error but Asad had been on the verge of abandoning his application and giving up on the appeal. The UNHCR had been confident enough of their intelligence from Afghanistan as to reject his bid for asylum. And yet, had the agency shown Asad their evidence, the file could have been corrected immediately.

Asad was relieved that the misunderstanding was now resolved, but, disturbingly, the issue of how it had happened in the first place was still unclear. The source of the problem could have been his adversaries back home. But he also recalled the scam he had heard about trafficking in files. Had his information been swapped with that of another case? Asad wondered if the Pakistani woman who had accused him of lying was part of some conspiracy or whether she genuinely believed he wasn't telling the truth. Whatever role she played in the muddle, the effect was hurtful. It's no wonder that the back door becomes attractive to refugees.

Asad asked them to put this "clarification" in writing but the UNHCR demurred, claiming it was unnecessary since the identity mix-up had now been cleared up. Asad didn't want to annoy the people who still held his life in their hands by pushing for a document and so he let it go. When the interview was over, the UNHCR staff were very friendly, ordering lunch for them all and afterward walking the Aryubwals to the gate of the compound, where they were sent off with friendly waves.

And then we waited.

Months went by, along with Eid al-Fitr, the celebration at the end of Ramadan; the Persian New Year of Nowruz; Christmas; then the arrival of 2010 followed by Easter along with many birthdays and anniversaries. All the events were acknowledged with a round of promises that these would be the last before we were able to celebrate in Canada. But the only news we received was that Asad's case was being reviewed by the UNHCR law department in Geneva.

Peshawar in the summer months is unbearable, with temperatures soaring into the mid-forties. Asad caught typhoid fever. When he called the UNHCR office in Islamabad he learned his case was "rapidly under progress." Since the Taliban attacks, life for Afghan refugees in Pakistan was growing more difficult by the day. The authorities had not followed through on their threat to expel the Afghans but the government found other ways to harass them. One day, it announced that the government would no longer renew identity cards, without which it was impossible to access any services.

I began to send money through the account of a Pakistani friend of the family since Asad was no longer allowed to do any banking with his expired documents. In the fall, just after Ramadan, the UNHCR finally reissued the ID cards that had been held up for months. Robina described a mob scene when Afghans tried to get their papers while Pakistani police beat them with sticks. Hossna, now nine years old, was with them in the crush and she went into an uncontrollable trembling fit after she saw a policeman slam a security door on a man's hand. A severed finger dropped to the ground in front of her.

In November, the UNHCR told Asad to report to Islamabad for an interview that would be with him alone. In the interview room, Asad met three foreigners: a man from Geneva whose nationality Asad could not discern, and a man and a woman, who were probably Americans. The Geneva man declared that he would conduct the interview.

Asad knew immediately that there was something highly unusual about this encounter. The interpreter usually sat next to whomever was asking the questions but in this case, the man was instructed to sit across the room, where he would have minimal eye contact with Asad. Asad found this arrangement disturbing, since the interpreter had been kind to the family and supportive over the many months of interrogations. He was the man who had told the Pakistani woman to back off when her questions had reduced the children to tears.

The questions in this meeting were also of a completely different nature, since almost all of them pertained to Rashid Dostum. The man from Geneva wanted to know whatever Asad could tell him about the Uzbek general and the events that took place at the Qala-i-Jangi fort in 2001, the story we had reported on CBC. What did Asad know, who did he know and how familiar was he with the people who were around Dostum? Asad answered in Pashto; the interpreter translated while the man from Geneva rapidly typed the responses onto his computer.

During the long translation periods, Asad had a chance to study the two other foreigners in the room. He had detected American accents when they were first introduced and he felt they didn't have anything to do with the UNHCR. The woman had a laptop and she was also rapidly typing Asad's translated responses. Asad remembers how unnerving it was to hear the fast clickety-clack of their keyboards all day. The other American sat silently watching Asad, his elbow on a desk and his head propped up on his hand. Asad knew that every word uttered was being studied while the lives of his family members relied on this performance. He had to stay focused. But he kept wondering why the Americans were there.

The interview went on all afternoon with hardly a question about Asad's case. Then at the end of the session, the American man spoke for the first time, posing a question that caught Asad off guard. "If Rashid Dostum was put on trial," he asked, "would you testify against him?" Asad didn't answer right away. In the CBC documentary, he had declared a willingness to help if Dostum were ever prosecuted. The Americans obviously knew that. But now Asad had to consider his answer more carefully—the question wasn't hypothetical. "If you ensure my safety," Asad finally responded, "I will tes-tify." The American said nothing though he seemed to smile. When I learned of this later I wondered if the Americans were actually there because they were hoping to find a witness for a possible prosecution.

The Geneva man had a few more queries and then, at the end of the session, the American declared that he had one more question. "Do you want to come and live in the United States?" he asked.

Asad was taken aback. Again he knew that the American wasn't just making small talk.

"I like the United States," he responded, slowly. "But I don't know anyone there. Carol Off is my friend. I want to go to Canada."

The interview was over.

When I learned of it later, I found the account to be quite troubling. Whoever these people were, they clearly wanted something from Asad, a refugee in a life-threatening situation. Were they trying to take advan-tage of Asad's vulnerability in order to gather evidence for a different case? Were his answers confidential? No one would tell him what the interview was really about and Asad had no time to worry about it. He was soon called back to Islamabad for an even more bizarre encounter.

In late November, Asad was told to return to the UNHCR and to bring his family. But upon arriving, the others were instructed to wait outside. Asad was ushered into a hearing room where, in addition to his interpreter, he was introduced to a tall man, possibly English from his accent. He was stern. "I am here for your case and only your case," Asad recalls him saying through the interpreter. "Do not lie to me. If I suspect you are telling even a single lie I will stop the interview immediately and that will be the end." Asad responded that he was happy to get a professional hearing and that he was prepared to answer any and all questions, "even if they reveal I did something wrong." The Englishman answered, "Don't try to manipulate me or make me emotional because it won't work." Asad noticed the man's computer had an image on the screen and he tried to see what it was. "Don't try to look at the computer screen either," said the man. "I will show you in time." The hearing lasted all day. Asad was allowed bathroom breaks but not permitted to speak to anyone outside the room. Food and beverages arrived from time to time while Asad answered what seemed like thousands of questions, most of them beginning with "Have you ever been involved with . . ."

Well into the afternoon, the Englishman finally admitted that they'd received information that Asad had been a commander with the Gilam Jam Brigade, and he stated for the record that the UNHCR now realized that the information was not true. Asad told him that he wanted the agency to do a thorough investigation. If he had done anything wrong, he would face the consequences. "But please don't get your information about me from my relatives," Asad told the Englishman. "If you do, all that you discover will be wrong." The computer screen image turned out to be from our CBC documentary and Asad was only asked to confirm that the statements he made in the program were accurate.

The Englishman then carried on with more questions and at precisely four o'clock, he stood up from his desk, announcing the interview was over. He had a flight to catch for Geneva. He was now satisfied with the case. "I am one hundred percent sure of you," Asad recalls the Englishman saying. "I have nothing but pluses."

Asad joined his family outside. Mobina and the others were anxious; they had received no news since nine o'clock that morning, apart from someone in the UNHCR office telling them that the people Asad was meeting were "very important." Asad animatedly began to tell them what happened in the interrogation room but he suddenly stopped when he noticed that the Englishman was at the door watching them. All the family stared back at the foreigner for several seconds trying to read his steady gaze. Suddenly the man gave them a thumbs-up. And then he was gone.

New Year's Day 2011 came and went with the now too familiar declarations that this was the last from opposite ends of this impenetrable process. The family was called back for more interviews, more questioning: Did Asad fight the Taliban? No, he left Mazar-e-Sharif before they arrived. Did he sympathize with the Taliban since they were fellow Pashtuns? No. Why had he married a Tajik woman? Because he loved her. Still there was no decision on his appeal. Asad attempted to call the Peshawar office routinely for a month without getting through to anyone even though a sign on the door of the building said they could be contacted only by phone.

And then, finally, on July 9, 2011, a letter: "We are pleased to inform you that you and your family members enumerated here have been determined as refugees." The family was ecstatic, and so was I, though it was strange to be so happy to know that they were now members of a club for the most desperate people in the world. Still, it represented tremendous progress. "We will now consider if any further action is appropriate in your case," the letter informed them. I took that to mean that the UNHCR might or might not determine that Asad and his family should advance to the elite level of the refugee society, those people found suitable for resettlement in another country. For my part, I was willing to help them go anywhere, but I thought my best shot was to get them to Canada.

In the three and a half years we had been nudging Asad's case along, all of our lives had changed. The Aryubwals had celebrated the news that my son was getting married and they mourned with me when my father died. Asad went out to buy sweets for the whole family when they learned I would be a grandmother. I toasted their birthdays and graduation ceremonies and shared their grief when Moscow finally released records that revealed what they had long presumed, that Asad's father was among those whom the Soviets had executed decades earlier. So many ups and downs, joys and tragedies. Our lives had melded together. I was involved, but not in a story anymore. This was life itself.

Asad's heart was now giving him problems and he suffered from panic attacks. Mobina's blood pressure was out of control and no one was able to get any exercise for fear of just about everything: suicide bombs, speeding cars, Dostum's people and the Pakistani police. But they were now refugees, a status we hoped would give them some kind of protection.

Two powerful human emotions governed the lives of this family. Their intense love for each other was the glue that kept them from coming completely apart. But they also had a tremendous capacity for hope. I often spoke to them late at night in Pakistan when I was able to get through to Ruby's cellphone. After the call, I'd picture them bedding down in their cramped apartment, together but each mentally alone, the children sensing their young lives ebbing away.

VII

When Home Lets You In

"Home is the place where, when you have to go there,
They have to take you in."

—FROM "DEATH OF THE HIRED MAN,"
BY ROBERT FROST

IN LATE 2010, THERE BEGAN A SERIES of events that would eventually culminate in the largest refugee crisis since the Second World War. It started in December, in Tunisia, with a simple yet horrifying act of protest.

Mohamed Bouazizi was a street vendor who sold vegetables from a wheelbarrow and struggled to support his mother, uncle and siblings on a modest income. Police teased and harassed him daily, demanding bribes that he couldn't afford to pay. Heavily in debt and feeling humiliated, Bouazizi didn't know where to turn. No one in authority cared to listen to the young man's grievances. And so, in desperation, he found another way to communicate. Mohamed Bouazizi set himself on fire.

Bouazizi's story spread and eventually inspired a massive protest. Throngs of Arabs marched in the streets of not just Tunisia but also Algeria, Morocco, Jordan, Egypt, Bahrain, Yemen and Lebanon. They occupied the public squares of their cities and demanded the resignations of their leaders. They wanted jobs, honest government, fair elections and control over their own destinies. No one can explain why it is that one man's shocking suicide had such an effect on so many people, except that a revolt against government in the region was long overdue. This was Arab Spring—the beginning of a revolution against decades of dictatorship in the Middle East.

The protests mobilized a generation of young people who wanted to escape the sense of futility that the vegetable-cart peddler presumably felt before he set himself aflame. It affected every country in the Middle East and spread deep into Africa. But the most surprising revolt was against Bashar al-Assad, the iron-fisted despot of Syria. Small acts of defiance in a few Syrian cities quickly escalated into all-out insurrection. The world watched first in fascination as a bastion of authoritarianism actually seemed to wobble, and then in horror as the Syrian regime rallied its forces to crush all dissent.

President al-Assad's crackdown on the protests was brutal. Those leading the movement were hustled away by secret police in unmarked cars. They were imprisoned, tortured and hanged. Subversive graffiti was quickly cleaned from walls, as was the blood that remained on streets after police shut down peaceful demonstrations. But the rebellion couldn't be suppressed. Instead, it went underground where it evolved into something far more deadly and unpredictable.

An armed insurgency began to displace the nonviolent street protests and Syria descended into civil war. President al-Assad deployed the air force and the army to attack his own people. He shattered his cities with missiles and killed civilians with crude barrel bombs filled with nails and razor-sharp shrapnel. And when that wasn't enough, he attacked them with chemical weapons, sending thousands of women and children to hospitals where many of them died. The violence in Syria became a lightning rod, attracting other armed groups with competing agendas and soon the original democratic cause of the uprising was mired in a battle for regional supremacy.

Syrian refugees escaping the carnage began to trickle into Turkey, then Jordan and Lebanon. Thousands found shelter with friends and families, but when the trickle became a river, the countries bordering Syria began to force the migrants through heavily controlled crossing points where they had set up camps. The number of displaced Syrians grew from thousands to tens of thousands and then exploded into millions, a massive movement of people seeking refuge from war. While covering the exodus, BBC correspondent Lyse Doucet reported that she had never met a single refugee who wanted to leave home.

The refugee crisis eventually engulfed Europe as hundreds of thousands of people flooded across borders. Their plight inspired empathy in some places but widespread hostility in most others. Europe had not seen such a wave of migration since the thirties and forties, and people feared the arrival of so many foreign Muslims in their cities. Governments, including those in North America, began to tighten border controls as the desperate refugees searched for any country that might accept them.

It was in this volatile global climate that I would try to bring a family of Afghans to Canada.

Asad Aryubwal was again routinely visiting the UNHCR office in Peshawar hoping to hear that his family had been accepted for resettlement. On occasion he would wait an entire day only to be told to come back again the next week. Sometimes the UNHCR staff never even called his name. Meanwhile, he frequently moved his family into new accommodations, trying to stay ahead of threats, perceived and verified.

In the years that the family lived in exile in Pakistan, Asad changed houses five times. He would have done so more often if there had been more landlords in Peshawar who would rent to Afghans.

The family could never be certain if the hit-and-run on Muhammad was a Dostum-inspired ambush or an act of malice by someone who knew he could hurt an Afghan with impunity. But there were other worrisome signs of danger. On one occasion, Asad noticed suspicious looking men loitering too close to their home, men who seemed to be watching him. The family packed up quickly and found another apartment. In another house, a rocket hit the building behind them. Asad was sure it wasn't aimed at him but he and Mobina suspected the apartment was only available for rent to Afghans because it was too close to a Taliban target for anyone who had other options to be willing to live there. They moved. Another flat was noisy and airless, with generators blasting on neighbouring roofs and light pollution from the busy street. Asad developed hives and the children all had rashes, either from bugs or heat or perhaps just stress. They moved again. Invariably the accommodations were cramped, usually no more than two rooms for seven people, all but Hossna now adults.

One apartment was directly across from a school. Hossna, seven years old at the time, cried each day as she watched Pakistani girls skip to their classes and frolic in the playground wearing their school uniforms. She couldn't understand why she was denied the privilege enjoyed by other children in the neighbourhood. Pakistani public schools will admit Afghan pupils though they have strict quotas. On one level, the restrictions are understandable since twenty-five million Pakistani children either can't afford to go to school or don't have schools to go to. But there are generations of Afghans living in Pakistan who have no formal schooling and no ability to lift themselves out of poverty. The illiteracy rate for Afghan refugee girls is 90 percent. Foreign aid agencies try to compensate by providing instruction to the Afghans, but those schools are established mostly in the refugee camps and the standard of teaching is rudimentary. With the money I was sending, Asad was finally able to enrol Hossna in the school across the street.

Ruby and Hossai went with Hossna each day, but as instructors, not students. The two young women had a higher level of education than many Pakistani women and they were proficient in both English and French. Hossai worked with the youngest children at the Montessori branch of the school, while Robina tutored children from grades 2 to 8 in English and science. They were paid a paltry salary and the administrators imposed numerous deductions that whittled

Big sisters Hossai and Robina with Hossna, at a school party in Peshawar, Pakistan, 2009.

away at their paycheques. Still the two young women were occupied and felt productive.

I started to send more money, thinking they might try to live a little more comfortably, but Asad used the extra funds to enrol his four older children in post-secondary education. Robina was now twenty-three; Hossai, twenty-two; Muhammad, twenty-one; Mujeeb, nineteen. Robina and Hossai joined Preston University, a private American-run business college. The primary school where they were teaching promptly dismissed them, claiming they would be less attentive to the students if they were, themselves, students. But the women didn't mind; the money they had been earning was negligible and they were more than content to concentrate on their studies.

At first, Muhammad was less ambitious than his sisters. He tells the story of Ruby grabbing the flesh around his waist and twisting it so hard he screamed with pain. She ordered him to find a school to attend and get an education before he moved to Canada and so he applied to study electrical engineering at one of the few universities that would accept Afghans. The admissions exams were extremely difficult and all in English, but he managed to pass.

Mujeeb was still in his teens where his education was at a halfway point between high school and college. It proved more difficult to find an institution that would accept him, so he began to study math and accounting online and he was home most of the time. It was just as well, since Asad and Mobina fretted each time their children left the house, wondering if they would be safe. The young people wanted to believe they were preparing themselves for gainful employment in Canada. I didn't have the heart to tell them that foreign degrees are rarely accepted by Canadian institutions and employers. I'm sure they suspected that would be the case, but it didn't matter. They loved school and their parents took pleasure in their successes.

I received monthly progress reports. As students they were often the highest achievers in their classes, which seemed to annoy some of their instructors, who didn't conceal their contempt for Afghans. When a bomb went off at Hossna's school, the other students and the teachers implied that it was somehow her fault. As Afghans, they had no option but to ignore the insults.

One day Mujeeb was robbed on the street—the thief put a gun to the boy's head then took his money and phone. His father didn't heed the advice of other Afghans who told him he should just let it go, consider Mujeeb lucky that it hadn't been worse than a simple mugging. Asad reported the incident to the police. The complaint went nowhere. A crime against an Afghan was not worth their time.

By the spring of 2012, we were all willing to accept any gesture as a sign of progress. I mentally kept lists of people who helped or hindered our advancement and developed sub-lists of those I labelled "Guardian Angels and Heroes." Within the ranks of the UNHCR, those who hindered are too numerous to mention. In general I found the senior agency staff to be anonymous bureaucrats from Western countries who seemed to come and go while remaining detached from the suffering found in their case files. Maybe that's the way it had to be; they maintained distance and objectivity within an institution that had an enormous responsibility. But now and then, there would be a spark of human empathy, a heartbeat, someone who dared to see a file as a genuine and often tragic human narrative.

Alice was one of those people. We never learned her last name, but she became the caseworker who was most responsible for nudging the

Aryubwal family file through the labyrinth of UNHCR bureaucracy. She conducted a number of interviews with everyone in the family and we understood that she would be the person who would prepare a file for the Canadian consulate to consider. There was a renewed lilt in Robina's voice when I called her, and in her emails she described Alice as a woman who seemed to understand their situation, who seemed genuinely impressed by them, their facility in languages, their academic efforts and their personal integrity.

The name Alice resonated with me and I seized on the possibility of divine intervention. Close friends and family members are named Alice including both my mother-in-law and newborn granddaughter Chloe Alice. My Aunt Alice had recently passed away and if there was any spirit capable of arranging miracles from beyond the grave it was she. Surely this meant we were on the cusp of a breakthrough. When I relayed all of this "evidence" to the family they concurred that supernatural forces were certainly in play.

Of course there was no breakthrough—only a brief departure from the usual indifference and skepticism in the person of a lovely, presumably French woman named Alice who believed in Asad and who seemed genuinely fond of Robina and her siblings. Nonetheless, we agreed that we now had a guardian angel in Pakistan and it was a small flicker of light.

I was rereading a book at the time that I had not picked up in years, *Man's Search for Meaning* by neurologist and Holocaust survivor Viktor Frankl, an account of his experiences in Auschwitz. He describes the overwhelming sense of futility and doom among the men with whom he was imprisoned. And yet he observed that they are able to intercept fleeting moments of bliss. Frankl recounts a dismal day spent on a prisoner transport train. As they travelled through a mountain range, the listless men jumped up and dashed over to tiny windows in order to catch a glimpse of the passing scenery. Frankl writes, "If someone had seen our faces on the journey from Auschwitz to a Bavarian camp as we beheld the mountains of Salzburg with their summits glowing in the sunset, through the little barred windows of the prison carriage, he would never have believed that those were the faces of men who had given up all hope of life and liberty."

They hadn't eaten in days, they were freezing and facing doom, yet the men still had a capacity to be inspired by nature's splendour. It gave them a feeling of hope, a sense that life still held promise. Such is the human spirit.

I first met Jeff Douglas in January 2011 when he became my co-host on *As It Happens*. He quickly joined the small roster of heroes in this story. Jeff had first-hand experience with the process of bringing refugees to Canada since his church had sponsored an Ethiopian family. He and his wife, Ana, had been the primary people in arranging the resettlement of a woman and her three small children who had been languishing for years in a refugee camp in Nairobi, Kenya. When I told him that I had lost my sponsor for a family of Afghans, he knew where to look for a replacement.

We met with a delegation from Jeff's west-end Toronto church, Runnymede United, and they agreed to raise money and provide assistance to help settle the Aryubwals in Toronto. But Runnymede wouldn't be the actual sponsor. We needed the United Church of Canada to provide what's called a Sponsorship Agreement Holder (SAH) permit to bring the family to Canada. This was necessary since Ottawa was now restricting the Group of Five program that the West Highland Baptists had offered. By now, the community of Canadians who help refugees to settle suspected there was a hidden policy on the part of the Harper government to place obstacles in the path of potential refugees. Restricting private sponsorships seemed to be part of that effort. The United Church of Canada, as a permit holder, became vital to our cause.

December 24, 2011, was a cold day with blue skies and blustery arctic air as Jeff and I travelled out to Etobicoke, the western edge of Toronto, and we walked several bleak windswept blocks, looking for the United Church of Canada's offices and a woman named Khwaka Kukubo who worked in the Refugee Program at the United Church of Canada.

Khwaka is a willowy, soft-spoken African-Canadian who works too hard. She was alone in the office and I was sorry to trouble her on Christmas Eve when everyone else had the day off. But she was the keeper of the SAH permit for the United Church and as such we needed her to provide a great deal of paperwork that all had to be completed before the end of the year. Khwaka was moved by Asad's story and she was determined to fill in the complex forms and gather the documents needed before the deadline. But she also warned us, as others had already, that SAHs such as the United Church of Canada were encountering roadblocks at every turn. She would do whatever was possible to help, but she couldn't guarantee success.

Khwaka's advice was to split the family up and attempt to bring Mobina and the girls to Canada separately. She believed we had a better chance if we based the asylum claim on the fact that the female members of the family faced specific persecution for having attended school. I desperately wanted to avoid doing this as my sense was that the family could only survive as a unit. Khwaka argued it was something asylum seekers did all around the world; families are dispersed like seeds, taking advantage of whatever wind would carry them best. But I wondered how many of those families ever reunited, at least in any cohesive way.

One of my closest friends had come to Toronto in 1996 as part of Canada's huge refugee resettlement program for Bosnia. Gordana Knezević had been an editor of *Oslobodjenje*, a newspaper that managed to publish every day but one throughout the entire siege of Sarajevo. At the beginning of the war, Gordana and her husband, Ivo, decided to put two of their three children on a bus that was leaving the city, having arranged for Igor and Olga to stay with family friends in Croatia for what they believed would be a few tense weeks or, at the very worst, a few months of conflict. Another son, Boris, remained with them in Sarajevo.

As Gordana returned from the bus station, shells began to rain down on neighbourhoods full of people and within hours of her children departing the city, Sarajevo was engulfed in war. It was almost impossible to leave again for the duration of the siege, though with enormous effort Gordana did eventually manage to get Boris to safety in the United States. Igor was eventually taken in by a widow in England who was looking to help Bosnian children. Olga stayed with friends in Zagreb.

Five years after that bus departed the city, the Knezević family finally reunited at Pearson International Airport in Toronto. The boys had become men; Olga was a teenager. Gordana and her husband were sick and exhausted from war and Ivo died not long after they all arrived in Canada. Each person had come through separate trials and ordeals and they understandably found it difficult to come together again.

As I sat in the United Church of Canada's offices on a blustery winter's day, conferring with Jeff and Khwaka, I thought of Asad, Mobina and the children sitting in their apartment, halfway around the world, with all of their expectations invested in what should have been a straightforward process but was really just a roll of the dice. I wanted to avoid breaking up the Aryubwal family. But in the end, with my consent, Khwaka sent the files for the male and female members of the family separately.

As the refugee process seemed to stall, Asad's children were resolutely focused on their academic work. It was in that frame of mind that Muhammad one day stepped out into the street in Peshawar, anxious to purchase a notebook in the nearby market for the start of his new semester. Without warning, he found himself confronted by plain-clothes policemen and then taken to jail. Muhammad had failed to bring his identification with him on what was to be a brief errand. It was a minor oversight, but in the perilous world of the refugee, a minor slip can lead to cataclysmic consequences.

He was only metres from his house when police arrested him, and by law he was entitled to retrieve the document. Muhammad assured them he had only to walk up a flight of stairs to get his ID, but the officers hustled him into the back of an unmarked car. He managed to make one fast phone call to his father before his phone was confiscated. Muhammad couldn't tell Asad where he was going; he wasn't even sure that these men were police officers.

Asad ran into the street, shouting for help, and a neighbour told him his son had been taken away in a white Corolla. No one had ever seen local police in such a vehicle before. Asad and his neighbours went to every nearby police station but couldn't find Muhammad. Mobina's blood pressure soared and the whole family was in a state of panic.

Asad finally tracked down his son in another precinct where he learned that the teenager faced a potential punishment of fifteen days in prison followed by deportation to Afghanistan. Pakistani neighbours, along with Muhammad's classmates, crowded the courtroom the next day, demanding that the judge release the young man, declaring it an injustice to arrest a student in front of his own house. Asad collapsed in the courtroom. Mobina appeared to be on the verge of a stroke. The only encouragement came from seeing how many Pakistanis had turned out to support them.

Muhammad spent two more nights in jail, crowded in with assorted thieves, drug dealers and killers, before one of Asad's neighbours swore an affidavit and paid to bail him out. Upon release, Muhammad slipped into a depression. He later told me that the greatest stress in the experience was his concern about what his parents were going through.

Asad wrote a scathing letter to the UNHCR—something he had never done before. "Is It Justice?" was his headline and he went on to tell the story of three days from hell, as he fought the system for his son's release. "I am not safe with all my family members," he concluded the letter. "Please help me as soon as possible. I am weak, I cannot bear any more pain."

Even with help from Alice, we still couldn't get the UNHCR to prepare a file to submit to the Canadian consulate. After many emails to various UNHCR officials, I finally heard back from someone quite high up in the ranks—Neill Wright, who was the head of the agency's Pakistani operation. His offer to help seemed genuine but the result of his intervention was only to add new names to the bureaucratic daisy chain—his, and now that he was passing on the file, a woman named Jeanette Zuefle with the UNHCR protection branch in Islamabad. She wrote back: "We can assure you that this case is well known to our office. It is currently undergoing an assessment of his resettlement eligibility in conformity with globally agreed criteria."

I understood the UN's reluctance to be hasty in recommending the Aryubwals for resettlement. We (and I now included Alice in that "we") were trying to get them into the 1 percent club, with its access to the world's richest nations, more specifically, Canada. The UNHCR's special resettlement program is carefully shielded. It can take years to persuade Western countries to accept the asylum seekers recommended by the agency, so the screening process has to be rigorous. One bad claim might spoil the entire stream and no amount of nagging from a journalist in Canada was going to shake the UNHCR from this position.

But I also wondered if the UNHCR had sensed a shift in Canada's willingness to accept refugees and had noticed that empathy levels had seriously diminished under the Harper government. The minister of Citizenship, Immigration and Culture at the time, Jason Kenney, had recently overhauled government policy in order to give himself extraordinary ministerial discretion in the selection of asylum seekers for resettlement in Canada. He imposed caps on the numbers of people who could be privately sponsored, even though the financial burden of caring for those refugees fell to ordinary Canadians in mostly faith-based communities. More and more churches, mosques and charities were moved by news reports about the growing global refugee crisis and—in almost unprecedented numbers—people were offering to help at their own expense. But Kenney's changes to the refugee selection process were reducing the pool of applicants who were qualified to come to Canada while steering sponsors towards refugee populations that the Harper government favoured. SAHs actually began to squabble with each other over access to diminished quotas, something they often found embarrassing. In fact Khwaka had battled a number of other groups in order to secure the seven spots she needed for the Aryubwals.

Refugee advocates declared 2012 to be among the worst years for settlement in Canada in three decades. As the government's priorities became more apparent, asylum support groups went on the offensive, disputing a Harper government claim that it was doing more than previous administrations to help refugees. When Kenney announced he had substantially increased the numbers of asylum seekers allowed into the country, the Canadian Council for Refugees (CCR) pointed out that he had actually reduced the number by 26 percent. When Kenney claimed he was admitting unprecedented numbers of refugees from Iraq and Turkey, his critics pointed out that his policies favoured Christians over Muslims and his gestures towards refugees based in Turkey had political, not humanitarian, motives. When Kenney declared he was giving priority to religious minorities because they were more threatened than Muslims in countries like Iraq or Turkey, even the UNHCR disputed his claim and begged Canada not to make its selection based on religious criteria. Under Kenney's changes, most applicants in some of the biggest refugee hubs in the world no longer qualified. Whether by coincidence or design, the Harper government had severely restricted applications from regions where refugees were overwhelmingly Muslim, including Nairobi (where Somalis take refuge), Cairo and, most relevant to the Aryubwals, Islamabad.

The Canadian Council for Refugees eventually got hold of documents from Kenney's department that revealed much of the Harper government game plan. The material was released through Canada's access-to-information laws and, though much-redacted, it shows that the government was looking for ways to fulfill its international obligations to the UNHCR while targeting refugees only from specific countries and ethnic groups. One memo discloses that the UNHCR had pointedly asked Canada not to abandon Afghans who were, at the time, the largest refugee population in the world (this is before the Syrian crisis peaked). But Kenney and his department decided to limit those numbers anyway, declaring, according to the documents, that Canada has already done its fair share for Afghans. The upshot was that Afghans who were applying through the Islamabad hub would have difficulty getting around Kenney's policies. Canada had spent billions of dollars and lost scores of lives in Afghanistan, but Ottawa was not going to acknowledge that large numbers of people continued to flee a country whose problems we had supposedly fixed.

In an email, the UNHCR's Jeanette Zuefle suggested that because Asad had only won his case on appeal, his file "might be scrutinized more critically by Canada" than normal. I got the sense that the Islamabad office of the UNHCR knew that Canada was becoming a difficult client and didn't want to poke the bear. Zuefle wrote, "The decision on whether or not a case is accepted for resettlement lies exclusively with the resettlement country. . . . To avoid a negative outcome, we need to invest more time in carefully assessing Mr. Aryubwal's complex and challenging case." From my point of view, the only thing that was complex or challenging was that the UNHCR had misidentified Asad, and that confusion was now part of the record.

I could feel the family's fatigue in my phone calls and correspondence with Robina. Since Muhammad's arrest, no one was functioning properly, especially as they now faced a deadline of July 2013 when Pakistan again promised that it would begin to deport refugees. "Day by day we are breaking down, especially my dad," wrote Ruby, in a moment of pure despair. "We are trying to be strong please don't worry everything will be fine." By the end of May 2013, Asad was in hospital. They didn't tell me until doctors began to discuss the need for heart surgery. "We hid this from you because you were getting worried," wrote Ruby when her father's blood pressure dropped alarmingly. "But they want to do an operation as soon as possible and we are afraid of an operation."

For the previous year, doctors had been warning Asad that his health was deteriorating even though he was only fifty years old. They wanted him to exercise, preferably to walk, but Asad never left home unless it was for urgent business. If anything happened to him, he knew it would be a disaster. During this medical crisis, I could see the utter terror everyone felt at the thought of losing him.

In the end, surgery was unnecessary. An angiogram revealed there was not, as the doctors had suspected, a blockage in his arteries. The severe pains in Asad's chest turned out to be the result of extreme stress. Everyone was relieved, but the diagnosis still indicated that Asad's health might be in jeopardy if his circumstances didn't change.

Alice eventually filed a positive recommendation and I began to lobby the UNHCR to transfer the files to the Canadian consulate as quickly as possible. Considering the recent incidents with Muhammad's arrest and Asad's health, there was a new urgency. Pakistan's deadline for deporting all Afghans was mercifully extended, and in late August 2013, the UNHCR informed Asad that he and his family had been recommended to Canada as good candidates for resettlement. Zuefle wrote: "I am pleased to be able to finally inform you that the family has been referred *in its entirety to Canada* [my emphasis]. . . . It is now for the Canadian authorities to examine the case and decide whether or not they accept the family for resettlement."

A week after we received Zuefle's email, a letter arrived for Robina from the High Commission of Canada in Islamabad informing her that she would be called for an interview in approximately forty-six to forty-eight months. Yes, *four years*. Surely it was a misprint. And the letter only referred to Robina. No one else was informed of any interviews.

I contacted Canada's high commissioner for Pakistan, Greg Giokas, who personally responded to my email. He told me that he had checked with the immigration department and had been assured that the Aryubwal file—including all members of the family and not just Robina—was in hand and progressing normally. They were in the pipeline. But by Christmas, we'd heard nothing more. Even officials at the UNHCR told us that such a delay was unusual. Normally, it was about forty-five days before the Canadian consulate formally acknowledges receipt of a UNHCR request, but in our case four months had passed. Alice's advice was that Asad should contact the Canadian embassy directly. But there was no way for him to do that. Khwaka could offer only this: "Welcome to our hell."

At least there was one development in Canada that I thought might prove helpful to the Aryubwals. Stephen Harper had shuffled his cabinet, moving Jason Kenney into the Defence portfolio. Chris Alexander became the new minister of Citizenship and Immigration. Alexander had once been Canada's ambassador to Afghanistan and had travelled extensively in the subcontinent. He had personal knowledge of the political realities in Afghanistan and Pakistan. Those who worked with refugees were convinced that the fate of asylum seekers applying to Canada would soon improve.

By the beginning of 2014 the war in Syria was out of control and a third of the country's population of more than twenty million people was on the move. Aid agencies were trying to help, but the sheer size of the humanitarian crisis soon overwhelmed them. By the time the international community acknowledged that it had an unprecedented emergency on its hands, neighbouring countries were swamped. Turkey, Lebanon and Jordan could no longer support the Syrian refugees; pledges from Europe and America never materialized; the ongoing war threatened to destabilize an entire region.

As though the movements of the Syrian refugees had sent out a signal, entire continents of people seemed to reach a crisis point at the same time. Wave upon wave of humanity was suddenly on the march. Afghans fled the violence of a newly revitalized Taliban; Eritreans joined the exodus from the Horn of Africa, escaping a regime that was now considered one of the worst human rights abusers in the world; Libyans bolted their failed state, left in ruins after Western democracies—Canada among them—had bombed the country and brought down Muammar Gaddafi; Iraqis continued to stream out of a region destroyed by a pointless war while thousands of others escaped violence, drought and poverty throughout North Africa, including Tunisia, the country where Mohamed Bouazizi had set himself on fire.

Once again, Asad found his own personal dilemma tangled with overwhelming world events.

Khwaka finally got confirmation from the Canadian government that it had received the United Church's application to privately sponsor the Aryubwal family, almost a year to the day after Jeff and I had made our Christmas excursion to Etobicoke. Khwaka was a bit concerned that the file was being routed through the federal government's screening department for privately sponsored refugees in Winnipeg. She told me that in the past, files from other offices were usually cleared in a few months. The new reality was that the process was taking longer. She didn't know why.

I located an internal audit of the Winnipeg bureau online, a seemingly innocuous document entitled "Operational Evaluation of the Centralized Processing office—Winnipeg," dated November 2013. It says in the document that the Winnipeg office was supposed to be able to communicate a decision in a refugee case within thirty days, but it was actually taking upwards of a year. The report's authors pointed out that since Winnipeg was in the process of taking over responsibilities for government-sponsored refugees, in addition to those applications from SAHs like the United Church, it would soon require two and a half years to make a decision on a single case. The auditors warned that staff would also need two years just to clear out the backlog of cases before the office could even begin reviewing those new cases. And that was before they could consider the future demands of the Syrian refugees who were now the world's priority.

The cause of this crisis, according to the document, was federal budget cuts. In the year before this review, the Harper government had closed nineteen immigration offices plus numerous visa offices abroad, creating the backlog that now clogged the system. When he was minister, Jason Kenney had claimed that he needed to reduce the numbers of refugees from certain regions because there were too many people already in the pipe but it seems the blockage he was trying to fix was of his own making. Most of the responsibilities for refugee processing had landed in Winnipeg, an office that was just recently assigned this task with no additional resources. It was a blueprint for how to fail human beings in desperate circumstances.

The planet was experiencing the largest movement of displaced people since the Second World War. The UNHCR head office in Geneva was looking to place as many as a hundred thousand people in countries that were part of its refugee resettlement program, and urged Canada to step up and do its share to relieve the burden. In the summer of 2013, Canada said it would accept 1,300 of the UNHCR's Syrians, but when CBC reporter Laura Lynch questioned the new minister of Citizenship and Immigration, asking him how the plan was going, Chris Alexander had to admit that by the spring of 2014, he had settled all of ten Syrians in Canada. It was becoming apparent that Canada's reaction to a growing international crisis was to reduce staff, freeze funds, close offices and put submissions on hold while claiming that it was stepping up its efforts to help solve a humanitarian disaster.

Alexander's stance surprised many people, including me. Following his years as the ambassador to Afghanistan, he'd worked for the United Nations in Kabul and I knew his reputation in the field. He was regarded by people I trusted as a thoughtful and genuine individual who seemed to know how the world worked in the midst of difficult times. I've since read his Afghan memoir—*The Long Way Back: Afghanistan's Quest for Peace.* While it does gloss over the international community's failure to put warlords such as Rashid Dostum in their place, the book is an otherwise candid and revealing assessment of a complex situation. How did an open-minded world traveller who seemed to have a beating heart come to be regarded as one of the most callous of Stephen Harper's cast of pragmatists?

Alexander kept insisting, in the House of Commons and during interviews, including interviews with me, that Canada was among the top countries in the world in accepting asylum seekers. He declared that Canada had accepted 10 percent of the UNHCR's refugees, though when pressed he would concede that he was referring to the

UNHCR's resettlement program which, as I've mentioned, amounts to about 1 percent of all the world's refugees. So Canada actually accepted 10 percent of the 1 percent.

To claim Canada was one of the most generous nations when the other 99 percent of homeless souls are living in camps in Africa or Asia and straining refugee programs in Europe to the point of breaking was, to say the least, disingenuous. At the same time, Alexander couldn't prove that Canada was accepting that 10 percent, since the government had temporarily stopped releasing the numbers of asylum seekers who were actually finding sanctuary here. The minister seemed to have embraced Stephen Harper's perception that the world was under siege by terrorists who were constantly trying to infiltrate our country, many of them disguised as refugees. According to their arguments, women in niqabs were sometimes in need of protection from their barbaric men-folk, but on other occasions, they themselves were the threat, attempting to show up at citizenship ceremonies with their faces covered for potentially sinister reasons.

Harper's people had fanned out across the country in 2014, well in advance of the federal election scheduled for the following year, to tell anyone who wanted to listen (while preventing journalists from asking too many questions) that Canada was at risk of becoming a terrorist haven, that we had to stop people who were determined to destroy our way of life. If the Conservatives were re-elected, Ottawa would pass laws that would enable vigilant public servants to strip people of their citizenship and toss them out of the country. Or better yet, prevent them from getting here in the first place. Syrian refugees might appear wretched and needy, but Canadians shouldn't let their guard down—there was no place in national security for sentimentality.

All of this played well with elements in the Conservative political base but was disheartening and disturbing for those who worked with refugees. I had to wonder about the reasons for the delays in processing the files of the Aryubwals.

We received some hopeful news in the spring of 2014 when the Canadian High Commission in Islamabad contacted Asad to tell him he would soon be granted an interview to discuss his claim for asylum in Canada. Then, suddenly, we learned the date was set for May 28, just weeks away, and that the consulate required detailed files and completed forms immediately. For six years, Asad had been waiting for the opportunity to present his case to the Canadian authorities and now we had seventy-two hours to pull together the story of their lives. In English.

Robina and I collaborated on the forms over Google Chat while I cared for my granddaughter, Chloe Alice, that weekend. The weather in Toronto was lovely and Chloe wanted to be outdoors. A young red-oak tree outside my home office window was almost in leaf. It had replaced the diseased ash that the city had removed years earlier during another conversation with Robina. On that occasion we had also believed we were on the eve of a significant breakthrough in their case. The new tree had been a sapling when it was planted, and now its branches reached my second-floor window.

Ruby and I filled out the documents and crafted testimonies that spanned a decade, laying out a story full of pain, violence, fear and exile. What differences flow from a simple accident of birth. In one country a man speaks his mind and his world falls apart; his children are left without a future and they live in abject terror for years. Here I was on the other side of the invisible divide, working in a profession where outspoken views are rewarded; my granddaughter, who was just learning to talk, would thrive in a society that encourages her and offers protection for those who speak out.

The task of filling out the forms was not half so difficult since Robina had prepared similar documents for the United Church, with the help of Khwaka. With news of the impending interview, Khwaka had decided it was prudent to withdraw the United Church's private sponsorship effort, hoping that the family would become government refugees and so be able to stay together. I suspect that the letter that only Robina had received promising her an interview at the Canadian consulate within the next forty-eight months had actually been the result of the United Church application. So I was glad that Khwaka could drop it.

Jeff's church had become frustrated by the length of time the process was taking—I couldn't blame them—and I was told they were now hoping to sponsor a Syrian family or to redirect their energies towards some other worthy cause. As Runnymede United Church moved on, Jeff remained involved and warned me that one should never celebrate until one's family is safely on Canadian soil.

Both Alice and Khwaka had told Robina that she should disclose everything in the documents, to anticipate what information would be required and provide it rather than appear to be obfuscating. Asad was well prepared by this point, having explained himself in countless interviews over six years. Ruby worked through several nights to gather all that was needed and she met the May 12 deadline for material to be submitted to the Canadian consulate. At 4:40 in the morning of May 15, I became a grandmother for a second time. It was a good omen that the child's second name would be Mae—the same as that of my late paternal grandmother, who had immigrated to Canada (illegally) when she was just a teenager. The entire Aryubwal family concurred that the newborn Clara Mae was definitely our latest guardian angel and her spirit would accompany them into the interview of a lifetime.

The family travelled to Islamabad a day early so that they could be punctual for their 7:00 a.m. meeting on May 28, 2014. The interview went very well. I don't have to take their word for it because I eventually got the transcript; it was clear they had made a good impression. A woman I know only from the transcript as "Mrs. LeBlanc" introduced herself and began the intense questioning, looking for inconsistencies and contradictions. This was meant to be a preliminary interview after which they might or might not be called back, but before it ended Mrs. LeBlanc declared that she was going to roll straight into the second interview without any delay. Robina told me later that "she liked us a lot."

In her report, Mrs. LeBlanc wrote: "ABILITY TO ESTABLISH: Family are good candidates, in my view. Children are educated, and have received more education than most applicants here. Most family members have work experience outside the home, with transferable skills. All applicants speak English. POSTIVE SELDEC [selection decision] ENTERED."

In person, Mrs. LeBlanc told them she had the authority to approve or reject and she was wholeheartedly going to approve. They would need to submit to background and medical checks that still might disqualify them. But from her point of view, they should go to Canada. They would be good for Canada and Canada for them.

That was it. So simple. So overdue. We knew there could be any number of delays and roadblocks ahead, but what mattered for the moment was a feeling of validation. They had told the truth consistently. They had put the details of their lives on paper for scrutiny and judgement. Mrs. LeBlanc had reviewed it all and decided on the spot that the Aryubwals were exactly the sort of people Canada was looking for. Few things mattered more to the family than that recognition.

I realized over the weekend of Google Chat and watching the red oak leaf out that Robina had become a woman. When I first met Ruby she had just turned fourteen. She was a funny, easygoing teenager who seemed far too optimistic considering what she had already endured in her short life. I met a more strained version of the same person in 2006, when she was eighteen, but I had only fleeting moments with her on that trip to Afghanistan with Glen. I can see now she'd been stressed by the constant coming and going of relations who seemed to be keeping a critical eye on her and the foreigners with whom she seemed too comfortable.

Along with the photo of Ruby in Paris, I kept another picture on my desk, of everyone sitting in their Kabul living room on that visit in 2006. Robina was in the middle as she always is, with her arms outstretched as though to take in the whole family, with one arm draped around my shoulders; the boys were trying hard not to smile, as boys do when they're teenagers; Hossai, a year younger than Ruby, had an old-soul look in her eyes. Ruby was wearing Western-style trousers and a shirt and all the other kids were in blue jeans. Asad and Mobina were in traditional clothing, looking somewhat perplexed. Little Hossna was not in the picture and was probably in bed as it appears dark outside.

Then there was the Ruby I met at twenty, at the Hotel Greenland, appearing as though she carried the world on her shoulders. And now this Ruby, a worldly wise twenty-six-year-old woman, whose best years seemed to be draining inexorably away.

As their English improved, I got to know the other children better and learned their thoughts and feelings. Hossai once wrote: "Honestly,

I am tired of this kind of living and so are my family members. Is being honest and educated such a big crime? Because of this we had to leave Afghanistan and come to another hell. I am thinking, crying, and seeing nightmares. If Dostum kills my father and brothers what will happen to us?"

Muhammad would occasionally write or take a phone call instead of Robina and I was surprised by the maturity in his voice but still the vulnerability that deepened after the abusive encounters on the street left a mark that I feared might be permanent. Mujeeb had now entered his twenties, his hunger for knowledge limited to the few schools and libraries where Afghans were allowed to study. Hossna was now almost the age Ruby had been when we first met.

The business college Hossai and Robina attended often wasn't a very welcoming place for Afghan refugees but the two women attempted to tackle the prejudice they encountered. Ruby thought that the conservative culture of the society prevented the female students from taking advantage of the knowledge they were acquiring in their business classes. It took a tremendous amount of persuasion, but she and Hossai were able to convince Preston University to conduct a one-day food festival at the school entirely prepared by the students.

The sisters organized the other women for a practical exercise in entrepreneurship—a small-scale trade show, selling pakoras, sweets and other food. Young men from the college helped with the booths and installed speakers for music and entertainment while Ruby took part in a press conference and interviews on local television. The other students seemed completely engaged in their business ventures while school administrators strutted, pleased with "their" success. Hossai and Robina were glowing when it was all finished.

I worried that there might be repercussions, given that Robina had encouraged the female students to act publicly in a way that Pakistani women rarely do, and I was surprised by my own conservative reaction. But Ruby had decided that if the public and the parents didn't like this modest display of feminine empowerment, then there would only be more and greater shocks ahead of them as the twenty-first century unfolded.

In 2014, sunbathers on the coast of the Mediterranean and beachcombers on Greek islands reported on a daily basis the unexpected arrival of strangers, both dead and alive. Corpses washed up on the shores while the beaches were clogged with discarded backpacks, shoes and life jackets, the whereabouts of their former owners unknown. Half of the asylum seekers were young men but the rest were women, children and the elderly. They handed over their life savings to criminal syndicates whose agents set them adrift on the Mediterranean and Aegean seas, often in leaky vessels or rubber rafts. Sometimes the coast guard rescued them before the boats capsized or they were plucked out of the sea by fishermen who described the horror on their faces, people who will rarely be able to close their eyes again without seeing their loved ones disappear below the waves. Once on shore, usually on foot, they would head for the large urban centres of Europe where they had friends or family members, or where there were government agencies that might have mercy on them.

Syrians were now the largest ethnic group on the move. Afghans were a close second but they faced almost insurmountable hurdles since the European Union had declared refugees from Afghanistan to be economic migrants and not qualified for asylum. European governments argued, as did Canada, that Afghans now lived in a safe country, since the US and NATO had gone to such great pains to make it so. Western governments conveniently ignored the fact that 2014 saw the highest number of civilian casualties from violence in Afghanistan since the American-led war in 2001. Even though the Afghan refugees were running from both a revitalized Taliban and the wrath of warlords, countries were dismissing their cases without even considering them.

I took some solace in knowing the Aryubwals were not among the people climbing into rubber rafts. Without their status as refugees in Pakistan and at least a theoretical possibility of moving to Canada, Asad's only recourse would have been to take his family out of the country by some other means. The slow squeeze on refugees in Pakistan was a huge factor in the number of Afghans clamouring to get into Europe. I could see Ruby, Hossai and Hossna joining other young women climbing into the rafts. I could picture Muhammad and Mujeeb among the men attempting to scale the wire fences constructed to keep the refugees out of the Balkans.

But beyond them, I could imagine my own family, in different circumstances, faced with the same frightening options. I pictured my son and his wife trying to get little Chloe Alice into a life jacket for a voyage she might not survive; the man I saw in a news clip, running through Balkan farm fields with his mother on his back, was my brother, Michael, carrying my own mother on his broad shoulders; the men trying to smash through the gates into Europe after having walked for days were my nephews, feeling not just fatigue and hunger but also humiliation, an emotion we don't always associate with refugees. And yet the feelings of shame—begging for food or shelter or simply a place to relieve yourself in private—are often the most overwhelming emotions that refugees experience. I had been in Macedonia when Albanians from Kosovo had poured over the border, escaping from Serb soldiers, only to be met by police with snarling dogs. I was watching the same scenes again on TV news as Macedonian police with their animals tried to intimidate these latest refugees.

Whatever impact the crisis was having on the hundreds of thousands of people who were trying to get somewhere else, it was also dividing public opinion in many countries, including Canada, driving a wedge between those who saw fellow human beings among the throngs of people walking across Europe and those who perceived an invading force. It wasn't always a simple debate between predictable ideological adversaries: Conservatives versus Liberals or Republicans versus Democrats, the "right" against the "left." The assumptions and opinions surrounding these migrants were dividing friends and family. For some, the migrants were evacuees fleeing violence; for others, they were potential terrorists. Perhaps it's necessary for a healthy society to be pulled in both directions, to have the gatekeepers and the gate-openers. In Canada, this divisive argument would become an emotional issue in the federal election campaign and refugees would be caught in the middle.

Journalists on Parliament Hill tussled with Chris Alexander, trying to get the minister to explain his government's refugee policy. He was still promising to resettle 1,300 Syrian refugees that year but he was never clear on the numbers of people who had actually landed in Canada, suggesting they were in the pipeline, even if they weren't here. He often included in his figures Syrians who had already been in the country when the war began, who had applied to stay in Canada, and it was a challenge to untangle his numbers. I tried to get him to explain it on *As It Happens* in an interview that quickly went off the rails:

CO: Well how many are here? We've been asking this for a year now. We've been asking you and Jason Kenney [the former minister of Immigration]. How many of them are here?

CA: And I'm telling you 1,150 refugees have received Canada's protection. Why isn't that an answer?

CO: But they're not in Canada. How many of them have come to Canada?

CA: The vast majority of them are in Canada. They are asylum seekers. Do you not have the decency and the politeness to admit that when these numbers change every day, I can't give you the precise number as of this day in June 2014. I can tell you we are well beyond the number of applications we expected to receive last year.

CO: The last time you got a number, how many—

CA: I'll phone you back and talk to you more about it, but I find your line of questioning . . . [phone line appears to go silent]

CO: Would you just please call us back and tell us how many of these 1,150 refugees are in Canada.

The *As It Happens* senior producer, John Perry, then tweeted that Alexander had hung up the phone during the interview. The retweet numbers immediately soared, and Alexander counter-tweeted that he'd disconnected because he didn't want to be late for Question Period. He did call back later, but we just continued with the same senseless back and forth.

I worried about what effect this interview, and some previous testy exchanges I'd had with Jason Kenney, might have on the Aryubwal case. Ministers were supposed to keep a distance from specific refugee files and they were to avoid any conflicts of interest. I had no reason to suspect them of meddling. But it's no secret that the Harper government disliked journalists in general and the CBC in particular: Might I be a liability? My name and the CBC's association with the case was all over their application, possibly presenting a red flag for political staff who had been warned by the Prime Minister's Office to look out for controversy.

The Aryubwal's interview at the Canadian consulate had gone well, but once again we were receiving no official word of the family's acceptance. The minister had insisted that it was good enough that refugees were in the pipeline even if they weren't in Canada. But I knew from my own experience with the Aryubwals that such status was almost meaningless. I was deeply troubled by the idea that one of the reasons Canada was taking so long to respond to the referral from the UNHCR might be because of me. This is exactly why my journalist colleagues claim you should never get involved with your stories. The two worlds, personal and professional, so easily become entangled.

Months passed after the meeting with Mrs. LeBlanc. We had now expanded the list of holidays for acknowledgement to include not just Eid, Christmas, New Year's, Nowruz and Easter but also Valentine's Day, International Women's Day and Halloween. And of course we recognized all birthdays. Any calendar event was an opportunity to declare that success was just around the corner.

I had sources in Ottawa and at the High Commission in Pakistan telling me that applications through the Islamabad office were now completely stalled and no one would be processed for the foreseeable future. Jeff Douglas asked a Member of Parliament, Pat Martin of the NDP, to inquire about the Aryubwal case. It was a timely intervention.

While checking the files, the immigration department discovered that paperwork for the family had not been submitted properly. It wasn't difficult to fix but definitely would have caused more delays if Martin hadn't flagged it. Other than that, all the MP had been able to learn was that there was an enormous backlog of cases at all the consulates, many of them more dire than the Aryubwals'. At least Asad and his family had a place to live and some support. Many of those who were waiting for news were in far more desperate circumstances.

But the situation in Afghanistan was becoming bleaker by the day. In September, the news from Kabul was that Ashraf Ghani had been elected to succeed Hamid Karzai as the president of Afghanistan. In the interest of stability, he negotiated a coalition government with his rival, the defeated candidate Abdullah Abdullah. The two men were sworn in as president and chief executive officer respectively. President Ghani then appointed his right-hand man. The new vice-president of Afghanistan, Ghani declared, would be Rashid Dostum.

Ghani claimed he had no choice if he was to successfully run the country since Dostum was in firm control of the northern provinces where he had the Uzbek minority in thrall. President Ghani needed Dostum in his corner.

By now, Dostum was a diabetic and probably an alcoholic. He was still known to be capricious and violent. Those who encountered him described a man who was becoming nostalgic, sentimental and often emotional—in short, more unpredictable and dangerous. He would sometimes break into tears during meetings or conversations.

There was no future in that country for Asad or for tens of thousands of others like him, notwithstanding all the best intentions and investments of blood and money by Canadians. Within the first year of the new Ghani/Abdullah/Dostum regime, the region witnessed an exodus of Afghan refugees not seen since 2001.

It was around this time that the family experienced another alarming incident. Hossna was stepping off a bus on her street on the way home from school, when she was attacked by a stranger on a motorbike who attempted to abduct her. She fought him off and called out for help. When other students responded to her cries her attacker sped away. Hossna was so shaken she could hardly walk. Her friends helped her home where she sat on the steps, crying, trying to breathe, determined not to tell her father, worried that he simply couldn't deal with another such episode.

But she was still a child, only thirteen years old, and she couldn't keep the secret. The whole frightening story came out that night. The family called me first thing in the morning and we discussed whether they should go to the police. One concern was that the man might return. But Asad concluded it was pointless and possibly dangerous to report the incident. They just couldn't afford to be on police radar at this point. We will never know if it was a random attack or a warning to Asad that he was still a wanted man, but this time the family didn't move apartments since they believed they were within shouting distance of Canada.

In December, Peshawar was the scene of one of the worst terrorist attacks Pakistan had ever experienced. Taliban jihadists entered the Army Public School on the outskirts of the capital and opened fire on the cadets, killing 141 people, almost all of them boys between the ages of eight and eighteen. The country went into a state of shock. I spoke with Robina and she and her family were as stricken as their Pakistani neighbours, except they knew what would come next. Two of the seven militants who were killed by police at the massacre were Afghans. If it were possible for the status of refugees in Pakistan to get worse, it happened now. Even those who had been kind to the Aryubwal family became hostile.

Just before Christmas 2014, it struck me that I might be the worst thing that ever happened to this family. I had put their lives in danger and influenced decisions concerning Ruby in a way that caused even more grief. But it seemed to me that where I had done the most harm to the family was by building up their hopes, leading them to believe that my efforts might expedite their file. I had been telling them since we first went together to the UNHCR in Islamabad that their problems would soon be solved, and now seven years had passed.

It was a thought that kept me awake at night. Time and time again, Asad and Robina had told me that I was their only hope. I was aware that they dissected each of my phone calls, emails and text messages for shreds of reassurance. Every word of encouragement from me was a drop of water in a parched throat. Each time I said, "There's light at the end of the tunnel," they rallied for another day. But now it struck me that this was simply wrong. There was no future for them through my efforts.

They'll learn for the first time when they read this that I actually contemplated cutting them loose. I hadn't given up on the Aryubwals, on their ability to survive, to find their way. I'd given up on myself. I decided that I would clean out my bank account, transfer the money to them and tell them they were on their own to go find another route, legally or otherwise. Run as fast as you can to safety, somewhere. Maybe with enough cash they would be more successful than the other refugees who were climbing into boats. Maybe they would all be living in the United States right now if they hadn't been misled by promises from me that turned out to be empty. I was within a whisker of following through with this plan when I had another idea. I called a lawyer.

Lorne Waldman was experiencing the fulfillment of the famous curse: "May you live in interesting times." When I went to see him in early 2015, he was embattled on every front. The Conservatives had turned immigration law on its head during their years in office and now they were spinning the refugee crisis into a re-election issue. Waldman was caught in the middle. He was the go-to guy for asylum seekers and suddenly all refugees looking for relief in Canada were troubled. He was confronting the Conservatives head on, challenging them by whatever means he could, as they attempted to pass statutes that limited the rights and freedoms of asylum seekers.

Waldman's office is in a peculiar little house, recessed from the street, among office buildings and condo towers in midtown Toronto. The door chronically sticks no matter the season; the waiting room is occupied mostly by new Canadians who, on the day I went to see him, probably had bigger problems than I did. But he listened to my story and, more than that, he agreed to work on the Aryubwal case pro bono.

As a reporter, I had encountered Lorne many times and I'd interviewed him on several occasions. I had never known him to be as fired up as he was now. One of his biggest cases was contesting a new law introduced by the Harper government that could strip people with dual citizenship of their legal right to be a Canadian, even if they were born in Canada. "Exiling someone who was born in Canada, and who has never been to the country they're going to be deported to, is a horrible punishment," Lorne told me.

He was also working on the case of Mohamed Fahmy, the Al Jazeera bureau chief who was then in an Egyptian jail and facing serious prison time on bogus terrorism charges. The Canadian government was doing little to help him. And Lorne was also representing Zunera Ishaq, a Pakistani immigrant who was insisting on her right to wear her niqab in a Canadian citizenship ceremony. "The case has nothing to do with the niqab," he told me. "It was about defending freedom of expression and opposing abuse of power on the part of the minister."

As if this wasn't enough, Lorne was assisting a legal challenge to new federal policies that removed health-care access for refugees who had been privately sponsored or had applied for asylum after they had arrived in Canada. Those refugees had to pay to see a doctor or even to get their children immunized. In the opinion of the minister, Chris Alexander, "Simply arriving on our shores and claiming hardship isn't enough. This isn't a self-selecting bonanza or a social program buffet." But the federal court sided with Lorne Waldman's argument that the federal measures amounted to "cruel and unusual treatment." Lorne believed that all of these Harper government policies and initiatives were designed to create an atmosphere of xenophobia that would in turn help the Conservatives to get re-elected. And that made his blood boil.

Lorne's passion for newcomers to Canada may have its origins in the fact that his own relatives were Jewish refugees. He tells the story of his maternal grandfather who was returning home one day to his village in what is now part of Poland. The local rabbi stopped him. Don't go, he instructed. The Cossacks were looking for him, trying to recruit men of fighting age. Lorne's grandfather fled without even saying goodbye to his pregnant wife, eventually arriving in Canada. It took another eight years before he could bring her and his children to Toronto. The year was 1920.

No one else on his mother's side of the family got out before the Nazis invaded. The Polish side of the family was wiped out during the Holocaust: "Of eighty or ninety people in my family, only three survived," Lorne says. His grandfather's synagogue tried to help Polish Jews emigrate. But they came up against Canada's anti-Semitic "none is too many" policy that disallowed Jewish refugees, even those who made it as far as North America, and sent them back to their deaths. Canada's response to Jews in the Second World War was seared into Lorne's psyche.

Lorne's first hunch as to why the Aryubwal case was not progressing was that the Canadian immigration department was trying to find something in Asad's background that would prevent him from being admitted to the country. He studied Asad's military record and concluded there was nothing bothersome in that area. Just about every man who had lived in Afghanistan during the twenty-five years of war had been involved, at some point, with the military. There were certain times in the country's history when any service was a red flag for those conducting security checks, but Asad had not been with Dostum in those years. In theory, Asad's assignment with Dostum shouldn't have set off any alarm bells. But Waldman had recently seen asylum seekers turned down for past activities that seemed even more innocuous. He was prepared to fight the Aryubwal case in court if he had to, but first we needed to find out what was in the Canadian government record.

In the early spring of 2015, Lorne filed an access-to-information request with the immigration department in Ottawa. It provided some revealing results, including the transcript of the "Mrs. LeBlanc" interview that had taken place in May of the previous year. The file confirmed that the family had been approved, pending background and medical checks, just as Mrs. LeBlanc had stated, but then nothing had happened.

In April, Waldman went to the Federal Court of Canada and filed a mandamus application demanding that Ottawa reveal its reasons for holding up the Aryubwal application. Before we even had a response to that request, Robina emailed to say that they had suddenly been called up for immediate medical examinations. I have no proof that Lorne got the ball rolling but it is often amazing how the threat of legal action will suddenly attract the attention of a bureaucracy.

From the access-to-information request, Lorne had obtained a sworn affidavit from Raymond Gillis, the senior immigration officer in Islamabad. The document showed that Asad, Mobina and Muhammad had all passed security and police checks well before Christmas of 2014. And shortly after that, Mujeeb and his sisters were also cleared. With the biggest impediments dealt with, the paper trail just stopped. We had been in the dark, trying to imagine what nefarious things were happening behind the scenes, envisioning all kinds of plots. But now we could see what had really been going on. Which was nothing. The government was simply ignoring the file.

Now that things were moving again, Lorne declared that he was finished his work on behalf of the Aryubwals, though he promised to be available if something else came up. I had to wonder how many refugees in life-and-death situations around the world were stuck in some bureaucratic backlog of the Canadian government, their files gathering dust while politicians decided that would play well to their base. We were lucky to have Lorne. So many others, especially the Syrians, had no advocates.

The *Globe and Mail*, along with CTV News, broke a story that shed light on some of the reasons why so few refugees were arriving in the country. In early 2015, the Prime Minister's Office had quietly instructed that the applications of Syrians be redirected from immigration personnel to Stephen Harper's political staff for vetting. Parliament Hill journalist Robert Fife reported that he'd learned from Ottawa insiders that the PMO was going through refugee records to ensure that certain religious minorities with communities already established in Canada were given priority. Fife's sources told him that people in those selected ethnic groups, principally Christian, were considered to be most likely to one day vote Conservative and that the Prime Minister's Office discouraged Citizenship and Immigration from accepting Muslims.

The PMO's audit also applied to refugees who had been referred by the UNHCR, as the Aryubwals had been. And the delay in the Aryubwal case corresponded to the time that the Syrian files were being diverted. Were the Afghans also caught up in this audit? Had their file been sent for vetting by political operatives?

The Parliamentary Budget Office revealed something just as troubling. A number of federal government departments had failed to spend money that had been allocated to them for programs and had returned the funds to the federal treasury at the end of the fiscal year. That gesture made it possible for the Harper government to declare a year-end surplus. These were two of the major planks in the 2015 Conservative re-election strategy—toughness on terrorism; balanced budgets. The immigration department had underspent their budget by $350 million over a three-year period, much of it money that was supposed to be used to process applications for refugees. While people's lives were kept on hold in unimaginable places, the immigration department was returning money, claiming it wasn't needed.

———

The Aryubwal family members were now down to the final screening for their health. More hurdles. The federal government had contracted out the task of medical assessments for refugee claimants to the International Organization for Migration, the IOM. Robina did some research and found that the fees for medical tests provided by the IOM were exponentially higher than those of other clinics she surveyed. Many of the refugees found that it took repeated tests, and fees, before the IOM would issue them a clean bill of health.

When the IOM suggested that Asad's wife, Mobina, might have tuberculosis, there was understandable alarm. It was a life-threatening diagnosis that could also sabotage their departure for Canada. Mobina decided to challenge the IOM opinion and she went to a private clinic where results from her TB tests came back negative. But the IOM argued that since its examiners met Canadian standards they alone would be the ones to decide if the family was healthy. Eventually the IOM doctors determined that Mobina didn't have TB but only after several more expensive trips to the agency's clinic.

The many hours they spent in the IOM's waiting rooms allowed Robina to do some snooping and she found many refugee claimants in the same situation as her mother. She spoke with a man who told her that he had been returning for repeated tests for the past three years. He was quite agitated during his conversation with Ruby and at one point yelled: "This is all bullshit. It's all about money." An IOM staff member told both of them to leave the premises.

Canada was among a number of countries that subcontracted the IOM to perform this service. It seemed to be a thriving business with perhaps a built-in incentive for offering negative results, and the tests could take place only in the organization's own facilities. Ottawa would pay the fees up front, but the refugees would be billed by the government for all these costs once they had arrived in Canada. The IOM was a respected agency, and its staff had helped me on stories in the past. But was the office in Pakistan acting in the best interest of the refugees?

As vexing as these delays were, I kept reminding them that they would soon be on a flight to Canada. It was difficult for them to believe that there weren't more obstacles to come, given their experiences of the past eight years, and I had my suspicions as well. But there was nothing more we could do.

I was on summer holidays in Cape Breton in August 2015, standing in the Port Hawkesbury branch of the Toronto Dominion Bank reading emails on my BlackBerry as I waited for a teller when a message popped up with a name I didn't know, and a slug line that made me go numb.

FROM: Ruffolo.Julie <Julie.Ruffolo@cic.gc.ca>
SUBJECT: Arrivals from Islamabad

Good Morning Carol,

Today, I received a DMR (Destination Matching Request) from our head office in Ottawa, listing one family of 4 + 3 singles. This is the ARYUBWAL family. They are requesting to be destined to Toronto, when they arrive in Canada as Government Assisted Immigrants.

Because there are so many clients who wish to be destined to Toronto, we will actually only destine clients here who have close family members residing in Toronto. These clients do not have any family here in Canada, but list you as a "contact" person in

Toronto. Also, we are quite close to meeting our yearly target of arrivals so our head office will not make exceptions.

At this time, I have been asked to inform you that these clients will be destined to Hamilton, Ontario.

This means that upon their arrival in Canada, at Pearson Int'l Airport, they will be then transported by ground to Hamilton and will be temporarily residing at the reception centre there. They will be processed in Hamilton and will start to receive their income support in Hamilton. Their counselor will then assist them in finding permanent accommodation in Hamilton.

I just wanted you to be aware of this, regarding these clients. If you have any questions, please feel free to e-mail me.

Have a great day,

Julie

Julie Ruffolo
C&I Counsellor | C&I Counsellor

I couldn't absorb this message. Could it be true? Could years of struggle end so innocuously? Where was the tickertape, the confetti, the balloons?

Outside, in a shopping centre parking lot, I called the number and spoke to Julie Ruffolo. For the first time since my calls to Michael Zwack ("well, that's the story he is telling you"), I was speaking on the phone to an actual person.

Julie Ruffolo immediately and, I thought, apologetically, started to explain the decision to send them to Hamilton instead of Toronto, as though this was the point of my call. She told me that she thought it was in their best interest: the city was cheaper to live in and the schools were great. And it was hard to find housing in Toronto. I told her Hamilton was wonderful—my biggest problem at the moment was that I was about to cry.

"Honey, you can't cry," said Ruffolo. "Because then I will cry and we won't get anything done here."

But then I did question the choice of Hamilton. The Aryubwals needed to be close to me in Toronto so that I could help them settle in. She listened patiently even though I probably sounded a bit over-wrought. Then she wisely replied, "Honey, I think these people might need a little distance from you."

I texted Robina and instructed her to look up Hamilton, Ontario, on a map—because that was where she was going to live. *They were coming to Canada.*

It would be weeks before the family officially heard the news that Julie Ruffolo had shared with me. They also learned the IOM would be in charge of making final arrangements for them, which inspired no one with confidence but our slogan had become "Keep your eye on the prize and don't sweat the small stuff."

It was not small stuff when the Pakistani police came calling. People emigrating from Pakistan needed to get exit visas, which apparently meant a home inspection from the authorities, ostensibly to ensure they were who they claimed to be and not felons escaping justice. It turned into another potential shakedown. The "vetting" usually involved a small conversation and the transfer of a wad of cash. I wired them extra funds to cover the "fees." The police were, for the most part, polite as they extorted the family, but one encounter with the security police was bluntly offensive and potentially dangerous.

It's not clear whether the agents actually had a job to do or just wanted a ride on what they saw as a gravy train. They teased and humiliated everyone in the family before insisting that Asad contribute a bigger payment than he was able, or willing, to make. On top of it, Hossna was in the midst of an appendicitis attack and they were just about to take her to hospital when the police pushed their way into the apartment.

The police rifled through their belongings while harassing the women with sexual insinuations. Mobina and her daughters were in tears, trying to comply quickly and to get Hossna to a hospital as the officers mocked them. They asked why the younger women weren't married, how excited they must be about the sexual adventures awaiting them in Canada. The police had all the power now and they could delay the trip for as long as they wished. Asad at last complied with their demands of payment, realizing that this was all part of the routine—just another step in the demeaning journey of the refugee.

Throughout the fall of 2015, I covered the federal election campaign while waiting for the family to arrive. Canadian politics got stranger by the day. Chris Alexander and his cabinet colleague Kellie Leitch declared that a newly elected Harper government would establish an RCMP hotline for citizens who wanted to report "barbaric cultural practices," presumably ones carried out by Muslims. It was widely perceived as a crass political gimmick and backfired on the government. But it caused an uproar in the media.

And then came the image that transformed the global perception of refugees in general and Syrians in particular. The photograph of three-year-old Alan Kurdi would become seared into the sensibilities of even the most cynical observers—a tiny corpse, curled up on a beach as though asleep, a little boy like millions of little boys around the world, in every culture. Except that this little boy was dead through no fault of his own or of anybody close to him. He was a victim of international politics and the indifference of his fellow human beings in a hundred countries—a hundred potential safe havens.

The death of one small boy transfixed the world and transformed the refugee issue in the Canadian election campaign. The boy's aunt lived in British Columbia and she had been trying to arrange for her brothers and their children to come to Canada. Tima Kurdi had made several petitions to the federal government, including one directly to Chris Alexander, with no response. Had she been successful, the assumption was that Alan Kurdi would not have died.

Alexander temporarily suspended his own re-election campaign and returned to Ottawa to handle the political fallout that was now threatening to derail the re-election strategies of the Harper Conservatives. The niqab issue and stoking the mindless fear of "barbaric" practices now seemed—as they had been all along—trite. Alexander vowed he would find out where the process had gone wrong. But after a few inquiries he declared that the story had been a case of inaccurate reporting and media sensationalism. The little boy's uncle, not his father, had been the one trying to come to Canada.

It was a moot point. Tima Kurdi had started the process for everyone in the family but the paperwork had only been filed for one of the brothers. The minister wanted to believe he had dodged the controversy. But now the overused and suspect word "refugee" had a face, a form, an identity that was distressingly familiar to people everywhere. Alan was a child and he was dead and it should not have happened. Alexander was soon back on the campaign trail in Ajax, Ontario. But this and other political realities would take a toll on his career. He, like the government he had faithfully and aggressively served, went down in a decisive and humiliating defeat.

A few days after the election, Alexander explained his predicament in a complaint to a television reporter. He insisted that he had done everything possible to help refugees, but during the campaign he was confronted with charges of being cold and callous. "I spent two weeks being called a baby killer," Alexander lamented. He also blamed the media: "Everywhere I went, people would say, 'You hung up on Carol Off.'"

The morning the Aryubwals were due to land in Toronto, Brian Kelly arrived from London, lugging camera gear as he had been doing for nearly forty years. His first encounter with Asad had been through a lens, and he would encounter him that way again that night. It was November 12, 2015, almost thirteen years since Brian and I had travelled through the Salang Tunnel with Asad as our escort, eight years since Robina had last been on an airplane, on a flight back from Paris; almost eight years since we met at Hotel Greenland. I checked online and their flights from Islamabad through Istanbul to Toronto seemed to be on time. As Brian loaded his gear into our vehicle, he bumped his head on the lowest branch of the red oak in my front yard. He didn't understand why I laughed.

Julie Ruffolo had told me that with government-assisted refugees— GARs—I was needed for very little. The people in her department would greet the family, process them, give them winter clothing, escort them through customs and drive them to Hamilton, unless I thought that it was important that I should handle this last, relatively straightforward detail. I told her yes, it was important.

My husband, Linden, drove our vehicle to the airport along with Brian and me. I anticipated a lot of luggage, in addition to the seven adults, and some friends had agreed to help with transportation: Robin Smythe, a friend from work, came to the airport with her hatchback. Paul Burk was another friend with a good-sized vehicle and he arrived along with his partner, Naomi Duguid. Naomi had counselled and comforted me over the many years that I navigated the international refugee system and she wasn't going to miss the victory lap of this long marathon. Jeff Douglas was already at the airport to pick up his mother who was arriving from Nova Scotia, and he came to the international arrivals area to share the moment. To pass the time, we chatted with a family of Sri Lankans, the women in niqabs revealing only their eyes. They were there to meet relatives but they were intrigued by the idea that "old-stock" Canadians such as ourselves would be waiting for a family of Afghans.

I had a contact inside the airport who agreed to tell me when the family had landed and were making their way through customs. It took hours and felt like days. The years since the ordeal started hung around me, years of anxious memories.

The automatic sliding door at the international arrivals gate repeatedly opened and shut as small knots of weary people emerged—tourists, business people, students, families reuniting. And there were newcomers wearing the garb of foreign places, every individual a narrative of trouble and survival. Then my contact called to say the Aryubwals had picked up their belongings and were headed to the final exit.

I saw Asad first, his hair now completely grey and his shoulders more stooped than I remembered. He was pushing a cart overflowing with baggage and he caught a glimpse of me just before the frosted glass panels shut again. Each time the doors opened he was closer and we waved frantically at each other, his face erupting with that infectious smile I had first seen at the Mustafa Hotel in Kabul. Asad was trying to keep the heaping pile of suitcases on his cart from toppling over as he made his way through the arrivals hall.

Then he was through the door, leaving his past life behind. He was in Canada. At that moment, he simply let the cart go, and it rolled away on its own momentum heading I don't know where because I was smothered in an embrace the intensity of which I had never felt before.

Asad wept inconsolably as he released the pent up frustration and suffering of years, perhaps a lifetime. I felt his fear, anxiety, humiliation, rage, frustration, delight and sorrow as he sobbed and sobbed.

The family arrives "home" at Pearson International Airport. The children have changed so much since I last saw them. Muhammad, Robina, Hossna, Asad and Mujeeb look on while I hug Hossai. [Photo: Lana Šlezić]

I caught glimpses of the others as they emerged; tired, happy, and also crying. Everyone around us was in tears; the Sri Lankans, the airport personnel, the people who had come to drive the family to Hamilton. But I held onto Asad, whispering to him over and over again words of comfort and also the truth: "It's okay now. You're home."

VIII

All We Carry Forward

. . . we are all related, we are family, we are kin.
Every story carries within it the seed of a thousand others and
it is only in the coming together that we discover the truth of that
and know that we are home.

—FROM "THE CANADA POEM," BY RICHARD WAGAMESE

IT WAS DECEMBER, SNOWLESS AND rather mild, but typical of Canadian neighbourhoods in winter in that there wasn't a soul to be seen outside. The low, late afternoon sun streamed through the front window, filtered by a few mature pine trees and leafless maples. I had been in the bustling streets of Peshawar where every square metre is dense with humanity but nothing else resembling nature. That scene couldn't be further from this quiet Sunday afternoon in Hamilton.

A pause in the chatter gave me a chance to take stock. We were crowded into the Aryubwals' small living room, already furnished and decorated just a few weeks after they had arrived. There were some cheap sofas provided by government services, but we sprawled on pillows and rugs on the floor that reminded me, painfully, of what it took to sit cross-legged for hours at a time. I was out of practice.

Hamilton Mountain is a residential neighbourhood you could find anywhere in Southern Ontario, constructed for a post-war population that came to the Golden Horseshoe looking for work. The streets are lined with box-shaped red-brick houses and well-kept yards with economy cars in the driveways. Hamilton was built by immigrants who came from everywhere in the world and I could imagine that, over the decades, several families, just like the Aryubwals, had sat in this little room wondering what was in store for them in this weird new place.

"Does this seem strange to you?" I asked, expecting to have to explain what I meant. But everyone laughed. Yes, they agreed, the whole experience was quite surreal. "Especially first thing in the morning," said Ruby, "when I look out my bedroom window and wonder where I am. How did I get here?"

The Aryubwals had spent their first month in a downtown Hamilton shelter for refugees where they experienced the good and the bad of Canadian generosity. Robina and Hossai immediately became involved with the other tenants—Somalis, Sudanese, Iraqis—to whom they offered advice and assistance. The federal government contracts out much of its settlement services to not-for-profit institutions that are always looking for ways to cut corners. Robina complained that the food that was provided was unhealthy and much of it had gone past its best-before dates. She warned the custodians that refugees were sometimes getting sick because of it. Their comings and goings from the building were restricted by the staff, and the tenants felt like hostages. Ruby, her sister and her mother reorganized the facility's kitchen, cooked, comforted confused newcomers and helped to interpret documents. Asad chain-smoked on the street outside while Muhammad restlessly walked downtown Hamilton, trying to make sense of where they were. Asad discovered that the building where they were staying also warehoused people in drug rehab and detox programs, some of whom, they were told, were recently out of jail. All of the refugees, including the Aryubwals, were shocked and disturbed to see the condition of people who had spent all their lives in Canada.

I went to Hamilton often in that first month and we explored the city together. There was a time when the steel mills and the factories there couldn't find enough people to fill the vacancies. Now the jobs had moved to cities and countries that were more willing to grind down labour costs. People who live in the city they bravely call "the Hammer" are fiercely proud and struggle to keep up appearances. But the Aryubwals considered the levels of poverty perplexing.

It wasn't long before Muhammad discovered Tim Hortons, and prominent in Asad's earliest English vocabulary is the term "double-double," the sugar-and-cream-laden coffee mixture that was to help him cut back on his smoking habit. We went on an outing to see the Santa Claus parade as it snaked through downtown, passing within blocks of

At the Santa Claus parade in Hamilton, November 14, 2015. Hossna in the foreground with Asad, Robina and Mujeeb.

the refugee centre. The family wore toques and mittens purchased for the occasion as they cheered on the floats. They found the event odd but delightful as we watched the majorettes with their batons, the bands playing Christmas songs (Hossna seemed to know the words), the antique cars and the clowns. Of course, we all waved to the jolly fat man in the sleigh bringing up the rear.

Hamilton's Gore Park in the centre of the city has an expansive and well-maintained memorial commemorating the dead from the world wars and Korea that now includes an installation honouring those who died in Afghanistan. Asad was deeply moved as he ran his hand down the lists of names of those Canadians who'd perished in his country, presumably for him and especially his daughters. When we encountered a statue of Canada's founding father in the same square, Robina already knew who he was: "That's Johnny Macdonald!" she declared, not realizing that it was John "A."

On another weekend, they all came to Toronto for a big lunch and a chance to meet those who'd helped along the way. Ruby was happy to finally speak with Jeff in person since they had become Facebook pals when she was still living in Pakistan. Over the years, Asad had often asked for Linden's advice as well as mine, and now the two men bonded over a whiskey. Naomi and Mobina took to each other as though they had been friends for decades or perhaps in another life. The Aryubwals met my son, Joel, his wife, Meredith, and their two girls—though Chloe Alice and Clara Mae were somewhat taken aback by the effect they seemed to have on those who cried at the sight of their young guardian angels.

The rental house in Hamilton was tiny and rundown but a good place to start. The government had provided basic furniture and housewares that were supplemented with some quality contributions from my former CBC colleague Mellissa Fung. In October 2008, Mellissa had been reporting for the CBC from Afghanistan when armed bandits abducted her just outside Kabul. The men chained her up and stuffed her in a cave-like hole eight feet underground where she was fed a diet of mostly juice and cookies and finally released twenty-eight days later.

You might think a person who had been kidnapped, held for ransom, deprived of light and assaulted before being released might not want to have anything more to do with that country. But Mellissa continued to be involved with foundations attempting to help Afghan girls and, at one point, she and I had even discussed trying to bring Robina to Canada alone, as a student. We abandoned the plan when the refugee process appeared yet again to be advancing.

Mellissa had recently moved to the United States, packing her worldly goods into a Toronto storage locker. When she heard that the Aryubwals had arrived in Canada, she shipped everything from the locker to the house in Hamilton and her contributions brought a touch of luxury to the house. Mobina had textiles she brought from Pakistan (the mountain of baggage we transported from the airport had contained mostly gifts for everyone in Canada and curtains for windows Mobina had never seen); she hemmed the draperies by hand. The mish-mash of décor all came together nicely.

Eno Causevic, my Bosnian friend who had introduced me to Alan Beech from the West Highland Baptist Church, came to visit. I contacted Alan since I thought he might want to know that the family had ended up in Hamilton. He became a frequent visitor and developed a bond with the Aryubwals almost immediately. Though he and Asad spoke no common language, they connected. Alan gave Asad a part-time job and offered to teach everyone how to drive. He quickly attained a high-level status in the hero department. Alan and his wife, Maria, put on a big holiday dinner for everyone where we met Alan's Italian in-laws, who told the Aryubwals about their own difficult struggle to settle in Canada many decades earlier. Asad declared later that he didn't realize how much Italians and Afghans had in common.

A month before the family landed in Canada the Liberal Party won the federal election, promising to dramatically increase the number of refugees coming to Canada from Syria and to expedite their arrival. Unprecedented numbers of Canadians immediately signed up to sponsor those refugees and within months, 25,000 Syrians were living here. Municipal governments and premiers of provinces competed with each other to welcome the new arrivals and the media produced warm and sympathetic features on people who said all the right things about their new home.

Where was the voice of those who had believed these asylum seekers were vectors for violence? The defeated Conservatives continued to caution, though not quite as strenuously, that the Syrians posed a danger to Canada. They argued that the refugees had not been properly screened, even as the country's security agencies were confident that they had been.

Elsewhere in the world, the warnings against refugees continued and in some places became more extreme. In their first year in Canada, the Aryubwals followed news from the US where the Republican presidential candidate, Donald Trump, became the champion of those who would build walls, impose severe restrictions on refugees, and ban Muslims from coming to the United States. They were distressed to hear he wanted to create a registry for Muslims already in the country. It seemed impossible to sane people that Trump would prevail, and Asad was sure that the election would end with the inevitable defeat of the Donald. Of course, Asad was wrong, as he often is when he believes that truth will triumph over mendacity.

The seething centre of the refugee debate is not really about policy; it's about perception. Either you identify with others or you don't. Either you see yourself in the eyes of others or you don't. The schism isn't limited to people in Western countries like Canada or the United States. Asad married a woman who wasn't from his clan; he opened his door to foreigners, even trusting them with his life. But his relatives eschewed contact with people beyond their sphere and punished Asad for his association with outsiders. Now he and his family were in a country where, with the exception of indigenous peoples, everyone originates from somewhere else.

My paternal grandmother came to Canada as a teenager from Poland. As the family legend goes, Mae's oldest sister was the one who was supposed to travel to North America to join their brother. The family's meagre savings had been invested in travel documents and tickets for her passage to a better life. On the night before my great-aunt was to leave she broke down and declared that she would not and could not go. She was in love with a young man and was determined to stay in Poland to marry him. Just before dawn, my great-grandparents shook their younger daughter awake and whispered softly, "Wake up, Mae. You're going to Canada." She was seventeen.

Mae arrived in Winnipeg with no money and her sister's passport. Her brother was already employed at the Royal Alex Hotel and he introduced Mae to a co-worker, a man of German descent, who had a job working in the kitchen. "George was nice and he knew how to dance, so I married him," my grandmother once told me. Decades later, Mae took advantage of a general amnesty for illegal migrants to Canada and registered as a citizen under her real name. On her first visit back home, in the 1960s, she found Poland depressing. The old country she had ached for as a teenager would have provided no future, whereas Mae had a successful life in Winnipeg. Her son, my father, married a woman whose own father had come from England and my parents provided her with seven doting grandchildren. As difficult as it had been to arrive in a strange country, Mae understood the advantages life had granted her.

Hossna, now fourteen, started high school not long after she arrived in Hamilton while the other Aryubwals found part-time jobs to supplement their government allowances. They attended English as a Second Language (ESL) classes where they ferociously competed with the other refugees and immigrants, including each other, for the highest marks. They approached ESL exams and assignments as though they were LSATs that might qualify them for limited spaces at Harvard Law School. They met newcomers from many other countries who complained about how difficult it was, who hinted that perhaps they would have been better off had they never come to Canada. In her forceful but polite way, Robina would tell those people to suck it up and get on with it. They had shed their past problems and inherited new ones, Robina argued, but at least these ones were surmountable. I wish Mae could have known her.

It didn't take long before the family outgrew Hamilton as the cosmopolitan charms of nearby Toronto beckoned. The energy and pace of the big city appealed to all of them, plus it had more opportunities. They'd struggled to find employment in Hamilton but Toronto held an embarrassment of riches for people willing to do any kind of job and to put in long hours. Within ten months, the Aryubwals had moved to a rented house in Toronto. They had a car in the driveway, busy social lives and as much work as they could handle. Asad found employment as a dishwasher at a high-end banquet facility called the Carlu, while the others worked for restaurants and delivery services. They accepted all the hours they could get since they were burdened with a large debt. The final bill from the IOM, for health checks and travel costs, was $10,000, payable to the Canadian government.

Naomi has two sons, Dominic and Tashi, recent graduates of the University of Toronto, who embraced their assignment of helping the Aryubwals with their academics. Dom wouldn't give up until he got the University of Toronto to take notice of a remarkable young woman who had wanted nothing more all her life than to go to school. Robina was accepted directly into the second year of a humanities program. Her plan is to go to law school.

Tashi researched grants and bursaries and as of this writing, the other Aryubwal kids are prying open the doors of colleges and institutions where they hope to register. Naomi's partner, Paul, is an engineer, and he took on the task of getting Muhammad's Pakistani degree at least partially recognized in Canada.

In the first few months after their arrival, I sometimes spent the night at the little house in Hamilton rather than drive back to Toronto. Breakfast was always interesting and I often got the best stories in the morning. That's also when I learned how much introspection was going on, especially on Asad's part—a man who is not given to self-analysis. He didn't sleep well at night, reviewing decisions and choices he made. How had he brought so many calamities on his family? Why did his own siblings treat his wife and children with so much contempt? These questions gnawed at him and he had no answers. I asked him many times to tell me his regrets. If he could live events again, what would he have done differently? I don't believe he was lying when he declared that he regrets nothing.

On the face of it, Asad had made a number of poor choices. He had married a woman he loved but had defied the will of his powerful siblings to do so. He had criticized a notoriously vindictive warlord on public television. He had allowed his unmarried daughter to travel to Paris, unaccompanied, bringing down the wrath of his relatives. All of these choices had terrible consequences. His wife had been abused; his extended family rejected him; he was forced to flee his country and rely on a complete stranger to rescue them. They had lived in terror for years.

Yet Asad had made all his decisions in good faith. He wasn't reckless in his actions. He spoke out against Rashid Dostum at a time when he believed his country was on the cusp of change and he talked to reporters he thought he could trust. He sent Ruby to a reputable school in the heart of Paris where he understood she would be properly cared for and he relied on the rock-solid character of his own child. Asad spoke truth to power and educated his daughters because he simply believed it was the right thing to do. And in a twist of fate, the choices Asad made that appeared to limit freedom had, in the end, landed his entire family in an environment of substantial liberty. Canada is a long way from utopia and the young Aryubwals know their struggle is far from over. But they're all finding their own way in a strange new society and, if they're fortunate, they will make choices with as much integrity as their father did.

No one in the family has ever asked me if I regret the role I played in their troubles, but I know they have wondered. Here's my response. Overall, I'm not sorry about anything because if we had not gone through this ordeal together, beginning with the interviews that landed Asad in hot water, I would not know these people and I would not have such friends. I'm sure that explanation is little comfort to those whose lives I turned upside down and I profoundly regret my role in their troubles.

If a journalist asks good questions she might win an award. If someone answers good questions it might get him killed. That's a crude analysis of what happened and it fails to reflect something important: motive. My role as a journalist is to expose things to the light of day and to be, within reason, disinterested in the consequences of that exposure. I do believe that it's part of human nature to want to share experiences, thoughts and feelings. People tell us things for a reason. They want journalists to broadcast and publish their experiences and insights. If we think a story might endanger someone, we decide not to report it, as I would have done with Asad had I known what Dostum was doing to him. But for the most part, people want to have a voice. It's our job to convey the essence and the meaning of what they tell us, and let the chips fall where they may.

I have no expectation that telling someone's story will fix anything because if I did, I would have an agenda and the truth would run the risk of being lost. I didn't return to Asad's side as a journalist; I did so as a human being. It was simply the right thing to do, a choice made in good faith. I appreciate that in my profession it's easy to become tangled in a cause and cross the line into advocacy. I understand why we have codes of conduct both in journalism and in society. But life is complicated. We do what we can and what we must.

One thing is clear to me, though, as I sit with the family; this is the conclusion of a journey that began with that first visit to Pakistan and the lessons that I learned during a dash across the tarmac at Jinnah International Airport. Be careful what you wish for.

————

On a warm day of their first spring in Canada, Ruby, Hossai and Hossna walked over to the playground they had seen on the first tour of their new neighbourhood, reflecting on their lost years of childhood. They exchanged a glance and a few giggles. Then they jumped on the swings and pushed off, their long hair blowing in the wind, free of burqas, chadors and the judgement of others. They laughed and shrieked as the swings took them higher and higher and they looked and sounded for all the world like happy little girls.

Timeline of Major Events

NOVEMBER 8, 1933 ... Mohammad Zahir Shah is crowned king of Afghanistan and rules for the next forty years, a period of relative stability for the country. Zahir Shah would be Afghanistan's last king.

SEPTEMBER 1953 .... Mohammed Daoud Khan, the king's cousin, becomes prime minister. He supports closer ties with the Soviet Union and questions the authority of the country's imams. Daoud Khan launches social reforms encouraging women to attend university and enter the workforce.

1965 .... Nur Muhammad Taraki and Babrak Karmal establish the People's Democratic Party of Afghanistan (PDPA), a Communist party.

JULY 17, 1973 .... King Zahir Shah is deposed in a bloodless coup by his cousin, Prime Minister Mohammed Daoud Khan, who abolishes the monarchy and declares himself president.

1975 TO 1977 .... President Daoud Khan launches constitutional reforms to grant women more rights. He also cracks down on the growing Communist opposition in the country.

APRIL 28, 1978 ...... President Daoud Khan is assassinated by forces loyal to the PDPA. This is the opening act of the Saur Revolution, a Moscow-supported coup d'état. Tens of thousands of Afghan civilians are arrested and many executed.

MAY 1, 1978 . . . . Nur Muhammad Taraki becomes president of Afghanistan. People in rural areas of Afghanistan immediately revolt against the new regime and begin to form anti-government militias. They call themselves mujahidin.

SEPTEMBER 14, 1979 . . Nur Muhammad Taraki is assassinated. Prime Minister Hafizullah Amin, another coup leader, becomes president.

DECEMBER 24, 1979 . . The Soviet Union invades Afghanistan.

DECEMBER 27, 1979 . . Soviets seize control of all government buildings in Kabul and execute President Amin. Deputy Prime Minister Babrak Karmal is appointed leader. Arrests and executions continue.

1980S . . . . Soviet armed forces, along with USSR-backed Afghan National Army troops are at war with mujahidin rebels. Osama bin Laden establishes himself in Afghanistan in order to direct Arab money and fighters to the mujahidin.

JANUARY 20, 1981 . . . . Ronald Reagan becomes president of the United States. He launches Operation Cyclone, supplying billions of dollars in weapons, training and cash to the mujahidin. The stated objective of the mission is to bring the Soviet Union to its knees.

1982 . . . . Afghans flee the fighting and the USSR's scorched-earth campaign. Nearly 3 million people escape to Pakistan. Another 1.5 million take refuge in Iran.

1986 . . . . The US covertly supplies the mujahidin with portable infrared homing Stinger missiles. The militants are able to shoot down Soviet aircraft, a turning point in the war that's often called "the Stinger effect."

APRIL 14, 1988 . . . . The Geneva Accords resolve the war and mark the beginning of the end of the Soviet occupation. Approximately 5.5 million Afghans—a third of the

Afghan population—have taken refuge in neighbouring countries.

SEPTEMBER 1988 ..... Osama bin Laden and his followers establish al-Qaeda—
"the base"—in Afghanistan. With the Soviet Union all
but dissolved, the terrorist group determines that the
United States is now its principal target.

FEBRUARY 15, 1989... The last Soviet troops return to the USSR. Afghanistan
begins its descent into civil war.

APRIL 24, 1992 .... Warlords (former mujahidin leaders) sign the Peshawar
Accord, a power-sharing arrangement that is almost
immediately shattered. The agreement establishes the
Islamic State of Afghanistan.

APRIL 24, 1992 .... Gulbuddin Hekmatyar (who didn't sign the Peshawar
Accord) launches a fierce attack on Kabul.

APRIL 1992 .... Kabul is engulfed in war. The United Nations gives
sanctuary to the last Soviet-backed Afghan president,
Mohammad Najibullah.

JUNE 28, 1992 .... Burhanuddin Rabbani becomes president of the newly
created, and unstable, Islamic State of Afghanistan.

AUGUST 1994 .... The Taliban takes control of Kandahar.

JANUARY 1995.......... The Taliban begins its campaign to conquer all of
Afghanistan, with the backing of Pakistan.

MARCH 13, 1995 ...... Taliban militants murder Abdul Ali Mazari, leader of
the Hazaras, a Shia Muslim minority.

SEPTEMBER 27, 1996.. The Taliban captures Kabul. Mohammad Najibullah
is apprehended, tortured, castrated and hanged on a
public road, alongside his brother. Taliban leader
Mullah Omar declares the Islamic Emirate of
Afghanistan.

SEPTEMBER 1996 ..... Warlords join together to fight the Taliban, establishing
the Afghan Northern Alliance, aka the United Islamic
Front for the Salvation of Afghanistan.

SEPTEMBER 1997 . . . . . . The Taliban is defeated in Mazar-e-Sharif.

AUGUST 1998 . . . . General Rashid Dostum flees to Turkey as the Taliban returns for another assault and takes control of Mazar-e-Sharif.

SEPTEMBER 9, 2001 . . . Ahmad Shah Massoud, the Lion of Panjshir, is assassinated by Tunisian suicide bombers posing as French journalists.

SEPTEMBER 11, 2001 . . Arab hijackers take control of four US commercial jet planes and direct them to attack targets in the United States. Two aircraft smash into the World Trade Center in New York City, another hits the Pentagon and a fourth crashes into a field in Pennsylvania. Thousands of people are killed. Osama bin Laden and al-Qaeda are accused of masterminding the attacks.

SEPTEMBER 21, 2001 . . The Taliban refuses US president George W. Bush's demand that Osama bin Laden be turned over to American authorities.

OCTOBER 7, 2001 . . . . . The United States launches Operation Enduring Freedom. Great Britain joins the US in a large-scale aerial assault on Afghanistan. Canada announces its willingness to join the US-led mission and launches Operation Apollo. HMCS *Halifax* begins counter-terrorism operations in the Arabian Sea.

NOVEMBER 2001 . . . . . . US Special Forces and the Northern Alliance, led by General Rashid Dostum, enter Mazar-e-Sharif and defeat the Taliban.

NOVEMBER 25, 2001 . . As many as eight thousand Taliban and al-Qaeda militants surrender to the Northern Alliance in Kunduz. Hundreds of "high-value" POWs are taken to General Dostum's fort, Qala-i-Jangi. The remainder are destined for Dostum's stronghold in nearby Sheberghan. The prisoners are packed into shipping containers for transport.

NOVEMBER 25 TO

DECEMBER 1, 2001.... POWs in Qala-i-Jangi Fort stage an uprising that turns into a bloodbath. Almost all the nearly five hundred prisoners are killed. Most of the prisoners sent to Sheberghan in the shipping containers also perish. Possibly as many as five thousand prisoners who surrendered to Dostum's militia are unaccounted for, and believed buried in mass graves at Dasht-i-Leili. Eyewitnesses claim that US Special Forces were aware of the botched prisoner transfer and the deaths.

DECEMBER 5, 2001.... UN Security Council authorizes the International Security Assistance Force (ISAF).

DECEMBER 20, 2001 .. During an international conference in Bonn, Germany, Hamid Karzai is chosen interim leader of Afghanistan.

AUGUST 2003 .... Canada contributes combat troops to the ISAF mission, basing its force in Kabul.

OCTOBER 2003 .... Chris Alexander becomes Canada's ambassador to Afghanistan.

OCTOBER 9, 2004 ..... Hamid Karzai is elected president of the Islamic Republic of Afghanistan.

SEPTEMBER—

NOVEMBER 2005 ...... Parliamentary elections in Afghanistan are held for the first time in three decades. Record numbers of women successfully run for office. A number of warlords are also elected.

AUGUST 2005 .... Canada takes over the Provincial Reconstruction Team in Kandahar.

2006 .... The Taliban launches an insurgency in southern Afghanistan.

JANUARY 2006 .... Canadian forces begin combat operations in Kandahar.

JANUARY 15, 2006 .... Canadian diplomat Glyn Berry is killed in Kandahar by a suicide bomber.

FEBRUARY 6, 2006 . . . . Stephen Harper takes office as Canada's prime minister.

FEBRUARY 2006 . . . . Canadian brigadier general David Fraser takes command of the multinational brigade in southern Afghanistan.

MAY 17, 2006 . . . . Captain Nichola Goddard becomes Canada's first female combat fatality and the sixteenth Canadian soldier killed during operations in Afghanistan.

SEPTEMBER 2006 . . . . . Canadian-led offensive Operation Medusa is launched with 1st Battalion, the Royal Canadian Regiment Battle Group.

DECEMBER 2009 . . . . . . US president Barack Obama declares the campaign in Afghanistan to be "a just war." He renews the US commitment with an additional thirty thousand troops.

JANUARY 4, 2011 . . . . . . Mohamed Bouazizi, a vegetable seller in Tunisia, sets himself on fire. His death is an inspiration for Arab Spring.

MAY 2, 2011 . . . . US Special Forces assassinate Osama bin Laden in Abbottabad, Pakistan.

JULY 2011 . . . . Canada's combat operations in Kandahar come to an end.

SEPTEMBER 20, 2011 . . Burhanuddin Rabbani is assassinated.

SEPTEMBER 29, 2014 . . Ashraf Ghani Ahmadzai becomes president of Afghanistan and appoints Rashid Dostum as his vice-president.

Cast of Characters

WARLORDS

Atta Muhammad Noor: An ethnic Tajik and a powerful northern commander of Jamiat-i-Islami. His militia clashed frequently with Rashid Dostum's forces but they fought together in the Afghan Northern Alliance. He replaced Rashid Dostum as the chief warlord of the north, becoming governor of Balkh province in 2004.

Abdul Rashid Dostum: Uzbek commander who established control of much of northern Afghanistan during the 1980s through his support of the Soviet occupation. During the Afghan civil war, Dostum aligned himself with Ahmad Shah Massoud and then Gulbuddin Hekmatyar. He became a principal commander in the Northern Alliance during the war against the Taliban. Dostum and his militia are accused of committing multiple human rights violations during the Soviet-mujahidin war, the Afghan civil war and the US-led invasion.

Mohammad Qasim Fahim: Tajik commander within the Northern Alliance and an ally of Ahmad Shah Massoud. He became vice-president in 2002 and again in 2009 until his death in 2014.

Gulbuddin Hekmatyar: Commander and founder of Hezb-i-Islami, perhaps the most ruthless of the militias that fought for control of Kabul during the civil war. He refused to sign the Peshawar Accord. Pakistan supported Hekmatyar until it shifted allegiances to the Taliban.

Ahmad Shah Massoud, the Lion of Panjshir: A Tajik commander of Jamiat-i-Islami and the Northern Alliance. He is perhaps the most controversial of Afghanistan's warlords; a hero to many who claim he pulled back from some of the most brutal campaigns of the civil war but a criminal to others who say he had command responsibility for a number of atrocities, including a massacre of Shia Muslims—Hazaras—in a region of Kabul. Massoud was assassinated two days before 9/11.

Burhanuddin Rabbani: A Tajik leader of Jamiat-i-Islami and closely associated with Massoud. A scholar and former professor, he was chosen to be president of Afghanistan by the signatories of the Peshawar Accord. Rabbani was accused, along with Massoud, for having command responsibility during a number of atrocities committed by Jamiat militiamen and their allies during the civil war. Rabbani was assassinated in 2011.

Abdul Rasul Sayyaf: Commander and leader of Ittihad-i-Islami. He is a Wahhabi and anti-Shia militant who has enjoyed strong backing from Saudi Arabia. He and his militiamen stand accused of multiple human rights abuses. Sayyaf helped Osama bin Laden to establish his base in Afghanistan and he supported al-Qaeda's attacks on the US. He is a prominent member of the Wolesi Jirga, part of the Afghan Parliament.

OTHER KEY PLAYERS

Mullah Mohammed Omar: A member of the mujahidin during their US-backed war against the Soviet Union. He founded the Taliban as a response to the anarchism and criminality of the mujahidin leaders who had become warlords following the retreat of the Soviets. Mullah Omar imposed a rigid and punishing form of Islamic law on Afghans under his control. He allowed Osama bin Laden to establish his al-Qaeda base in Afghanistan.

Osama bin Laden: A Saudi Arabian construction company heir and founder of al-Qaeda. He helped Saudi Arabia to supply arms, money and fighters to the mujahidin during the war against the Soviets and established a permanent base in Afghanistan after he was forced to leave Sudan. Bin Laden was found hiding in Abbottabad, Pakistan, and assassinated by US Special Forces on May 2, 2011.

Ayman al-Zawahiri: An Egyptian surgeon and member of the Muslim Brotherhood who joined al-Qaeda following his brutal incarceration in an Egyptian prison. Al-Zawahiri became bin Laden's deputy and is considered responsible for shifting al-Qaeda's focus to attacking the United States. He now leads al-Qaeda.

POLITICIANS

Chris Alexander: Former Canadian ambassador to Afghanistan and a minister in the Conservative government of Stephen Harper.

Hafizullah Amin: An Afghan Communist who helped to lead the Saur Revolution. He became president of Afghanistan for one hundred days in 1979 before he was assassinated by the invading Soviets.

Benazir Bhutto: Former prime minister of Pakistan and leader of the Pakistan People's Party. She was assassinated in December 2007.

Leonid Brezhnev: Head of the Soviet Union's Communist Party from 1964 to 1982. He ordered the invasion of Afghanistan.

Ashraf Ghani Ahmadzai: Became president of Afghanistan (in a power-sharing arrangement with his opponent, Abdullah Abdullah) in September 2014. He appointed Rashid Dostum as his vice-president.

Stephen Harper: Became prime minister of Canada in February 2006.

Babrak Karmal: Moscow-appointed leader of Afghanistan following the Soviet invasion in 1979.

Hamid Karzai: Appointed interim leader of Afghanistan in 2001, following the US-led invasion of the country. Elected president in 2004.

Jason Kenney: A minister in the cabinet of Stephen Harper.

Mohammad Najibullah: The last Soviet-appointed president of Afghanistan. Took sanctuary within the UN compound during the civil war. He was captured by the Taliban in 1996, tortured and hanged.

Nur Muhammad Taraki: An Afghan Communist and a founder of the People's Democratic Party of Afghanistan. He was a leader of the Saur Revolution. He became president in 1978 and he was assassinated in 1979.

Acknowledgements

My biggest and most important thanks goes to the Aryubwals: Asad, Mobina, Robina, Hossai, Muhammad, Mujeeb and Hossna. It goes without saying that I could not have written this book without them—but their patience with my questions and endless requests for clarifications was much appreciated. I have endeavoured to tell the story accurately and any failure to do so is entirely my responsibility. This is not a complete account of their lives but rather my understanding of their experiences. I look forward to one day reading their own version of events.

It takes a village to make a book and the people at Penguin Random House Canada worked very hard on this one. Many people played a role but I want to single out some of the most important villagers. Anne Collins was the first to tell me that this story merited a book and she was beside me every step of the way, as she has been for many years. Pamela Murray tirelessly read and edited many drafts and has provided abundant advice and guidance. Scott Sellers is the best companion any writer could ever ask for on the journey of writing and selling a book.

Deirdre Molina coordinated all the comings and goings in the background of this project, attending to details that I can't even imagine. Mathew Sibiga doesn't just market books; he champions them. Angelika Glover and Tilman Lewis brought sharp attention and insight to the copy-editing of the manuscript. Big thanks to all of you.

A special nod goes to my literary agent, Shaun Bradley, who is always such a support for me but especially on this book where there were so many personal obstacles. Shaun got me through while providing vital assistance with the storytelling. As always, thank you.

Trying to find clarity in this story while collapsing decades of history, both global and personal, was a massive task and some key people helped me with that. Naomi Duguid provided her skilled attention and much advice at every stage of the project. Sarah Cooper contributed invaluable research that informs the book, and she also gave timely feedback after reading of some of the drafts. Robin Smythe supported the project every step of the way, allowing me time off work from the CBC in order to write and then providing expert editing guidance on the book itself. Brian Kelly and Heather Abbott mined their memories and their photo collections to help with the editorial. And they were always there for advice and encouragement.

There are some people who didn't assist with the book per se but without whom we wouldn't have the story you've read here. I want to acknowledge Alan Beech, Eno Causevic, Khwaka Kukubo, Jeff Douglas, Lorne Waldman, Heather Conway, Peter Oliver, Dom and Tashi Duguid, and Paul Burk. Each of them contributed to the success of bringing the family the Canada and/or helping them to settle. It gave me such pleasure to see many of them meet the Aryubwals for the first time, people they had supported when they were complete strangers. You all have my undying gratitude.

Thanks to my family members who put up with my absences and my distractions, especially my mother, Shirley Off, and my son and his wife, Joel Harrison-Off and Meredith Burley. And thanks to Chloe Alice and Clara Mae for all of their inspiration, divine and otherwise.

There are few words that can explain how grateful I am to my husband, Linden MacIntyre. He supported and coached me during the years as we stickhandled the Aryubwal refugee file through the Byzantine bureaucracy; he helped me to shape the narrative; he read many drafts and provided shrewd editorial advice. I can't thank him enough.

Finally, a special posthumous thanks to Richard Wagamese, poet and storyteller. Shortly before he died, I had a chance to interview Richard about his writing and his Ojibway heritage. The title for this book, plus a number of quotes, come from "The Canada Poem," Richard's tribute to our multiracial society and his understanding of what it means to be Canadian. The poem could only have come from someone whose ancestors lived here with their own culture for hundreds of generations before the first European settlers arrived. Indigenous people have been accepting new Canadians to their lands ever since. In Richard's words:

> ". . . so maybe this is what it comes to mean
> this word, this name, this Kanata
> the Huron word for village that has
> come to mean 'our home'
> maybe in the end it's a word for one fire
> burning where a circle of people gathers
> to hear the stories that define them"

—FROM "THE CANADA POEM," BY RICHARD WAGAMESE
OCTOBER 14, 1955–MARCH 10, 2017

Index

CAROL OFF is the host of CBC Radio's *As It Happens*, the network's flagship evening radio program. She has extensive radio and television experience covering stories in Canada and around the world. Off reported the fallout from the 9/11 disasters with news features and documentaries from New York, Washington, London, Cairo and Afghanistan. She has won numerous awards and accolades for her CBC documentaries in North America, Asia, and Europe, and is the author of three previous books, most recently, *Bitter Chocolate: Investigating the Dark Side of the World's Most Seductive Sweet*, a finalist for the National Business Book Award and nominated for the prestigious Shaughnessy Cohen Award for Political Writing. She lives in Toronto.